# PSYCHOEDUCATIONAL GROUPS

# PSYCHOEDUCATIONAL GROUPS
## *Process and Practice*
### *Second Edition*

## NINA W. BROWN

BRUNNER-ROUTLEDGE

New York and Hove

Published in 2004 by
Brunner-Routledge
29 West 35th Street
New York, NY 10001
www.brunner-routledge.com

Published in Great Britain by
Brunner-Routledge
27 Church Road
Hove, East Sussex
BN3 2FA
www.brunner-routledge.co.uk

Brunner-Routledge is an imprint of the Taylor & Francis Group.
Printed in the United States of America on acid-free paper.

10 9 8 7 6 5 4 3 2 1

Library of Congress Cataloging-in-Publication Data

Brown, Nina W.
    Psychoeducational groups : process and practice / Nina W. Brown.— 2nd ed.
        p. cm.
    Includes bibliographical references and index.
    ISBN 0-415-94602-6 (pbk. : alk. paper)
    1. Mental health counseling. 2. Group counseling. 3. Small groups.
    4. Life skills—Study and teaching. I. Title.

    RC466.B76 2003
    362.2'04256—dc21

                                                            2003009519

*This book is dedicated to my colleagues and friends from the Mid-Atlantic Group Psychotherapy Society: Beryce Maclennan, Barry Bukatman (deceased), George Saiger, and Mary Dluhy.*

# Contents

| | | |
|---|---|---|
| Dedication | | v |
| Preface | | ix |
| Acknowledgments | | xi |
| 1 | Psychoeducational Groups: An Overview | 1 |
| 2 | Group Leader Self-Factors, Competencies, and Skills | 25 |
| 3 | Group Leadership and Instructional Style | 47 |
| 4 | The Group: Process and Progress | 69 |
| 5 | Planning the Psychoeducational Group | 87 |
| 6 | Evaluating Psychoeducational Groups | 107 |
| 7 | Membership Problems, Concerns, and Skills | 119 |
| 8 | Managing Conflict and Guidelines for Confrontation | 139 |
| 9 | Leading Psychoeducational Groups for Children | 153 |
| 10 | Leading Psychoeducational Groups for Adolescents | 177 |
| 11 | Leading Psychoeducational Groups for Adults | 195 |
| 12 | Psychoeducational Support Groups | 221 |
| 13 | Therapy-Related Psychoeducational Groups | 239 |
| References | | 253 |
| Index | | 261 |

# Preface

Psychoeducational group leadership has not received the attention it needs to effectively prepare group leaders. Indeed, many practicing leaders have not had any formal training in group work, nor specific instruction for leading these groups. This book is intended to present some of the basic information about groups, and their leaders to help educate and guide you in understanding the structure, needs, dynamics, and specific techniques for leading these groups.

However, no one book can offer all the needed background information you will need, and was written with the assumption that you would have some needed formal instruction in the selected area, and basic communication and relating skills. Suggested areas include human growth and development, tests and other appraisal procedures, diversity and cultural issues, and an understanding of how to critically review the literature. This information is central to a deep understanding of the group, its members, and how to facilitate progress for both.

Another important point is that a psychoeducational group is not a collection of activities. I've noticed group leaders focus on forms, exercises, and games, and who seem to have a goal that members complete these without highlighting and enhancing members' personal learning. In other words, the leader has decided what is best for group members, is intent on accomplishing the leader's goals, and not attending to the members' goals. Some activities can be helpful at times, and information is presented in this book to guide you in selecting and effectively using them to help members achieve their goals.

Your personal development is also necessary as your self is one of the most important pieces you bring to leading psychoeducational groups. This is why there are personal development exercises included in the first eight chapters. I encourage you to use these to become more aware of your self, and to seek out other avenues for personal growth and development. This will make you more aware and sensitive to group members, reduce the potential for negative countertranference, provide you with confidence, and guide you to understand what to do and say in the group.

Leading any group can produce considerable anxiety for the leader, but your knowledge, understanding, and skills can help you contain and manage your anxiety. That is the greater part of what this book is intended to do, that is to give you leader enhancing information, as well as a deep understanding that will guide and support you when you facilitate any kind of psychoeducational group.

# Acknowledgments

Much of what I know about groups is due to the teaching and guidance of Fred Adair, my doctoral advisor and dissertation chair; the conferences and clinicians for the Mid-Atlantic Group Psychotherapy Society and the American Group Psychotherapy Association; and students in my classes throughout the years. Thanks to all of you. Special thanks to Charlie Fawcett and Nial Quillan who helped with the literature search.

# Chapter 1

# Psychoeducational Groups:
## *An Overview*

Major Topics and Concepts

*Knowledge Factor*
>  Knowledge, Art, Science, Skills, and Techniques Model (KASST)
>  Definition, classification, and categorization for psychoeducational groups
>  Major ethical issues
>  Culturally sensitive group leaders

*Art Factor*
>  A guide to completing personal development exercises

## INTRODUCTION

Creating and leading psychoeducational groups demands a considerable amount of expertise and knowledge. A variety of groups fall into the category of psycho-educational, the conditions addressed are vast and emotionally sensitive, and there is a wide range of intended audiences. The leader of these groups has to be extensively prepared with information, skills, and a deep understanding of the group topics and the intended audience. Leaders are not just presenters of information. They are also facilitators who are responsible for the following:

- Guiding participants' personal learning
- Showing group members how to interact to reduce isolation and to help each other
- Providing opportunities for emotional expression in a safe place

- Capitalizing on and fostering development of hope
- Directing and implementing learning for members
- Implementing strategies to promote members' self-understanding
- Creating opportunities to practice new learning

The extensiveness of what needs to be learned, practiced, and understood in order to lead effective psychoeducational groups was the groundwork for the development of the KASST Model. This model is related to much of the material presented in this book and is intended to guide your learning. Each chapter presents information on one or more components. For example, Chapter 2 discusses leaders' skills and some art factors. Use the model as a guide for gathering knowledge, learning skills and techniques, and understanding the group.

## KASST MODEL

This book is organized around the Knowledge, Art, Science, Skills, and Techniques Model (KASST). The categories in the model are blended when facilitating a psychoeducational group but are presented here as separate descriptions. Each is important in a different way and can help guide you in your development as a group leader. It can be difficult to recall and use all the information during the group session, but that expertise can be developed with practice so that it is implemented naturally. Your group members will greatly benefit from your careful leadership preparation.

All the chapters in the book address one or more components of the model. A brief overview of each component describes its essential importance (Table 1.1).

## KNOWLEDGE

Group leaders need a body of knowledge about groups, topics or conditions that are the focus for the group, and how to teach and facilitate the group. All this information is important, but this book focuses on knowledge about group development, helpful group factors, methods and principles of instruction, and other information about the group itself.

One major assumption that underlies much of the information presented in this book is that the group is an entity just as each member is an entity. It is essential for the group leader to also understand the group as a whole. Chapters 2, 3, and 4 present much of this information.

## KASST MODEL FOR PSYCHOEDUCATIONAL GROUP LEADER COMPETENCIES

| KNOWLEDGE | ART | SCIENCE | SKILLS | TECHNIQUES |
|---|---|---|---|---|
| Group dynamics | Core self | Planning | Facilitating | Exercises |
| Stages of development | Feelings | Task needs | Teaching | Role-play |
| Therapeutic factors | Empathy | Directing | Modeling | Discussion |
| Process | Ego strength | Evaluation | Conflict resolution | Lecture |
| Ethics | Cultural sensitivity | Literature review | Anxiety management | Media |
| Instructional principles | Inner experiencing | Target audience | Process commentary | Activities |
| Condition or topic | | | | |

BLENDED

Develops feelings of safety and trust among group members

Capitalizes on process

Helps to decide when and how to intervene

Guides members to self-understanding

Allows the leader to hold and contain affect for members

Assists in providing constructive feedback

Fosters attending to both task and relationship needs

Increases the leader's recognition of transference and countertransference

Empowers members to aid in dissolving resistance

Enhances the leader's awareness of individual members,
the group as a whole, and personal inner experiencing

Maximizes learning and retention

TABLE 1.1

## Art

The art of group leadership relies on the inner experiencing, self-awareness, and extent of personal development of the group leader. It is your essential self that conveys to members your warmth, caring, genuineness, tolerance, and respect. Words are not enough, because members can sense the real you behind the words. They may not be able to articulate what they sense, but they will act it out in many ways.

The extent of your personal development is crucial for cultural sensitivity, constructive use of your countertransference, and the reduction of its unconscious negative impact. Your unresolved family of origin issues and unfinished business can play major roles in your group leadership style and ability, and you are encouraged to be self-reflective, increase your self-awareness, and continue to work on your unfinished business and other issues. The personal development exercises in every chapter and some information in chapters 2 and 3 are related to the art component in the model.

## Science

The framework and support for successful psychoeducational groups are found in the science component. This component, more than any other, is specific, objective, and logical. Guidelines for planning, organizing, directing, structuring, and evaluating are presented in Chapters 5, 6, 7, and 8.

These tasks are essential for optimal functioning of the group and attend to many members' needs. This is especially important, as there is a considerable instructional part to psychoeducational groups. The teaching-learning task should not be minimized, as it is one of the distinguishing features for these groups. You will learn to be both a teacher and a group facilitator.

## Skills

Teaching and facilitating skills are both important but should not be emphasized over any of the other components. There may be a tendency to focus more on skills, since these can be taught and practiced more easily than can some other more complex components, such as process commentary or group dynamics. Skills are helpful but are not a substitute for knowledge, understanding, and the essential self of the group leader.

Further, since the focus for this book is on groups, it is assumed that you have already received some preparation in basic interviewing, communicating, and counseling skills. The information presented here is intended to enhance your existing knowledge and to expand your knowledge of some group facilitation skills. Chapters 2 and 7 through 13 address the skills component.

## Techniques

Techniques are specific strategies used for teaching and facilitating groups. Activities such as games, exercises, and role-play; teaching approaches such as lectures, discussions, and media; and facilitating procedures such as conflict resolution and what to do about problem behaviors are examples of techniques. These are described in some detail to help you understand their strengths, limitations, and use.

Techniques are a vital part of psychoeducational groups and can help in learning and retention. Some techniques are designed to promote active involvement of participants as an aid to their learning. Other techniques are used to maximize information presentation and to assist in understanding the material. Still other techniques can help personalize learning for each participant and show individualized applications.

The major constraint for techniques can be an overreliance on them. Overusing techniques can give an illusion that you, as the group leader, are promoting learning when you are actually using activity to substitute for reflection, integration of information with personal material, and a deeper understanding of personal issues and relationships. Activity for the sake of doing something so that the leader can feel useful and less anxious is not an adequate reason to use techniques. The material presented here emphasizes thoughtful and judicious use of techniques.

## PSYCHOEDUCATIONAL GROUPS DEFINED

There are a variety of groups conducted every day for many different audiences. Many are counseling or therapy groups, but most fall into the psychoeducational group category. Psychoeducational groups usually are defined as groups where the primary focus is education about a psychological concept or topic (Gladding, 1995).

The term *psychoeducational group* is used in this book to include a broad spectrum of groups that have a significant educational component in addition to the psychological component. Such groups are used with children, adolescents, and adults in all kinds of settings, including hospitals, businesses, universities, governmental and social service agencies, and the military. They may consist of one session or many sessions.

The definition of psychoeducational groups adopted by the Association for Specialists in Group Work (ASGW, 1991) addresses the importance of educational and prevention goals in such groups. These groups serve to educate those facing a potential threat or a developmental life event (e.g., retirement), or to teach coping skills to those dealing with an immediate life crisis. ASGW defined the goal for such groups as "preventing an array of educational and psychological disturbance from occurring" (Gladding, 1995, p. 436).

This book focuses on the theory and practice of psychoeducational groups and starts with the assumption that these groups are provided for all ages and educational levels in practically every setting. Another basic assumption is that the groups emphasize education or learning rather than self-awareness and self-understanding. The cognitive component takes precedence over the affective component; indeed, for some groups the affective component may be completely absent.

Psychoeducational groups are a hybrid of an academic class and a counseling group, and have many characteristics of each. They are like classes in which there are numerous participants, principles of instruction are applied, the presented material is intended to be learned and retained, and the leader is the expert/instructor. Classes and psychoeducational groups tend to emphasize cognition first and feelings or actions second.

These groups are similar to counseling groups in that member interactions are important, attention is given to group dynamics and group process, skills such as communication and relational skills can be topics or the focus, and the leader is a facilitator at times. There are other points where the two types of groups converge, but there are some major points. Psychoeducational groups can be easier to plan and lead, as there is less ambiguity and uncertainty about the material to be covered, expected learning outcomes, sequencing of material, and members' information needs. In contrast, counseling groups have more ambiguity, emphasize emotions, and learning outcomes are individualistic, not for the group as a whole.

## PSYCHOEDUCATIONAL GROUPS IN THERAPY

Psychoeducational groups are primarily educational and emphasize skills training. However, they also can contribute significantly to group counseling/therapy and to group psychotherapy, as demonstrated by the following studies: In a meta-analysis of 191 studies, Devine (1992) confirmed the efficacy of psychoeducational care for adult surgical patients. La Salivia (1993) proposed enhancing addiction treatment through psychoeducational groups. Gamble, Elder, and Lashley (1989) reviewed studies on the use of psychoeducational groups in the treatment of eating disorders, depression, and alcohol abuse. Although the studies lacked adequate control groups, the treatments were found to be effective. Forester, Cornfield, Fleiss, and Thomas (1993) used a psychoeducational component in their group work with cancer patients, as did Fawzy and Fawzy (1994) and Fawzy, Fawzy, Aront, and Pasnau (1995).

Psychoeducational groups also can be used in pregroup preparation sessions, in which prospective group members are taught what to expect in therapy and how to be effective group members. Yalom (1995) reviewed research on the efficacy of pregroup preparation and found that prepared members exhibited less anxiety, participated more, had lower dropout rates, showed an improved ability to communicate, expressed more emotions, and had better attendance rates.

These are but a few examples showing the usefulness of psychoeducational groups in therapy. While such groups are not considered to *be* therapy, they do have therapeutic usefulness. Chapter 13 presents information on therapy-related psychoeducational groups.

## CONCEPTUALIZATION OF PSYCHOEDUCATIONAL GROUPS

The Association for Specialists in Group Work (ASGW), a division of the American Counseling Association, has developed separate lists of skills and knowledge for leaders of task and work groups, psychoeducational groups, counseling groups, and psychotherapy groups. In addition, ASGW (1991) has developed basic guidelines for core group work training in specialty areas. The association's definitions for psychoeducational groups and for task and work groups have been combined in this book under the umbrella of psychoeducational groups. Support and therapy-related groups are included as well, as many of these have strong, significant educational components.

Before discussing the knowledge and competencies needed to conduct psychoeducational groups, it is helpful to distinguish between psychoeducational groups and counseling/therapy groups. Table 1.2 presents an overview of major differences between the two group types.

TABLE 1.2

Comparison of Psychoeducational and Counseling/Therapy Groups

| Psychoeducational Groups | Counseling/Therapy Groups |
| --- | --- |
| Emphasize didactic and instruction | Emphasize experiential and feelings |
| Use planned, structured activities | Little use of planned, structured activities |
| Goals usually defined by leader | Goals defined by group members |
| Leader operates as facilitator, teacher | Leader guides, intervenes, protects |
| Focus on prevention | Focus on self-awareness, remediation |
| No screening of members | Screening and orientation to group expected prior to beginning group |
| Cannot set limits on number in group | Can set limits on number in group |
| Group can be very large (e.g., 50) | Usually limited to 5 to 10 members |
| Self-disclosure accepted but not mandated | Self-disclosure expected |
| Privacy and confidentiality not primary concerns or emphasis | Privacy and confidentiality critical, basic elements |
| Sessions may be limited to one | Usually consists of several sessions |
| Task functions emphasized | Maintenance functions emphasized over task |

## DIFFERENT PSYCHOEDUCATIONAL GROUPS

Psychoeducational groups range from discussion groups to self-help groups. Sessions may be held in organizations, businesses, churches, schools, detention homes, jails, colleges and universities, community centers, governmental agencies, or even private homes. These groups cover all ages, from children through the elderly, and they may be preventive or remedial in focus. Leaders of psychoeducational groups should have basic preparation to lead a variety of groups for different age levels in practically any setting. A process for extending knowledge and learning new skills is discussed in Chapter 2.

*Educational/task groups* are formed around a common purpose, usually a task to be achieved. The emphasis is on increasing members' knowledge about a particular topic or subject, and the group includes considerable discussion of opinions and ideas. Examples of groups in this category are discussion groups, study groups, task forces, volunteer groups, civic organizations, and committees. Most of these groups have designated or elected leaders. Leaders who have an understanding of group dynamics and leadership skills can help educational/task groups conduct their business more effectively and efficiently.

*Educational/guidance groups* focus on providing information to help participants cope with a crisis, developmental issues, or prevention of problems. Dissemination of information is important for these groups, and the information usually is focused on a particular topic, such as job search skills. Examples of groups in this category are career education groups and groups focused on alcohol education or learning about an illness, such as cancer, choosing a college major, or developing study skills. Leaders must have teaching skills in addition to understanding group dynamics and group leadership skills.

Psychoeducational groups whose primary focus is teaching cognitive-related material are classified as *educational groups*. Some examples are discussion, study skills, career education, alcohol and drug education, and parent education groups. In a sense, these groups are classes. They differ from classes in that the goals and objectives are more limited, the time frame is more flexible, no tests or other evaluations of learning are expected, and participants usually are free to exit.

Educational groups are some of the most structured of the groups discussed in this book, in the sense that the goals and objectives are predetermined and the materials and strategies are preselected by the leader. Participants have little or no agenda input, although the leader may decide on adjustments to meet participants' needs. Further, these groups are seldom limited to one session. Each session should be self-contained, however, so that participants can take increased or new knowledge with them. Even parent education groups address a specific topic at each meeting. Having self-contained topics means it is not necessary to know one topic before learning another. The topics are not hierarchical, but they may be sequential for other reasons, such as increasing sensitivity.

*Training/work groups* are initiated to meet work expectations or demands. They usually provide information on work processes, structuring for team development, or how a job or task can be performed more efficiently. Often these groups are formed around a perceived need identified by the employer. Such groups might focus on time management, team building, specific skills such as computer networking, or other task-related activities. Leaders have a significant teaching role for all of these groups and a strong facilitative role for some, such as team building.

Work-related psychoeducational groups may be called professional development workshops or seminars, managerial training, or organizational development training. These groups are intended to help workers at all levels learn new skills or processes that will increase productivity. The primary focus usually is on workers learning better ways to perform their jobs more effectively and efficiently.

Work-related psychoeducational groups typically are designed for adults. Some focus on teaching adolescents work-related skills, but these are more often found in schools or other training facilities, such as group homes and vocational schools.

*Training/relations* groups may stand alone, or bridge training/work groups or training/social skills groups, as these groups can have subject matter germane to all three. An example of common subject matter is communication skills. Both communication and interpersonal relations play parts in training/relations groups. The leader teaches new ways of communicating and relating. These groups may focus on parenting, communication skills, interpersonal relations, work relationships, getting along with supervisors, changing personal relationships, divorce, and so on. There is a significant information dissemination component and a significant personal issues component. The leader needs to have knowledge and expertise to balance both.

*Training/social skills groups* focus on developing social skills and can be either preventive or remedial. Most are formed in response to observed detrimental behaviors, such as violence. These groups tend to have both education and personal issues components and rely in part on experiential activities, such as practicing new behaviors. They may focus on conflict mediation, anger management, social skills development, and so on. Leaders need expertise in setting up and conducting experiences (e.g., role-play) and in presenting information and facilitating the group process.

Social or life skills smooth and enhance our interactions with others. They range from basic communication skills to complex ones, such as developing and maintaining relationships. Skills training groups teach people how to increase their effectiveness in relationships ranging from brief, impersonal interactions, such as buying an ice cream cone, to more complicated interactions, such as conflict management.

All of us learned what social skills we possess from direct and indirect teaching and modeling. Parents, other relatives, teachers, ministers, neighbors, and friends all participated in teaching us social or life skills. Some individuals, for one reason or another, do not receive adequate teaching or modeling early in life, and their daily functioning and interactions with others are impaired. This impairment promotes feelings of alienation and isolation, leading to a poor quality of life. Skills training usually involves a small group (5 to 10 members) that meets for several sessions over time.

## BASIC CHARACTERISTICS OF PSYCHOEDUCATIONAL GROUPS

Groups can be classified by their primary purpose: education, skills training, or self-understanding/self-knowledge. There will be considerable overlap of purposes for some groups (e.g., communication skills), but it is helpful for the leader to remember the primary purpose for the group so that the focus can be maintained.

Education, as a primary purpose, refers to learning new material via the *cognitive* mode, through lecture, discussion, and observation/participation. Dissemination of new material is the focus, with the leader doing much of the presenting. New ideas, concepts, and facts form much of the content for education-focused groups.

Skills training groups have a strong *experiential* component. Participants are expected to practice the emphasized skills. The group leader is expected to model the desired skills and to structure experiences to help participants practice them. Feedback on progress is another important component of these groups.

Groups focused primarily on *self-understanding/self-knowledge* begin to overlap with counseling/therapy groups. However, these purposes are considered somewhat differently for psychoeducational groups. The gained understanding and knowledge are on a more superficial level, self-disclosure is not a requisite, resistances are not identified or worked through, and past relationships are not explored. The gained understanding and knowledge are expected to reassure the members, to give feedback on the impact of their behaviors on others, or to build self-confidence.

### Group Structure

The variety of psychoeducational groups also leads to very different structures for various groups. Structure includes the following:

• Size
• Management of content
• Length and duration of the group
• Leader responsibilities
• Severity of the problem
• Competence of the leader

## Group Size

Psychoeducational groups range in size from 5 to 50 or even 100 members. Some workshops and seminars that fall into the category of psychoeducational groups can have 50 or more participants. These larger groups are included because most of the characteristics of psychoeducational groups apply (e.g., goals, content, and expected outcomes). Counseling/therapy groups usually are limited to 5 to 10 members, even when there is a coleader. Groups with fewer than 5 members will find it difficult to develop a sense of cohesion.

## Management of Content

All groups have some content. How that content is managed refers to the mode of presentation, the initiator, and processing. Modes of presentation can include lectures, role-play, and demonstrations.

Leaders of all kinds of groups have responsibility for preplanning. In psychoeducational groups, the leader may solicit input from others for setting goals and structuring activities. Initiators of topics, concepts, skills, or process may be leaders. Individual members, supervisors, or the group as a whole may have a leadership role. Processing and reflection are the depth and extent to which emerged material is talked about in the group.

## Group Length and Duration

The length and duration of psychoeducational groups can vary widely, from one session lasting 1 to 2 hours to long-term, ongoing groups, such as self-help or support groups. Generally, education-focused groups have fewer sessions than skills training or self-help groups. However, psychoeducational groups are characterized by the brevity of their sessions: most employ short sessions over a brief time period.

## Group Leader Responsibilities

Leaders of psychoeducational groups have the primary responsibility for determining goals and objectives, forming the group, selecting activities, and monitoring the functioning of the group. There is some variation of leader responsibilities among the different types of groups, and group leaders may engage outside experts to help set group goals and select activities—for example, supervisors may help with team-building groups, probation officers with anger management groups, and counselors with career education groups. These experts may make suggestions or identify needs for participants.

Members seldom participate in goal setting for psychoeducational groups as leaders rarely have the luxury of a pregroup interview session. This is unfortunate, since members are more likely to be willing to work on personally relevant goals. The group leader is put in the position of trying to guess what will be personally relevant for prospective group members.

*Severity of the Problem*

Not all psychoeducational groups are problem focused the way counseling and therapy groups are. Although some counseling groups are seen as prevention groups, the idea that there is a potential problem helps give these groups a problem focus. Although some psychoeducational groups do have a problem focus, such as anger management, many others do not. For purposes of classification, problems also will encompass topics and concerns. Severity includes impact on relationships and functioning, with considerable impact referring to an unaddressed problem or concern. Groups that have prevention as a focus will be classified as moderate to slight, because some members in these groups may have already experienced a negative impact on relationships and functioning.

*Competency of the Group Leader*

The competency of the group leader is determined by many factors, including the following:

- Knowledge of group dynamics
- Basic counseling, communication, and group leadership skills
- Knowledge of human growth and development issues
- Specialized knowledge and skills—for example, in substance abuse, career development, or characterological disorders
- Training
- Supervised clinical and/or field experiences

Leaders of psychoeducational groups need the same knowledge base and many of the same skills as leaders of counseling and therapy groups. However, they use these skills in somewhat different ways.

Leaders of psychoeducational groups use their knowledge and skills to understand participants and their needs, whereas leaders of counseling/therapy groups build on their understanding for interventions, facilitation, and resolution of personal concerns, problems, and issues. Further, leaders of counseling/therapy groups need more extensive preparation than leaders of psychoeducational groups.

## ANOTHER GROUP CLASSIFICATION

Groups can also be classified by their level of need for intervention, facilitation, or resolution of personal problems and issues. Prevention assumes that there has not been a manifestation of behavior that is cause for concern, but there is a need for expanded knowledge. The justification for prevention is that developmental issues are likely to arise, and these issues can be dealt with more easily if the individual knows what to expect and what processes to use. Prevention-focused groups are useful in such areas as learning to use time wisely, selecting a career, and learning parenting skills.

Remediation assumes there is a deficit. Deficits usually result in negative relational, self-satisfaction, self-efficacy, and self-confidence outcomes due to ineffective behaviors, attitudes, or skills. Once the deficit has been identified, specific remedial procedures are implemented. Examples of remedial groups are self-help groups, anger management groups, and groups focused on building self-esteem.

Personal issues involvement (PII) for psychoeducational groups ranges from low or slight to high or intense. Groups are classified by the extent of need (see Table 1.3)—for example, little personal issues involvement is needed to be a member of a discussion or time management group; more involvement of personal issues is needed to be a member of a self-help or anger management group.

The level and extent of expected self-disclosure rise with the level and intensity of PII. Participants are encouraged to engage in appropriate self-disclosure in all groups. However, self-disclosure is more intense in counseling/therapy groups than in psychoeducational groups. When there is expected self-disclosure along with PII, the leader needs more expertise in order to use the information effectively, link it to the group process, and protect and support the group member.

## CATEGORIES OF PSYCHOEDUCATIONAL GROUPS

Psychoeducational groups can be categorized in several different ways: structural versus unstructured, personal versus abstract, developmental versus remedial, and open versus closed. All of these polarities can be combined to form even more categories. Categories fall along a continuum, and some types of groups can bridge categories.

TABLE 1.3

Classification by Extent of Personal Issues Involvement

| Personal | Combination | Abstract |
|---|---|---|
| Support groups | Guidance groups | Discussion groups |
| Social skills training | Conflict mediation | Seminars |
| Communication | Training groups | Staff development |
| Relationship training | Committees | In-service |

## Structured Versus Unstructured

All groups require planning if they are to run smoothly and accomplish members' objectives, but some are more structured than others. In *structured groups* the leader selects the activities, each activity has a particular goal, and the activities are primarily paper-and-pencil tasks designed to facilitate discussion. Group members have little or no involvement in selecting objectives and tasks.

*Unstructured groups* are at the other extreme. The leader (if there is one) does minimal structuring—just enough to ensure that the group gets off the ground and that members' objectives are addressed. Group members make most decisions about what they will do. Few, if any, paper-and-pencil activities are used. Self-help groups are good examples of unstructured groups. Table 1.4 lists psychoeducational groups by their degree of structure.

## Personal Versus Abstract

*Personal groups* deal with issues of self-awareness and with the individual's issues or concerns. Self-disclosure is expected and encouraged. While a personal focus may be more closely associated with counseling/therapy groups, psychoeducational groups such as support groups and social skills training groups also have significant levels of personal involvement. In fact, leaders of all groups have to be prepared to deal with personal issues.

*Abstract groups* deal with topics that may hold personal interest for participants, but they do not ask for the same level of self-disclosure or self-involvement. Abstractness suggests an emotional distancing. The topics can be talked about with only mild emotional involvement or with none. Discussion groups, training groups (e.g., team building), and other educational groups cluster toward the abstract.

## Developmental Versus Remedial

*Developmental groups* build on members' strengths, whereas *remedial groups* focus on overcoming weaknesses or deficits. Developmental groups are more

TABLE 1.4

Classification on a Continuum of Structure

| Structured | Elements of Both | Unstructured |
|---|---|---|
| Training groups | Guidance groups | Support groups |
| Staff development | Discussion groups | |
| Team development | Social skills training | |
| Seminars | Conflict mediation | |
| | Communication/relationship training groups | |
| | Committees | |
| | In-service | |

preventive in nature but are not limited to prevention. Capitalizing on existing strengths is much easier than remediating deficiencies.

A unique problem for the leader of a remediation group is that many of the participants are there involuntarily. Some members even deny having deficiencies and resent having to attend the group. Examples of remediation groups are social skills training and conflict mediation groups. These same types of groups can be developmental if the participants are voluntary attendees and have not evidenced deficiencies in the areas, for example, by fighting.

## Open Versus Closed

*Open groups* usually meet over an extended length of time with changing membership—that is, some members leave and new ones are admitted. *Closed groups* also can meet over extended times, but as members leave, no new ones are admitted. Groups that are short term usually are closed. Although there may be no prohibition against admission of new members, it is rare that new ones attend.

Support groups, skills training groups, and discussion groups are examples of open groups. With open membership, the group is constantly renewing itself, or, in some instances, remaining in or reverting back to the initial stage with the introduction of new members. A prime challenge facing the leader of an open group is making new members feel welcome, as the new member is faced with the task of fitting into an already existing group. Table 1.5 presents categorization by open or closed membership.

## ETHICAL ISSUES

Leaders of psychoeducational groups should follow the same ethical guidelines as leaders of counseling and therapy groups. Although not all of the guidelines

TABLE 1.5

Classification by Degree of Open Structure

| Open | | Closed |
|---|---|---|
| ◀————————————————————————▶ | | |
| Support groups | Social skills training | Seminars |
| Committees | Communication | Training group |
| Discussion | Relationship training | Guidance groups |
| | Conflict mediation | |
| | Team building | |
| | Staff development | |

are applicable to psychoeducational groups (e.g., screening), most have relevance. I encourage you to study the Association for Specialists in Group Work (ASGW, 1990) guidelines and to incorporate them as part of your practice in group work. There are 16 categories for ethical guidelines in psychoeducational groups:

1. Orientation and providing information
2. Screening
3. Confidentiality
4. Voluntary/involuntary participation
5. Leaving the group
6. Coercion and pressure
7. Imposing counselor values
8. Equitable treatment
9. Dual relationships
10. Use of techniques
11. Goal development
12. Consultation
13. Termination from the group
14. Evaluation and follow-up
15. Referrals
16. Professional development

*Orientation.* Group members should be adequately prepared to participate fully in the group experience. You can reduce much of the confusion and ambiguity that exists for all beginning groups by providing as much information about the experience as possible prior to beginning the group. Group members should know what to expect so that they can make informed decisions about participation. Guidelines are presented in the section on "Planning" in Chapter 5.

*Screening.* Screening group members to determine their suitability for the proposed group has limited application for psychoeducational groups. Groups that emphasize development, social skills, life skills, or those that involve personal issues may benefit from screening members. However, groups for team building, time management, and other training functions probably will not derive much benefit from screening, nor will the leader be in a position to determine group membership. It is possible to screen via a written questionnaire, but if you do not have the authority to exclude members, the questionnaire serves no useful purpose.

*Confidentiality.* As an ethical issue, confidentiality has many of the same constraints as screening. Psychoeducational groups usually do not deal with matters that demand confidentiality. Some groups do deal with personal issues, however, and the group leader should emphasize confidentiality. You can approach the issue by assuring members that discussion of content outside the group is acceptable, but identification of members and their issues is not. Confidentiality is more of a concern for group counseling/therapy than for psychoeducational groups.

*Participation.* Voluntary/involuntary participation is a complex issue. What constitutes voluntary participation? For example, students preparing for a degree in counseling are expected to participate in a growth group. Is this voluntary or involuntary? Because this is a complex ethical issue, it is addressed more fully in the section on "Ethical Guidelines for Involuntary Participants" in Chapter 7.

*Leaving the group.* As a group leader, you must sometimes provide the opportunity for a member to leave the group in a constructive way that takes into account the feelings of that member and the feelings of the members who remain. It is assumed that members have the right to leave a group, although there may be consequences for doing so. This ethical issue may apply more to counseling/therapy groups, but it has implications for any group that meets over time. Leaders of psychoeducational groups should be prepared to cope with premature termination for a variety of reasons. Although it may not be as much of an issue for these groups, leaving still has an impact on group members.

*Coercion and pressure.* Leaders have the moral, legal, and ethical responsibility to protect members from "physical threats, intimidation, coercion, and undue peer pressure" (ASGW, 1991). Although such acts may be more intense and dangerous in counseling/therapy groups, the potential for harm is present in psychoeducational groups. Presenting clear guidelines for expected group member behavior, blocking inappropriate behaviors, and assessing the effects of exercises and activities will help you meet this guideline.

*Imposing counselor values.* Knowing your values, attitudes, and beliefs allows you to understand the potential impact they may have on others. It is acceptable for a leader to appropriately disclose his or her values, attitudes, and beliefs; it is not acceptable for the leader to insist that group members follow them. Although psychoeducational groups are more task focused, values play an important role in many aspects of the group. Therefore, it is important for you to be aware of your personal values and to be careful not to impose them on the group.

*Equitable treatment.* It is important to recognize and respect the differences of all group members. Differences such as gender, religion, race/ethnicity, lifestyle, age, and disability are important. The group leader should know enough about cultural and diversity issues to be sensitive to these differences and to ensure that members are not discriminated against because of them.

*Dual relationships.* The issue of dual relationships is a troubling and complex one. Some dual relationships are easy to identify—for example, sexual, supervisory, and family. Others are not so easy to define—for example, student–teacher and social contact. The leader of a psychoeducational group may also be in a work relationship with one or more participants in the group. Does this constitute a dual relationship? There is no easy answer. It depends on whether there is the potential for the leader's objectivity and professional judgment to be negatively affected or for it to have a negative impact on a group member. Leaders of psychoeducational groups should give careful consideration to the issue of dual relationships and do everything in their power to ensure that these do not impact the functioning of the group, or the progress of individual members.

*Use of techniques.* Group leaders should not use techniques for which they have not received training. It may be tempting to try new techniques, but doing so may imperil group members in ways that the leader did not anticipate. This ethical guideline is somewhat tempered for psychoeducational groups when you are using structured exercises that are new but similar to those for which you were trained. Techniques usually refer to a category (e.g., gestalt games, imagery), not to a variation. The primary concern is that group members not be put in situations that are dangerous for them.

*Developing goals.* More learning and greater satisfaction occur when goals for the group are consistent with individual members' goals. Leaders of psychoeducational groups generally set the goals, sometimes in collaboration with the organization for which the group is being conducted (e.g., team building), and there are occasions when goals are set in consultation with group members. Most often, however, it is up to the leader to set the goals.

This ethical issue appears to be more relevant when groups are small, personal issues are the focus, and there will be more than one session. However, leaders of all psychoeducational groups should be aware that the group is enhanced when members help set the goals and that goals are more likely to be achieved if members have vested interests. Even when you must set the goals yourself, it may be useful to review them at the beginning of the group, telling members that the goals can be changed if they feel the goals are not meeting their needs or expectations. If you have adequately researched the subject and know relevant information about the participants, probably only a few changes will be recommended.

*Consultation.* The ethical issue of consultation applies when the leader is in training, there is more than one session, and personal issues are the focus of the group. Consultation refers to the leader receiving supervision, establishing rules for between-session meetings with members, limiting what the leader can discuss with others (e.g., case management), and having a dual role—that is, responsibility to the members and responsibility to the agency (e.g., a probation office). However, members need to know in advance what content will be discussed or shared with others who are in authority or outside the group. That way, members can be more self-governing.

*Terminating a member.* There are times when a member must be terminated from the group for his or her own good or for the good of the group. Disruptive members, those who have overwhelming personal or emotional disturbances that impede their participation, and violent or abusive members are some examples. Leaders of psychoeducational groups are unlikely to run into this situation often. If, for some reason, a member does have to be terminated, you must arrange for a constructive termination that takes into account the needs of the member being terminated and those of remaining members. You may need to bring in a consultant to aid in the process, especially if you are not experienced in this situation.

*Evaluation and follow-up.* Provisions for evaluating the group should be made during the planning period. It is useful if the evaluation is in written form, although oral feedback also can be solicited. If the group is an open-ended one, you can use formative evaluation to help make adjustments to the process. There may also be opportunities to have follow-up evaluation. Usually, the return rate for evaluation forms in psychoeducational groups is poor. Once participants have returned home, other activities take priority and the evaluation does not get completed. You should complete some form of evaluation, but follow-up may not be possible or necessary.

*Referrals.* Referrals can help participants, and leaders should have some knowledge of community resources, especially those relating to topics being presented in the group. If you are unfamiliar with the community or resources available, you should refer members to an individual who does have that knowledge.

*Professional development.* Professional development is expected for group leaders. While the leader may be an expert in the topic, there is always more information, new techniques, and more understanding of group dynamics to be learned. It is important for group leaders to continue to prepare themselves to conduct groups, and this can occur through classes, seminars, workshops, conferences, and home study. The primary responsibility for continued professional development lies with the leader.

## CULTURALLY SENSITIVE GROUP LEADERS

Every group has diversity, even those that appear to be homogeneous. After all, the members are only homogeneous around one or two characteristics, such as gender, age, or race. When trying to understand and accommodate group members who are multicultural, ethnocultural, transcultural, or minorities in the group, the tendency seems to be to consider them as "different"— different in the sense that they bring diversity to the group. What is not often consciously considered is the degree and extent of diversity present in every group.

Effective group leaders will have education, training, and an understanding of diversity, including racial and ethnic diversity. However, this will not be the full extent of their knowledge. They will also know and understand the need to be culturally sensitive; their personal issues around racial, ethnic, and cultural diversity; and strategies for inclusion for diverse members.

Before presenting that discussion, an example of what is meant by all groups having diversity around many different characteristics other than race and ethnic group may be helpful. Two student groups from my group counseling class are described.

The first group consisted of six females and one male. Two females were African-American, one female was Chinese (from Taiwan) and the other three females were white Americans. The lone male was black. Two of the white females were in their 30s and the other females were in their early to late 20s, one just having completed her undergraduate degree. The male was in his late 30s. On the surface there was considerable racial, gender, and age diversity. However, the difference that ended up playing the most significant part in the group involved religion. One of the African-American females was a very conservative born-again Christian, the Taiwan Chinese woman was a Seventh Day Adventist, another woman was a non-church-attending Catholic, and the male was antagonistic against all religions.

The second group was composed of seven females. Two were African-American, one was Hispanic, and four were white Americans. Most of the group members were in their mid- to late 20s, but one African-American woman was in her early 40s. Thus, there were three racial/ethnic groups in this one small group of graduate students and one minority member because of age, and all were U.S. citizens. Topics in the group that highlighted other kinds of diversity were religion and one member revealing that she was a lesbian.

Even though all these graduate students had many characteristics in common, they were more different than they were alike, especially in attitudes and perceptions—not just the more visible characteristics such as race and age. Some clashes arose because of cultural differences, but the deepest conflict emerged between the two African-American women in the first group, both of whom were around the same age, both Christians, and both with similar developmental experiences. Yet they were different in some meaningful ways that produced disagreement.

All this is to emphasize and highlight the need for all group leaders to realize the important role that diversity plays in the group. Sue and others (1999) describe the "changing complexion of society" (p. 1063), race, gender, and sexual orientation in support for developing multicultural psychology. They present arguments that a single focused multicultural course is insufficient for educating mental health professionals who will increasingly work with more diverse clients, and there is a need for more education, training, and personal work in preparation programs. Salvendy (1999) echoes this stance by pointing out that all mental health preparation programs need to "establish a much more comprehensive transcultural awareness" (p. 457).

Becoming culturally sensitive is both an intellectual and an emotional endeavor. Cultural sensitivity incorporates diversity (e.g., age and gender; race and ethnicity) and multicultural, intercultural (e.g., socioeconomic class), and other status variables. The group leader has to recognize that all these variables can be combined in an infinite number of ways and that it is risky to try categorizing group members on the basis of the seemingly dominant variable (e.g., race). For example, the two black women in the first example previously presented appear to be very similar. They are in the same age group and degree program, both are U.S. citizens, and they belong to the same race. Their major conflict was around religion, although both were of the Christian faith. Within the characteristic of religion, there is also considerable variety or diversity. Evaluating, judging, or responding on the basis of race alone for these two women would not be advisable. Race does not unite or divide them. Do not jump to conclusions on the basis of surface characteristics.

Cultural sensitivity means knowing some important information about the group members' use of language, customs, politics, history, gender roles, child-rearing practices, status and class, and so on. Even if all group members are native-born U.S. citizens, you can find considerable differences in their cultural experiences. However, all U.S. citizens also have numerous shared experiences—for example, schools, TV, and language (even if another language is spoken at home).

Cultural sensitivity also means suspending judgment, accepting and appreciating differences, understanding that being different does not mean being wrong, having firm clear boundaries, possessing ego strength, having carefully chosen values but not imposing those values on others, and developing an ability to accept and relate to individuals as they are. These are internal states, and group leaders have to stay in touch with their attitudes, beliefs, values, and feelings as well as continuing to work on their personal development. Group leaders who are culturally sensitive will consider their personal development to be very important and will do the following:

- Work to understand their biases and prejudices
- Understand their feelings and reactions to cultural differences
- Become aware of and question their cultural assumptions
- Explore the important components of different cultures
- Have a plan for learning about cultural differences and diversity

Personal issues play a vital role in cultural sensitivity for the group leader. Understanding one's personal issues and continuing to work on unfinished business is basic in the education and training of mental health professionals. Its importance for the group leader cannot be overestimated or overemphasized. Unresolved issues can significantly impact the therapeutic relationship, cause of therapy, and outcomes. Since most of this takes place on an unconscious level, there is no awareness of what is happening and no conscious intent. However, the absence of awareness and intent does not lessen the negative influences and impact, which can be considerable.

## GUIDE FOR COMPLETING THE PERSONAL
## DEVELOPMENT EXERCISES

Chapters 1 through 8 have personal development exercises that are designed for self-reflection and self-exploration. These exercises are not a substitute for personal work with a trained counselor/therapist. They are simply one way to begin to know and understand yourself better and to increase your awareness of your unresolved issues and unfinished business. It is important to remember that everyone has these issues, many are in your unconscious, they can impact your functioning as a group leader, and they have a powerful influence on your ability to form and maintain the needed relationship with group members. These are the major reasons for engaging in continual personal development.

Each exercise has a primary objective that sets the focus. Just examine whatever emerges. You are encouraged to personalize these exercises.

You can explore the personal material that emerges from an exercise by yourself or with someone else. You can write the answers to the reflection questions at the end of each exercise and any other thoughts, ideas, and feelings that come to mind. Or you can talk about these things with someone, such as with a class group supervised by the instructor, with a supervisor, or with a trained therapist.

### Personal Development Exercise: My Past

**Objectives:** Learn important facets of "self"; Try this exercise to help you understand some of your unfinished business or issues.

**Materials:** Sheet of paper 16 by 20 inches or larger, pencil, felt markers in a variety of colors or crayons, three sheets of writing paper.

**Procedure:** Sit at a table in silence where you will not be disturbed. If music will help you concentrate, play something quiet and soothing, not an energizing piece. Close your eyes if you want and let your thoughts go back over your life. You can begin with the present and reflect backward to your earliest memory, or begin with the earliest memory and move forward. Do not force memories; just let them emerge. If they are not in chronological order, do not try to put them in order at this time.

When you are ready, open your eyes and on a piece of paper list 10 or more events, changes, decisions, and so on, that have seemed important to you during your life. After listing these points, go back and write your age at the time of each event alongside each item. Try to become aware of the period of your life that is most featured on the list. For example, you may have more events between the ages of 10 and 13 than before or after those ages.

After noting your ages, place the large piece of paper in front of you. Use a pencil or felt marker to draw your lifeline beginning with birth and continuing to the present. The line may be curved, zigzag, spiral-like, with straight lines, or any shape that seems appropriate. Go back and record your list of events on the lifeline by drawing a picture that illustrates the event, drawing a symbol that describes it for you, or however you wish to record it.

On a separate sheet of paper, list the emotions aroused in you as you listed the events and drew the lifeline. Pay particular attention to any intense feelings you remember having at the time that were rearoused while recalling the event. Place a star by these feelings and on the list of events. Be sure to record your emotions that you experienced, or are experiencing as you read and record your lists.

**Processing:** The final step is to review all the lists and the drawing for your lifeline and to write on a separate piece of paper either a summary of what emerged for you, your thoughts and feelings, although they may not necessarily be in any order, or just your feelings tied to a particular event. As you end, complete this statement: "I still feel strongly about ____." Or, "I did not do or say what I wanted to when (name the event) happened." These events are some of your unfinished business that have an influence on you and your life today.

As you completed the exercise, you probably became aware of several pieces of unfinished business—for example, relationships that ended without you wanting them to end, people who may have moved or died before you got a chance to say all the things you wanted to say or to say goodbye, times people did or said things that hurt you, decisions you wished you had made but did not, relationships with friends or family that changed for the worst, satisfying achievements, and so on. You may also remember some events that changed your life or your perception of yourself—for example, parental divorce, emotional or physical abuse, the breakup of your family, illness of a sibling or family member that was life-threatening, your own illness, difficulties in school, and so on. Just as your life events have played a part in forming you as you are at present, so too have your clients' life events influenced their development. Understanding how you came to be gives you some basis for being more sensitive and understanding of how they came to be.

# Chapter 2

# Group Leader Self-Factors, Competencies, and Skills

Major Topics and Concepts

*Art Factors*
    Personal growth, countertransference, and self-absorption
    Basic leader characteristics

*Skills Factors*
    Group leadership skills
    Group level skills
    Developing skills
    Specific leader skills

## INTRODUCTION

Some group leader skills are relatively easy to learn, such as attending. Others can be learned with practice and feedback, such as active listening and responding. However, none are effective without the art factors for group leadership, and these cannot be taught; they have to be developed by each person individually. For example, you can be taught the nonverbal behaviors that portray warmth and caring, but you cannot be taught to be warm and caring, since these traits come from your inner self. The skills are important, but the self-development is also important, regardless of the kinds of groups you lead or your theoretical orientation.

This chapter presents the rationale for continuing personal development to increase your effectiveness as a group leader. Also presented are descriptions for basic characteristics that help group leaders establish core conditions, such as warmth and caring; how skills used with individuals also have applications in group settings; and group-level skills such as linking. Although much of the emphasis is on skills, the art of group leadership factors contributes significantly to their effectiveness.

Mindless use of techniques and skills is not helpful for group members. These can give the illusion of progress and growth, as there can be much activity. But, if there is no understanding that accompanies the use of techniques and skills, the most important part of learning for group members will be lost. It is strongly recommended that you become more aware of both your inner experiencing and of external events that are occurring simultaneously in the group and use this information for the benefit of the group and its members.

## RATIONALE FOR PERSONAL GROWTH EMPHASIS

An integral part of any preparation as a group leader is your personal development. This is very important for both you and clients. It plays a significant role in preventing burnout and countertransference as well as promoting skill development, knowing and understanding what to do in sessions, better understanding of clients' issues, and feeling confident about how you deal with clients. The literature is clear that your personal development impacts your work with clients in direct and indirect ways.

At the beginning, it may be difficult to understand how working on your personal development will result in helping your group; you may need to suspend disbelief and have a little faith that this self-exploration is needed to become a more effective group leader. In time, you will realize that you are gaining a deeper understanding of just what your clients are struggling with and how hard it is for them to become aware of their personal issues so that they can work on them.

An example may help to highlight the importance of learning more about your self, your unresolved issues, and your unfinished business. Answer the following questions:

- How do you react to and manage criticisms?
- Do you become defensive when criticized and deny the charge?
- Do you attack the person who criticizes and point out how wrong he or she is?
- Do you ignore the criticism and the person?
- Do you shrug the criticism off outwardly but seethe on the inside?
- Do you agree with the criticism to get the person to shut up?
- Do you become hurt and angry but do not say anything?

Any and all of these responses can be easily traced to childhood reactions to criticism from a parent, if not totally, then in some way. This example is only one of many behaviors, attitudes, or reactions that can be traced to past events that influence you in the present.

Life events also play an important part in determining self-perception. Your family of origin experiences, and past experiences interact with your personality to form your perception of your adequacy, efficacy, worth, and value. Your beliefs, attitudes, and values are developed from your family, the larger culture, and other experiences. The more you understand who you are, how you developed, and your relationships, the more you can understand your clients, and reduce the potential for countertransference.

## POTENTIAL FOR NEGATIVE COUNTERTRANSFERENCE

Unfinished business and unresolved personal issues have potential for causing countertransference or transference. Transference and countertransference refer to the process by which thoughts, feelings, and wishes from the person's past are put on—that is, transferred—to another person. *Transference* is the term used when the process goes from the group member to the group leader, and *countertransference* is used when the process goes from the group leader to the group member. Both occur on an unconscious basis, so they may be difficult to identify.

Countertransference can be especially destructive to the relationship between the leader and group members because it can influence how you perceive and react to the client, affect the direction of the sessions, and impair the leader's ability to be objective. An example may help to clarify this concept. Suppose you and your mother were very close, but she became ill and died when you were in your early teens. You still feel hurt every time you think about her, and you wish and yearn for her to be with you today. You may have worked through some of your grief, but you still cry on special occasions such as her birthday. A group member who is a few years younger than you tells you how much she detests her mother because the woman is emotionally abusive. As the client is talking, you find yourself becoming angry but try to hide it or suppress it in some way. You listen to the client and nod your head. When you respond, you focus on how the client's mother may be trying to help her to not go astray or get in trouble, which is why her mother seems to be nagging. You gently chide the client for not being more understanding of how hard it is to be a good parent and she should appreciate what her mother is trying to do. At that point, the group member clams up and seems to withdraw.

This is not a subtle example of countertransference. Most of the time the issues are buried so deep that reflecting will not bring them to awareness. There may be numerous life events that have the potential for countertransference, and because it takes place on an unconscious level, you are not aware of when it is happening. Bringing your unfinished business and unresolved personal issues to awareness can do much to prevent countertransference that has a negative impact.

Parental messages from your past may continue to influence your thoughts, behaviors, feelings, and attitudes. You are probably aware of many of these messages but remain unaware of others and their current impact on you. These parental messages did much to influence your self-concept—that is, your perception of your "self." The way you feel about and perceive your self has its roots in how you were responded to and whether your needs were met by your major caregiver.

Some pieces of your psychological development were influenced by the degree to which you completed other expected developmental tasks, such as separation and individuation, and how your parents responded or guided you through these tasks. Research seems to show that children of depressed mothers do not get the positive encouragement needed to move through these developmental tasks, because these mothers cannot be emotionally present with their children due to the depression. Overprotective parents, rejecting parents, neglectful parents, abusive parents, and absent parents also have an effect on psychological development.

Parents play a major role in the development of your self-concept. How you perceive yourself is, in part, a reflection of how your parents reacted to and perceived you. They communicated in direct and indirect ways their feelings about your abilities and worth; their expectations for your behavior, values, and attitudes; and their satisfaction or displeasure at your ability to meet their expectations.

You also had some reactions and feelings about your parents' expectations and responses, and it can be important for you to become aware of what these are as they continue to impact your current functioning and relationships. You may find that you are still trying to obtain a parent's approval, trying to get a parent's attention, hearing parental disapproval of you in words from others, reacting with hurt feelings to any perceived criticism, expecting to be chastised, competing with siblings for parental love, and trying to get a parent to understand and respond to your feelings.

## UNDERDEVELOPED NARCISSISM OR SELF-ABSORPTION

Narcissism is a focus on the self or love of self. Kohut (1977) not only described in some detail how the self develops but also proposed that there is age-appropriate and healthy narcissism. For example, it is age appropriate and healthy for toddlers to consider almost everything and everyone an extension of their self, to act as if everything belongs to them and that everyone is in service to take care of their needs. However, it is neither age-appropriate nor healthy when an adult feels and acts this way. Kohut (1977) also described healthy adult narcissism. He proposed that healthy adult narcissism is characterized by humor, creativity, and empathy. Less than healthy narcissism has its roots in empathic failures in infancy and childhood where the child's primitive self was not positively responded to by the primary caregiver, or when the child was expected to take care of and meet the needs of the parent instead of having his or her needs met by the parent.

Two examples of underdeveloped narcissism are extensions of self and lack of empathy. Some people with underdeveloped narcissism can have an incomplete differentiation of "self" and "not self" as demonstrated by their insensitivity to others' boundaries and/or lack of empathy. Examples of insensitivity to others' boundaries include the following:

- Entering someone's room without knocking or asking for permission to enter
- Using someone's possessions without asking
- Making personal comments about someone's appearance
- Interrupting an ongoing conversation
- Touching someone without his or her permission
- Sending children to get something for you when they are busy with their own activity

In each instance, there is an unconscious assumption that the other person's space, possessions, or activities are of lesser importance than your needs and that you are entitled to violate these boundaries. Remember, boundaries are both physical and psychological, and they distinguish between what is "you" and what is "not you." When you cannot or do not have a clear understanding of your own boundaries, you are less able to differentiate between where you end and others begin.

Examples of lack of empathy include the following:

- Changing the topic when others are talking, especially if they become emotional
- Expressing false sympathy or empathy
- Failure to respond to others
- Ignoring what people say when they are talking to you, especially if they have intense emotions
- Focusing only on your needs
- Discounting the impact of an event on someone else
- Minimizing the other person's feelings
- Feeling or saying that the other person's feelings are wrong or irrational

Lack of empathy is an inability to reach out and get in touch with what the other person is experiencing. With underdeveloped narcissism, there is an insensitivity to others because of the impact their emotions will have on you or because you cannot understand what all the fuss is about. The insensitivity is not a conscious act; it is part of the person's developmental delay or failure to complete a major developmental task in infancy or childhood.

## BASIC LEADER CHARACTERISTICS

The most effective leaders of psychoeducational groups possess certain characteristics and skills. Characteristics refer to what you are and skills to what you can do. Some of these characteristics can be developed, but they must be internalized and become an integral part of your personality in order to be effective. Skills can be more easily taught, although they may not be easy to learn or to master.

Major characteristics of an effective group leader include the following:

- Belief in the group process
- Confidence in yourself and in your ability
- Courage to risk
- Willingness to admit your mistakes and imperfections
- Organization and planning abilities
- Flexibility
- Ability to tolerate ambiguity
- Self-awareness
- Sense of humor

Other characteristics that are helpful are those you would need for leading counseling or therapy groups, including caring, warmth, positive regard, and genuineness.

### Belief in the Group Process

A leader's belief in the group process provides an atmosphere of safety for group members. While the issues may not be openly addressed, many members of psychoeducational groups have safety and trust issues. They wonder if the group will be of any benefit to them, if they will be accepted and respected, and if the leader can take care of them. Leaders who have a deeply held belief in the efficacy of the group provide reassurance to these members on a unconscious level. This reassurance is conveyed in the preplanning the leader does, in how members are prepared for group, in how their spoken and unspoken questions are addressed, by the leader's ability to contain and manage personal anxiety, and in the leader's flexibility.

## Self-Confidence

Confidence in yourself and in your ability is almost self-explanatory. The leader who models self-confidence teaches group members by example. Developing self-confidence happens over time through positive experiences—that is, the quality of your experiences affect your acceptance of your ability. For some, positive experiences include approval and praise from others. While everyone needs some feedback on how they are perceived or on how well they have learned to do something, some people gain more confidence when there is consistent, positive feedback from many others, which can happen in a group. Confidence also is enhanced when a member tries out a new skill and the desired results occur. Again, it must be noted that confidence develops over time. Confidence in your group leadership skills also develops over time with appropriate feedback.

## Courage to Risk

Taking a risk means being willing to expose yourself to possible failure or to criticism from others, to seek new experiences, to be in error, to grow, and to develop. An effective group leader is dynamic—always growing, always changing. While he or she may be teaching the same content to many different groups, the leader should always be searching for better methods, more participant learning, and so on. Risk taking also comes into play during sessions. Leaders need not be perfect, and sessions sometimes can be enhanced if the leader will take a risk.

## Ability to Admit Mistakes

A willingness to admit mistakes and imperfections can be helpful under certain conditions. By admitting mistakes, the leader models an acceptance of self and conveys an attitude of acceptance of others. When you can show that you accept yourself and own your mistakes and imperfections, group members can believe that you will accept them and not expect them to be perfect. This does not mean that apologies are always needed; it simply means that you should own and take responsibility for your errors or imperfections without denigrating yourself, feeling shame, or turning on others and blaming or criticizing.

## Being Organized

Being organized and having a planful nature constitutes a hybrid of characteristics and skills. It is possible to teach organizational and planning skills, but the desire for organizing and planning is an internal one. Effective leaders do considerable work before group sessions to ensure the efficacy of the group for members. Planning and organizing help ensure the safety of members, promote participation, reduce anxiety for the leader and for members, and enhance learning. How to plan and organize is addressed more extensively in Chapter 5.

## Flexibility

Flexibility is a result of confidence and the ability to tolerate your own and others' anxiety. The willingness to change a planned process or activity is not something that can be taught, but it is a characteristic of confident group leaders. The ability to look at a changing situation and make appropriate adjustments can facilitate the progress of the group. When the group leader lacks flexibility, members may feel stifled, controlled, and overdirected. The flip side is that too much flexibility promotes anxiety, as members are unable to judge what is expected or what will happen next. Striking the proper balance is a learned trait or skill.

## Tolerance of Ambiguity

In planning a group, it is useful to know educational level, abilities, emotional concerns, and physical conditions of members. However, since many psychoeducational groups do not allow for prescreening, leaders often do not know much about members prior to the first session, so they must prepare in a vacuum. Furthermore, some groups have involuntary membership and the leader may not even know it. Leaders who feel comfortable and confident in the face of knowing little about members are better able to conduct effective groups.

## Self-Awareness

Self-awareness is an ongoing developmental process. It is an important characteristic for leaders of all types of groups. Countertransference issues arise even in psychoeducational groups, and the effective leader knows enough to be aware of personal issues, recognize countertransference when it appears, and understand its impact on the group and on individual members.

Personal ownership of attitudes, behaviors, opinions, and feelings is both a characteristic and a skill. Ownership is a characteristic because it is basically internalized. In order to genuinely take responsibility for your attitudes, behaviors, opinions, and feelings, you must accept that they are yours and are not imposed on you by others. Feeling that someone else has provoked any or all of these characteristics means you are not accepting ownership of them. Mere lip service to assuming ownership is not enough; it has to come from within.

In addition to being a characteristic, there is also a skill component: conveying to others that you accept personal ownership. Another aspect is respect and toleration of differing points of view. Skill in conveying your attitudes, opinions, and feelings in such a way that others do not feel compelled to adopt them is important. Members will be turned off if you come across as dogmatic and as having all the right answers. While members are attending the group to learn, they are not blank slates on which you can write.

## Sense of Humor

A sense of humor allows leaders to take themselves less seriously and models for members the ability to see the humorous side of a situation. People who can laugh at themselves usually are healthier than those who cannot. Additionally, seeing the humor in something relieves tension, promotes a sense of playfulness, and contributes to a general sense of well-being.

## Basic Inner Self Characteristics

The usefulness of basic inner self characteristics—that is, caring, warmth, positive regard, and genuineness—has been well documented. While there are nonverbal behaviors that convey these characteristics, it is difficult to fake them; they must come from within and are an integral part of one's being. Even in psychoeducational groups, the leader needs to have these characteristics, as they tend to promote learning, which is the goal for these groups.

Caring is shown through attending, listening, and directly responding. Physically orienting yourself to the speaker, maintaining eye contact, and hearing the meaning (not just the words) all convey caring. Warmth is shown through some of the same behaviors but adds a facial expression of concern for the other person. Smiles or other appropriate facial expressions convey warmth. Positive regard means being open to the speaker and willing to hear his or her point of view without judging the person to be good or bad because that viewpoint is different from yours. Positive regard assumes the worth and uniqueness of the other person. Genuineness (or authenticity) is being willing to let yourself be known to the other as you really are: no false pretense; no reluctance to share thoughts, opinions, or feelings; and a real appreciation of the other as he or she presents him- or herself to you.

## GROUP LEADERSHIP SKILLS

Basic task and maintenance group leadership skills include the following:

- Attending
- Reflecting

- Summarizing
- Active listening and responding
- Clarifying
- Supporting

In addition, the leader needs some group leadership facilitation skills, including linking, blocking, tuning in to process, confronting, and terminating. All of these are important and may be used in other than traditional ways. With practice, these things can become an integral part of your skill set. These skills are described below and suggested strategies for developing them are given in the section titled "Skill Development" later in this chapter.

Preparation to listen, respect for others, and interest in others are conveyed by *attending skills*. These are primarily nonverbal behaviors, such as a slight forward lean, eye contact, orientation of the body toward the speaker, and not allowing yourself to be distracted from the speaker. Attending to members when they are speaking makes them feel valued and that you are interested in what they have to say.

*Active listening and responding* means being able to hear and understand direct and indirect communications and to convey your understanding to the other person. Tuning in to feelings, hearing the metacommunication, and understanding the role of nonverbal behaviors in communication all play important roles in active listening and responding. Self-awareness is important to the extent that you understand your personal issues and how they may affect your listening and responding skills.

*Reflection* is a useful skill with psychoeducational groups because members do not always say what they mean, and leaders do not always understand what they mean. Reflecting back what was heard allows for correction of misunderstandings and can produce further elaborations.

*Clarification* is a part of reflection and active listening. This is the skill of understanding what was meant, illuminating intent, clearing up misconceptions and misunderstandings, and providing clearer direction.

*Summarizing* the key elements of a session helps members tie the many parts of the experience together. Sessions usually begin with objectives. Summaries show how or if the objectives were met, remaining questions or concerns, other emerging issues, and qualitative judgments about the session. So much has transpired that members may have forgotten what they set out to do, and the summary reminds them that they accomplished the objective(s).

*Support* by the group leader must be done with care. You must not rush in to provide support but instead should judge when members need support and when they can be left to work it out on their own. Learning when support will be productive or counterproductive comes with experience.

## Group-Level Skills

There is a category of group leadership skills that includes linking, blocking, tuning in to process, confronting, and terminating. These skills are complicated, making them difficult to define, describe, and develop. Each skill is briefly described here. Confronting is discussed in greater depth in Chapter 8.

*Linking* involves relating what members are doing and saying among the group. Seeing and pointing out commonalities, similarities, and patterns is an advanced skill that comes with practice and experience. The leader has to really listen to discern such commonalities and patterns. Illuminating them promotes growth and development for the group and for individual members. The group can become more cohesive and members can relate to each other in meaningful ways to gain self-awareness.

*Blocking* involves intervening to stop intellectualizing, storytelling, inappropriate responses, or any behavior that negatively affects the progress of the group or the well-being of group members. Blocking must be done so that it cuts off the undesired behavior without blaming or criticizing. You must take care not to make members feel chastised or wrong.

*Tuning in to process* involves evaluating the ongoing progress and process of the group, which generally is left to the leader. Most of the other skills discussed here can be manifested by group members, but evaluation requires a knowledge of group process generally not held by members unless they have had education or training in it. Understanding the stages of a group and the process taking place in it are skills developed by the experienced group leader.

*Confronting* is a skill that is misunderstood by many people. It has come to be synonymous with attack. The accurate meaning of confrontation, however, does not involve attacking, telling someone off, or force of any kind. Confrontation is an invitation, not an imposition. The receiver is invited to look at an aspect of him- or herself and its impact on others. Confrontation is extended tentatively, not forced on the other person. Telling someone what you think he or she needs to know is an attack, not a confrontation. The giver of the confrontation must be clear about his or her personal motives before taking action. Wanting to retaliate, tell someone off, or discount another person are inappropriate reasons for confronting. Guidelines for constructive confrontation are discussed in Chapter 8.

It is important to have *constructive terminations* for sessions and for the ending of the group. Too many times experiences are simply stopped, not ended in such a way as to provide closure for participants. You should take time to decisively end sessions. Constructive termination ensures that loose ends are tied up, important and intense feelings are dealt with so that members are not left dangling, and participants have an opportunity to say goodbye to one another.

Knowing what is effective and what to avoid is important for group leaders. Many of these skills seem relatively easy to master in isolation. It is much more difficult to use them when so much is happening in the group at every moment. All groups are dynamic, and the effective leader recognizes and accepts that fact and does not attempt to ignore the complexity.

Further, an effective leader is aware of his or her personal needs and uses these in constructive ways to facilitate the group. Group members are valued as worthwhile, unique individuals, not as pawns to be manipulated for their own or for the leader's good.

## Skill Development

Many group leadership skills can be described and easily understood. Others are more complex, and even their descriptions may not do them justice. Some examples of the more complex leadership skills are linking, blocking, and summarizing.

Basic communication skills form the foundation for group leadership skills. The leader must be able to attend, paraphrase, and reflect as a part of active listening and responding; question appropriately; and confront in a constructive way. These skills allow the leader to be facilitative and to structure and perform task and relationship functions that help groups progress and be successful. Further, these basic skills are the foundation on which more complex skills are developed. The leader calls on all of the basic skills to link, block, and summarize.

### Elements of Effective Communication

A leader is more effective if he or she uses clear, concise, direct, and open communication. The effective leader takes steps to ensure that he or she understands and is understood. Some characteristics of effective communication are two-way active listening, feedback, lack of listener stress, clarity, and focusing on the core issue.

*Two-way communication* means that ideas, information, opinions, attitudes, and feelings flow between communicators. For psychoeducational groups, the leader and members each contribute to the functioning of the group. An effective leader uses the resources in the group, as well as his or her own knowledge and expertise, to attain the goals of the group. You should never assume that members also have little or nothing to contribute. While the leader is, or should be, more knowledgeable, members also need to feel competent.

*Active listening* cannot be overemphasized. Hearing what was said and understanding what was meant are skills an effective leader must develop. Messages involve both feelings and content, but most listening focuses only on content, with little attention to feelings. This is a critical mistake, as the primary part of the message is the feeling part, not the content. Because psychoeducational groups usually are content focused and task oriented, the focus tends to be on those aspects, and feelings often are overlooked or discounted. No matter how important content is, it is important to hear and respond to the metacommunication of feelings.

*Effective feedback* has several components: active listening and responding, attention to nonverbal behaviors, recognition of the impact of the feedback on the other person, and the amount and timing of the feedback. Feedback is effective when the receiver can absorb and use it. It is ineffective if the receiver feels overwhelmed or attacked, rejects or resists the feedback, or has an undesirable reaction to it (e.g., withdrawal). As the leader, you should give only the amount of feedback a receiver can tolerate or use, not the amount you wish to give. Specific guidelines are given later in this chapter.

*Lack of stress* refers to communicating without having to worry about being understood. The leader uses vocabulary appropriate for the audience, concepts that are generally understood and jargon-free, and limited amounts of information. Nothing is more disagreeable to group members than to feel the leader is talking down to them. Effective leaders gauge the comprehension level of participants and communicate in terms that promote interactions and understanding. As the leader, you have enough variables to consider without worrying about whether members understand what you mean.

It is not possible to have all communication be *clear and unambiguous.* However, effective communication strives for that ideal. This is particularly important in groups in which considerable activity is taking place and intense feelings are apt to be present. One problem is that everyone tends to hear or understand through a perceptual filter—that is, past experiences, relationships, sense of self, and level of emotionality interact to filter what is heard and understood. In some instances, the perceptual filter distorts what is communicated. You can help by clarifying what was said or meant.

Focusing on the core issue is a complex skill that incorporates active listening, linking, summarizing, and understanding issues and the indirect ways they may be communicated. This skill is learned over time.

## DEVELOPING LISTENING AND RESPONDING SKILLS

Tables 2.1 and 2.2 are designed to help you become aware of your listening habits and communication style. You may find it helpful to record your answers to the scales and to ask someone with whom you interact on a regular basis to rate you as well. The items also provide a list of behaviors you might want to increase, decrease, or eliminate.

Paraphrasing is restating what has been said, without parroting, in order to give the speaker your understanding of what he or she said. This way, the speaker has an opportunity to clear up any misunderstanding. Paraphrasing refers to content and is a part of reflecting, which includes both content and feelings.

TABLE 2.1

Listening Habits Scale

**Directions:** Rate the frequency with which you do the following.

| Listening | Almost Always | Usually | Some-times | Seldom | Almost Never |
|---|---|---|---|---|---|
| 1. Calling the subject uninteresting | — | — | — | — | — |
| 2. Criticizing the speaker's delivery or mannerisms | — | — | — | — | — |
| 3. Getting overstimulated by something the speaker says | — | — | — | — | — |
| 4. Listening primarily for facts | — | — | — | — | — |
| 5. Trying to outline everything | — | — | — | — | — |
| 6. Faking attention to the speaker | — | — | — | — | — |
| 7. Allowing interfering distractions | — | — | — | — | — |
| 8. Avoiding difficult material | — | — | — | — | — |
| 9. Letting emotion-laden words arouse personal antagonism | — | — | — | — | — |
| 10. Wasting the advantage of thought speed (daydreaming) | — | — | — | — | — |
| 11. Interrupting the speaker | — | — | — | — | — |
| 12. Becoming distracted by others | — | — | — | — | — |

Paraphrasing reduces confusion and misunderstandings that can easily occur. We tend to hear what is said through a perceptual screen influenced by our physical and emotional state as well as by our reaction to the speaker. In addition, there are times when speakers do not say what they intend to say. Paraphrasing allows for early corrections.

Learning to restate what you hear may be difficult and uncomfortable at first. Thinking of what words to use so that the speaker does not hear his or her exact words quoted back takes some practice. Judging when paraphrasing is needed is another skill that must be developed. In order to be effective, paraphrasing must be practiced.

You should use paraphrasing when a speaker is being overly general and you want more specificity. For example, if the speaker says that he or she would make a good counselor, you might paraphrase to see if your perception of a good counselor is the same as his or hers. In this case, you might say something like, "You see yourself as being able to guide others to help themselves?"

Another time paraphrasing is helpful is when the speaker's comments are general and examples should be suggested. For example, if the speaker says "We are not getting qualified students in the program," you can paraphrase by saying, "Do you mean that too many students are failing, or that the quality of work in your class has decreased, or that test scores are lower than those of a few years ago?"

TABLE 2.2

Effective Verbal Communication Behavior

**Directions:** Rate yourself on the items below using the following scale:
  **5** = I do this most of the time, or all of the time.
  **4** = I do this often.
  **3** = I do this sometimes; more often than not.
  **2** = I seldom do this.
  **1** = I do this infrequently, or not at all.

| | | | | | |
|---|---|---|---|---|---|
| 1. Restate what others say without parroting | 5 | 4 | 3 | 2 | 1 |
| 2. Restate what others say without adding to the meaning | 5 | 4 | 3 | 2 | 1 |
| 3. Make clearer what others mean in what they say | 5 | 4 | 3 | 2 | 1 |
| 4. Check with others to ensure clear understanding | 5 | 4 | 3 | 2 | 1 |
| 5. Focus on underlying feelings | 5 | 4 | 3 | 2 | 1 |
| 6. Focus on underlying issues | 5 | 4 | 3 | 2 | 1 |
| 7. Bring conflicting thoughts/feelings into focus | 5 | 4 | 3 | 2 | 1 |
| 8. Identify commonalities between self and others | 5 | 4 | 3 | 2 | 1 |
| 9. Combine, tie together, or identify themes in verbal interactions | 5 | 4 | 3 | 2 | 1 |
| 10. Ask questions only for information, not to get my point across | 5 | 4 | 3 | 2 | 1 |
| 11. Try not to bombard others with questions | 5 | 4 | 3 | 2 | 1 |
| 12. Make more statements than questions in conversations | 5 | 4 | 3 | 2 | 1 |
| 13. Focus my questions on *what* and *how*, rather than on *why* | 5 | 4 | 3 | 2 | 1 |
| 14. Allow others to express difficult feelings without interrupting | 5 | 4 | 3 | 2 | 1 |
| 15. Let others interpret their behavior | 5 | 4 | 3 | 2 | 1 |
| 16. Reflect feelings accurately | 5 | 4 | 3 | 2 | 1 |
| 17. Sense what feelings others are trying to express | 5 | 4 | 3 | 2 | 1 |
| 18. Refrain from giving advice | 5 | 4 | 3 | 2 | 1 |
| 19. Provide concrete feedback to others that they can use | 5 | 4 | 3 | 2 | 1 |
| 20. Am comfortable with silence | 5 | 4 | 3 | 2 | 1 |

Situations when paraphrasing is useful include when complex or complicated directions are given, when the speaker has used vague or general terms, when an example provides clarification, and when either the speaker or the receiver has strong emotional involvement. It is not necessary to paraphrase every statement. However, it is a component in active listening.

Reflection involves both the content and feelings involved in the message. It has the same purposes as paraphrasing: reducing misunderstandings, promoting clarity, and conveying understanding of meaning to the speaker. The most important thing to remember is that the perceived feelings should be clearly identified and labeled.

Effective reflection involves attending, an openness to experiencing, and an ability to describe or label feelings. Learning a feeling language is an important part of developing reflecting skills. To get started, you can work on expanding your vocabulary with particular attention to words describing mild forms of intense emotions. For example, if a speaker is annoyed and you term the emotion as anger, he or she will probably reject the label and feel that you have misunderstood him or her. Here are some guidelines for reflecting:

- Identify the underlying message (usually an emotion) and name the emotion you hear.
- Be tentative and paraphrase to check for accuracy.
- Be alert to connections or links to other verbalizations.

### Ineffective Communication

There are some communication behaviors the leader should avoid, including speaking for others or the group as a whole instead of making personal statements, asking inappropriate questions, using clichés, and exhibiting defensiveness. These kinds of communication promote inaccuracy of perceptions, game-playing behavior, hiding of the real self (a kind of deception), and feelings of being manipulated.

Following are some ineffective communication styles that tend to arouse hostile feelings and promote resistance. Some of these styles have positive points, as they can be used for appropriate circumstances. For example, in the military there are times when an authoritative response is called for. However, a psychoeducational group leader has little or no need for any of the styles described below.

The authoritarian is ineffective because he or she assumes a status differential. The authoritarian gives orders and expects those orders to be followed and becomes impatient if there appears to be any questioning of the "orders," and this attitude tends to dampen interaction between other group members.

The criticizer points the finger of blame, criticizes, and moralizes. This style of communication uses *oughts* and *shoulds* and tends to arouse guilt feelings in others. The criticizer does not seem pleased with anything or anybody and tends to alienate others by making them feel inadequate no matter what they do.

The expert knows *all* the answers and is not shy about imposing them on others. Experts do not wait to be asked for an opinion but rush in and overwhelm others with their "expertise." Experts tend to think they know a lot about everything.

The analyst always wants to tell others about their motives and underlying reasons for their feelings and behaviors. The person who tries to analyze is even more dangerous when he or she knows a little about human growth and behavior, especially personality theory. Other group members tend to avoid the analyst because his or her communication style arouses hostile, angry feelings. Analyzing can be of use in a therapy session but is not useful and may be dangerous outside of the therapeutic relationship.

The optimist, while seemingly benign, is a problem communicator. We all like to interact with upbeat, optimistic people. They make us feel good and promote hopefulness. However, the eternal optimist is off-putting, because he or she uses this optimism to avoid seeing or dealing with real problems and seeks to minimize or ignore his or her own and others' feelings.

The protector is especially problematic in a group. People who have difficulty dealing with anxiety-provoking situations and those who are emotionally expressive naturally tend to rush in to soothe, rescue, or protect in some way. The message they send is that others need their help. The truth is that protectors are unable or unwilling to deal with their own feelings of discomfort and seek to minimize others' feelings in an effort to minimize their own. This style is difficult to deal with, because when their help is rejected, protectors feel hurt and others feel guilty, making for a real catch-22 situation.

The interrogator puts others in the hot seat because his or her questioning and probing, ostensibly used to get at the facts, makes others uncomfortable. Questions have their role, and this is addressed in the section on "Questioning Skill Development" later in this chapter.

The magician is a lot like the eternal optimist. He or she tries to make problems, issues, and concerns disappear by refusing to acknowledge their existence. Whereas the eternal optimist brushes aside concerns by minimizing their impact, the magician tries to make them disappear completely by not thinking or talking about them. When the problem resurfaces, the magician shifts the topic to something less threatening. Others feel put down or discounted when the magician communicates with them.

The generalizer frequently uses words like *always* and *never*. Generalizers tend to categorize and make judgments about *all* instead of seeing others as individuals or situations as varied. Generalizations are rarely appropriate when talking about people's behavior.

The accuser arouses hostility in others by calling names, labeling, and putting others on the defensive. Communication is ineffective or ceases completely when people feel attacked or labeled in some way. This kind of accusing communication is designed to put others at a disadvantage and to put the accuser at an advantage.

When you do not use personal statements but instead use terms like *we, the group,* or *all of us,* you are modeling and encouraging the use of indirect and ineffective communication. It is much more effective for the leader and members to take responsibility for their own communications by making personal statements. There are times when you will point out what the group is doing; this is not speaking for the group.

### Questioning Skill Development

Questioning can be used effectively if certain points are used to make a conscious choice on when to question. All too often, questions are used inappropriately, leading to ineffective communication. There are three major uses for questions:

1. To obtain data and information
2. To clarify and avoid misunderstandings
3. To pinpoint something in order to take immediate action

Statements usually are more appropriate in other situations.

The primary rule of thumb for a question is to obtain needed data. The word *needed* is emphasized, because in most counseling situations, additional data are *not* needed. For example, a group member may be talking about an argument with a boss. Often, another group member or the leader will ask, "Has this happened before?" or "What kind of person is he?" or "Who else was there?"

This information is not needed. You are dealing with the speaker's experience and his or her feelings. When I point this out to students in my group counseling classes, the response is generally, "I was trying to understand." We then explore that objective further to determine how the questioned information aids in understanding. Most of the time, it does not give any further information of use. This questioning serves to keep the focus off the speaker and his or her reactions.

There are times when questions are useful for clarification, of course. Verbalizations may be vague, rambling, ambiguous, or confusing. In these cases, questions can help us focus on the essentials and promote understanding of the message and the intent of the speaker. By asking the speaker if our identification of the point is correct, we help to clarify his or her communication. The group leader needs to develop this skill and use it effectively.

Pinpointing is needed in situations where prompt and precise action should be taken. These usually are crises, such as an accident in which someone has been hurt. Group leaders may never face this purpose for questions.

Benjamin (1987) proposed five types of questions: direct, indirect, open, closed, and double. *Direct questions* are most easily identified. They are specific and to the point. The group leader uses the direct questions most often—for example, "How did you respond?" or "What did you do?" or "Is the agenda meeting your needs?"

Indirect questions usually can be reframed into statements. Making a question into a statement may involve something as simple as changing the inflection at the end—for example, "You are leaving?" becomes "You are leaving." In the group, you could say, "There seems to be a lot of tension" instead of "Is there tension in the group?" Indirect questions are usually somewhat rhetorical. The speaker either knows the answer or has an opinion. But instead of saying so directly, he or she puts it in the form of a question—in part so that personal ownership of the answer or opinion does not have to be assumed.

*Open questions* allow the responder the freedom to decide what information to share. These questions may produce unintended results, be confusing or threatening to the receiver, and open the door to storytelling. Open questions are genuinely seeking information, and the speaker has no preconceived ideas about what information he or she wants but is willing to use what is presented.

*Closed questions* seek to limit the response to specific information or answers. When specific information is needed, a direct, closed question is appropriate. One difficulty with closed questions is that the answer may not

give the questioner the information he or she needs because it is too limited—
for example, asking someone if he or she has finished an activity allows only
a yes-or-no answer. It does not take into consideration that the person may
never have engaged in the activity at all (e.g., the classic "Have you stopped
beating your wife?"). Closed questions may have the unintended effect of
making the receivers feel you are trying to trick them or that you are not interested in their answer if it has the potential for clashing with your opinion or
preconceptions.

*Double questions* put people in a bind by limiting the choice of answers
to one out of two when there may be others available—for example, asking
people if they want to eat at X or at Y restaurant limits their choices. There
may be dozens of other eating places available and one of these could be more
to their liking. Limiting choices can be useful if these are, in fact, the only
choices (e.g., asking a child if he or she wants to wear the green shirt or the
yellow one when those are the only two that coordinate with the rest of the
outfit).

Become aware of how often you ask questions. One helpful exercise is to
tally the number of questions you ask in a day. Another exercise is to go an
entire weekend without asking questions, except as facts are needed.

The next step is to become aware of the type of question you ask most
frequently and to determine how many of your questions are genuine requests
for information—for example, when you ask someone, "How are you?" do
you really want to know, or is it just your way of being polite? How can the
person know if you are really interested or just being polite?

Begin to make a conscious evaluation of the need for asking a question.
Can you make a statement instead? What advantage is there in asking a
question?

Along with the growth in self-awareness, observe your own behavior and
that of others when asking questions. It is not unusual to ask many questions
of the same person. In a sense, you bombard the person with questions. This
can produce feelings of being attacked, and the resulting behavior is a defense,
an attack, or a retreat. None of these behaviors promote effective communication.

There is an art to encouraging members to actively participate, and stimu-
lation of good questions is a good leadership skill. Good questions show interest and relevancy, encourage participation and interaction, and point out the
need for elaboration or clarification. The leader, however, cannot count on
getting good questions from members, so an additional skill you need to develop is turning inadequate questions into good questions.

Your first task as group leader is to examine your reactions to questions.
Some common reactions are to become defensive, see questions as threats to
your expertise or leadership, rush in to answer quickly, answer indirectly or
with a question, and ignore the question. Responding appropriately to questions involves self-awareness, observation of the questioner, judging the ap-

TABLE 2.3

Reactions and Modifications to Receiving Questions

| Reaction | Modification |
| --- | --- |
| Become defensive | Do not take questions personally. Do not explain or apologize unless called for. |
| Questions perceived as threats | Suppress your anger. Identify why or what about the question is threatening. Do not express the anger, cut the person off, or discount him or her in any way. |
| Answering quickly | Mentally count 5 seconds. This gives you time to make sure you understand the question. Use clarification before answering. |
| Answering indirectly | Increase consciousness of answering indirectly and make a conscious effort to give direct answers. Indirect answers leave people confused and frustrated. |
| Answering with a question | If you are not sure you understand, this may be appropriate. If, however, you do this under other circumstances, ask yourself what you are seeking to do. Some motives are to make the other person feel inept, to show off, or to change the topic. Reduce this behavior. |
| Ignoring the question | This is very similar to answering indirectly but does not show as much respect. You may not wish to answer the question and should directly say so. |

propriateness of a response, as well as other communication skills. Table 2.3 presents some suggestions for modifying reactions to questions. The subsequent discussion focuses on when it may be appropriate to use some of these reactions.

There are few rules or guidelines that are appropriate for all situations. The same is true for how to field questions from members. Becoming defensive or perceiving questions as threats speaks to characteristics more than skills. These reactions are unique to the individual and usually have their antecedents in past personal experiences. Some of the other reactions may be appropriate under unique or differing circumstances.

Answering quickly may be useful for blocking undesired or inappropriate behavior. It may relieve tension and provide members with a sense of security. Indirect answers can be useful if some members lack the verbal facility or the confidence to ask direct questions. What they ask is not what they want to know, and the leader is aware of this. An indirect answer addresses the *real* question, and thus it can be more rewarding to the questioner than a direct answer.

Ignoring a question is tricky. You run the risk of alienating the speaker by having no response. But there are a few circumstances where it may be more helpful to act as if the question had not been asked—for example, when the question is rhetorical, when it is asked and answered almost at once, and when basically the same question is asked by several members at the same time.

Rather than ignoring questions, you could refocus, reframe, or explore implications.

Once you have worked through your awareness of questioning behavior and reactions, it becomes easier to field questions from members. A larger concern then becomes how to encourage and stimulate questions. Some suggestions are presented below.

*Determine your expectations.* How do you want questions to be asked? Only when you give space for and request them? At any time? How do you want participants to ask questions—by raising their hands and being recognized or by jumping in? This is your group and you call the shots.

*Inform group members of your expectations.* Don't expect members to read your mind and know your expectations. If you are giving a minilecture during which questions will be a distraction, ask that questions be held until the end. If you do not mind being interrupted, say so.

*Ask if members have any questions and pause a few seconds before continuing.* There are some points at which a leader should open the floor to questions—for example, after reviewing the objectives and schedule, after giving directions for an exercise or activity, after disseminating information (e.g., a minilecture), and after a discussion.

*Do not ask for questions just before a break.* Questions and answers have a way of generating discussions. Sticking to the agreed-upon schedule is important, and these discussions can easily run over the time period. If one or two members have burning questions, you can remain a few minutes after group to answer them.

### Inappropriate Questions

Inappropriate questions fall into several categories: limiting, putting someone on the spot, hypothetical, demands, reflected, rhetorical, and trapping. These are all ineffective ways of communicating. Questions should be limited to asking for needed information; they are not to communicate a position or a point.

Limiting questions seek to contain or narrow the range of responses. The questioner is trying to obtain a particular response and asks questions in such a way that the desired answer is the most likely one or the only one that can be given. Examples of limiting questions are "Don't you think that . . . ?" or "Wouldn't you rather . . . ?"

It is relatively easy to put someone on the spot with questions. The purpose is to punish the speaker rather than to obtain needed information. Leading the speaker with questions is a form of manipulation. Some individuals think that if they ask a series of questions, the other person will come to a desired conclusion. It is a kind of herding or locking in, to get your own point across in an indirect way. It is much more effective to simply state your opinion or position, however, rather than to ask unnecessary questions designed to put someone on the spot.

Hypothetical questions are seldom used to elicit new information. If used to present a possible scenario in order to see how the other person would respond, a hypothetical question is useful and legitimate. Most often, however, the hypothetical question is used to probe for an answer to a question the speaker is afraid to ask directly.

Questions such as "When are you going to . . . ?" are implied demands. The questioner is not really interested in gaining new information; the question is a goad or a command to do something. Some people are reluctant to state what they want. They disguise this with questions about what the other person's wants or preferences are. There are times when both parties wind up doing something neither wants because of indirect communication through questions.

Rhetorical questions usually are followed by a phrase that assumes approval in advance (e.g., "Right?" "Okay?"). Such statements or requests also may be preceded with "Don't you think that . . . ?" or "Isn't it true that . . . ?" Rhetorical questions are framed in such a way that the desired response is assured not to elicit new information or opinions.

Some people have developed the habit of asking questions instead of making statements. Group leaders need to become aware of their communication behavior and take steps to limit questions to requests for information.

## Personal Development Exercise: The Color Wheel

**Objective:** To help identify the differing intensities of feelings, focus on feelings, and learn additional adjectives for expressing feelings.

**Materials:** A variety of different-colored paper cut into strips, a sheet of paper, a pen or pencil.

**Procedure:** Spread the variety of colored paper strips on the table. Taking each color in turn, give it a name—for example, light yellow. Associate each color with a feeling and write the feeling on the colored strip—for example, red could be associated with love.

Review your color choices and associations, and see if there are any patterns—for example, the cool colors may have personal associations that are peaceful. Note where you have gaps and if the gap is because you could not think of a feeling.

**Processing:** If you have many gaps or cannot think of feelings for strips, it may indicate that you are limited in the feelings you experience. This is an area where you can increase your range of emotional expression. You may also want to note if there is a group of feelings where you have difficulty with associations. This, too, can be an area to work on.

# Chapter 3

# Group Leadership and Instructional Style

Major Topics and Concepts

*Knowledge Factor*
Theories of leadership
Learning levels and leadership style
Basic principles of learning
Transfer of learning
Retention of material

*Techniques and Skill Factors*
Methods of instruction
Principles of instruction
Techniques of instruction

*Art Factor*
Guide to your personal leadership and instructional style
Personal development exercise

## INTRODUCTION

Unless you participated in a teacher education program, you may not know how to teach. Psychoeducational group leadership demands that you know how to lead a group and how to teach. Therefore, this chapter presents theories of group leadership as well as theories about how people learn and how to teach.

If you are like many people when confronted with having to present or teach something, you think about what was most effective and what was least effective for your personal learning, using that as your guide for what to do and how to do it. You may even think about individual differences but do not know how to accommodate these. As a leader of psychoeducational groups, this would not be an effective approach. You need to teach and lead based on your audience's needs and characteristics, not on yours. Therefore, this chapter presents group leadership theory, and you are encouraged to read and learn more about the different ways in which people learn, how to accommodate various learning styles, and the effective ways to present material so that it is learned and retained.

Also very important is your preference for instructional style, as this will be a major determinant for how you teach. For example, if you prefer a lot of movement and activity, you will tend to plan your groups to use a lot of these. Suggestions are presented to help you integrate your instructional style with various learning needs.

## THEORIES OF GROUP LEADERSHIP

Theories of group leadership include the following:

- Leaders can be identified by certain traits and characteristics.
- Leaders can be identified by a style, such as democratic.
- Leadership demands a distribution of actions and is not dependent on one person.
- There are different styles of leadership for different stages or group situations.

### Traits and Characteristics

Numerous studies have been conducted to identify the traits or characteristics of effective leaders as compared to followers. The results to date do not reveal any clear-cut set of characteristics. For example, Bird (1940) concluded that high intelligence, initiative, a sense of humor, and extroversion were traits of leaders. Mann (1959) reviewed 125 studies on leadership and concluded that intelligence and personal adjustment were correlated with leadership.

Stogdill (1974) reviewed two sets of leadership studies: studies conducted from 1904 to 1947, and studies conducted from 1948 to 1970. The review revealed two different sets of characteristics, with persistence, responsibility, and initiative as the only overlapping traits. Johnson and Johnson (2003) noted that great leaders seem to be identified in retrospect, not in advance, and that there needs to be a match between conditions and the person for leadership to emerge.

## Styles

There are several leadership theories based on style. Two such theories are charismatic and person centered. Charismatic leaders inspire and motivate on the basis of personality alone. These leaders seem to be able to touch something important in a number of people, who are then willing to follow and obey them. They have extraordinary powers of persuasion and communication, and are generally very goal focused.

Person-centered leadership encourages members' participation in decision making, the leader shows concern for members' welfare and comfort, and role differentiation is maintained. This style of leadership is not consistently related to productivity.

## Distributed Actions/Functions

Distributed actions and functions theory perceives leadership as members having vital functions to perform, not just the leader. Leaders provide structure—for example, integrating information, coordinating, and summarizing. It is the leader's responsibility to provide for the well-being of group members—for example, relieving tension, attending to the emotional climate of the group, and building relationships. Fiedler (1978) proposed a distributed function for group leaders based on group needs. He proposed two functions: task and maintenance.

Task-oriented leaders take responsibility for the direction and functioning of the group. They make decisions and group members are willing to follow. Tasks are clear, unambiguous, and can be structured.

Maintenance-oriented leaders concentrate on having members participate in shared responsibility and decision making. These leaders are most effective when the task is somewhat clear (although there may be some ambiguity) and members are willing and able to assume some responsibility for the functioning of the group.

Both functions can be used effectively in psychoeducational groups. Task functions are most important in pregroup preparation and in the beginning stages. As members become more comfortable and trusting of themselves, the group, and the leader, they assume more responsibility for the functioning of the group and the leader assumes a maintenance function. It may take time and experience to know when to shift functions, but both are useful and can be detrimental if used inappropriately.

## Situational Leadership

Hershey and Blanchard (1977) proposed a theory of situational leadership that classified leadership behaviors along two dimensions: task and relationship. They used the two dimensions in conjunction with the maturity level of group members. Task behaviors are telling, explaining, and clarifying, and are primarily one-way (i.e., leader to members). Relationship behaviors are those the leader uses to give emotional support and to facilitate group progress. They are characterized by two-way communication.

Hershey and Blanchard (1977) defined maturity in terms of a person's extent of achievement motivation, degree of willingness to assume responsibility, past experiences, and educational levels. The degree of maturity also is related to the newness or novelty of the task—for example, a highly educated adult may have little or no knowledge of a given task and thus would exhibit low maturity.

These categories produce four interactions of task and relationship, with four related leadership behaviors: (1) high task–high relationship uses telling behaviors; (2) high task–low relationship uses selling behaviors; (3) low task–low relationship uses participating behaviors; (4) low task–high relationship uses delegating behaviors.

Both of these leadership theories take into account the variations in needs and abilities of group members, the tasks, and the group itself. However, neither describes how to recognize learning levels in the group and what the leader can do to facilitate group development.

## LEARNING LEVELS AND LEADERSHIP STRATEGIES

Leaders of psychoeducational groups need to use a combination of learning theory and group development. Theories of learning, including principles of instruction, provide a framework for presenting material for the intended audience so that they can understand it, apply it, and retain it. Theory presents a basis for learning and suggests strategies.

Knowledge of group development allows you to make optimal use of techniques and strategies. Group development stages suggest when and how to present material so that it can be effectively received and used.

Table 3.1 presents an overview of the leadership and learning levels most often encountered in psychoeducational groups. These levels were developed using theories of learning and stages of group development. They are not dependent on members' intelligence or amount of education, although these factors may come into play for the advanced levels. The table presents simplified ways of identifying levels, associating them with behaviors, and suggesting leadership strategies. I strongly encourage you to learn more about typical behaviors expected at different ages, and in different stages of a group.

Table 3.1 is more useful if these points are kept in mind:

• Age plays a role but is not critical in determining participants' level of learning.

- Members may move through all levels in one group session, or may only move through one or two levels.
- The leadership strategy must be consistent with the leader's personality, but all leaders need to use some form of each leadership strategy.

## Learning Level Classifications

### Low Level

When participants are behaving at a low level, you must do more directing and structuring. Decisions about what to do and how to do it are beyond members' capabilities at this point. All participants are dealing with issues of safety, trust, inclusion, and competence, regardless of their educational or experience level. Explaining, clarifying, and reflecting are useful for reducing ambiguity and answering unasked or indirect questions about the real issues. Some members may be so fearful that they never move beyond this level. You should neither push them nor expect more than they can do.

### Low to Moderate Level

When participants reach a low to moderate learning level, some of their real issues have been sufficiently addressed, so less resistance is encountered. Members appear willing to give you and the process a chance to meet their needs. Participation is still tentative and there is an air of wariness, but many members mask these feelings and wear a facade of cooperativeness and involvement. You can increase participation and involvement by encouraging and motivating.

Again, your major focus is not on the task but on the indirect and unspoken feelings of participants. Nonverbal behaviors are useful here. Eye contact with head nods, a slight forward lean, warmth, and showing interest and respect can contribute to participants' feelings of encouragement and motivation. You should plan activities that can be easily understood and accomplished with little or no frustration. You will be very active and busy with participants at this level, as responses need to be immediate and directed to individuals.

### Moderate Level

Few participants begin a group at the moderate level. If you have members at this level, you will find them to be of immense help. Their modeling of desired attitudes and behaviors, confidence in the process and the leader, and willingness to participate promote feelings of trust and safety for other members.

However, most groups will not have this benefit. The good news is that the group can get to this level in a short time if you facilitate the process. Building confidence in the group process and leader while attending to safety and trust issues encourages development to the moderate level. Once this level is attained, you can become less active, since members will interact with each other more and communications will not be primarily to and through you.

TABLE 3.1

Guide to Psychoeducational Group Leadership and Instructional Styles

---

**Directions:** Rate yourself on the items using the following scale:

5 = Considerably like me.
4 = Very much like me.
3 = Somewhat like me.
2 = A little like me.
1 = Not at all like me.

1. I enjoy and learn from sharing information in a small group.
2. I need to see a personal connection in order to learn.
3. Pleasing other people is important to me.
4. Pleasant relationships and harmony are highest in my priorities.
5. I have difficulty accepting criticism.
6. I like to get things settled and finished.
7. I need to know what to expect, and I do not like surprises.
8. There is a "right" way to do things, and I want to do that.
9. It bothers me if things are not orderly, organized, and systematic.
10. I value structure and predictability.
11. I am often spontaneous in my actions.
12. I begin many projects but do not always finish them.
13. I put off doing tasks but can accomplish much in a burst of activity.
14. I enjoy dramatizations and like to perform.
15. I am very curious about many things.
16. I tend to work better independently than in a group or team.
17. I am not good with chitchat or small talk.
18. I value having information presented briefly and concisely.
19. I am very task oriented.
20. I very much need to know why and how something is done, or how it works.
21. I am intrigued by tasks that call for me to use my imagination.
22. Routine bores me.
23. I tend to work in spurts of energy and activity.
24. I very much enjoy learning something new.
25. I am not as attentive or concerned about facts as I should be, and I sometimes get them wrong.
26. I like to use what I already know instead of learning something new.
27. Presenting material step by step is preferable to me.
28. I enjoy tradition, rituals, and custom.
29. Experience is more important to me than theory.
30. I am good with details.
31. I prefer individual activities to group ones.
32. Ideas energize and intrigue me.
33. Disruptions annoy me.
34. I am good at screening out distractions.
35. I am often accused of not communicating my thoughts and feelings.
36. Variety and action are important to me.
37. I enjoy talking about ideas, and it helps to clarify them for me.
38. I get a lot of energy from being with other people.
39. I am impatient with long and slow projects.
40. Many times, I act before I think.

**Scoring:** Items are clustered as follows. Add your ratings for each cluster.

| | | |
|---|---|---|
| Personal Relationships | Items 1–5 | _____ |
| Consistent-Precise | Items 6–10 | _____ |
| Flexible-Spontaneous | Items 11–15 | _____ |
| Logical-Rational | Items 16–20 | _____ |
| Creative-Imaginative | Items 21–25 | _____ |
| Factual-Realistic | Items 26–30 | _____ |
| Reflective-Thoughtful | Items 31–35 | _____ |
| Energetic-Distractible | Items 36–40 | _____ |

Identify your top three clusters and your bottom three clusters. These behaviors and attitudes impact your leadership style for psychoeducational groups—for example, if your top three clusters are Logical-Rational, Creative-Imaginative, and Reflective-Thoughtful, your leadership style tends to emphasize individual participation, being task oriented, incorporating new and imaginative materials, being skimpy on presenting facts, and getting irritated with interruptions.

Next, identify your lowest three clusters. You will encounter these behaviors and attitudes with some group members and you need to take them into consideration when leading a group. You need to be able to understand and handle them, not discount, ignore, or dismiss them as unimportant—for example, if your three lowest clusters are Factual-Realistic, Consistent-Precision, and Energetic-Distractible, you should design your group activities and leadership style to accommodate some of these behaviors and attitudes, such as attending to the need for personal perspective, valuing relationships and harmony, presenting material step by step, minimizing theory, and including variety and action. For a brief description of clusters, see the section on "Leadership Strategy Clusters."

A leader must have confidence and trust in the group process and in the group members in order for this level to be satisfactory. You must relinquish some power and control and let members assume some responsibility for the functioning of the group. This means a switch in strategy and roles, becoming less directive and structuring and more mutually participatory.

### High Level

When participants reach the high level, they can effectively function independently as team members. This level is attained over time with considerable interaction of members. They have to know each other well and feel accepted, cared for, and respected. You can facilitate this process, but it cannot be hurried. Each and every member might attain this level, but some members will take longer to arrive than others. You must take care not to become discouraged when a group fails to reach this level. There just may not have been enough time.

## Leadership Strategy Clusters

### Personal Relationships

Your tendency is to perceive, learn, and appreciate in terms of your value system, and making personal connections is very important to you. You are not motivated or intrigued by an intellectual or cognitive approach until the personal connections and associations have been made with you.

Thus, you may tend to overemphasize harmony, pleasing others, and other relationship issues when leading groups. You may ignore or dismiss any signs of conflict, alternative approaches, and suggestions, and may minimize the educational component.

### Consistent-Precise
You value order, predictability, and a sense of accomplishment—you like to finish things. These characteristics allow you to plan and organize well, and can be valuable assets for creating a psychoeducatonal group. You do not care for surprises and work hard to ensure that you prepare for contingencies.

Your insistence on order may lead you to overemphasize structure at the expense of spontaneity, creativity, and flexibility. Since groups are unpredictable, you may try to exert more and more control and become very frustrated when these efforts are not successful.

### Flexible-Spontaneous
You get excited about new ideas, projects, and the like, but may fail to follow through until completion. Your excitement can be contagious and can energize the groups you lead. Your on-stage persona can also be enticing and interesting, which is an asset for engaging group members.

Your tendency to become distracted by something new and exciting can lead you to losing the focus for the group. There can be many surprising things that emerge in groups, and you can be accepting of these and easily capitalize on them. The real drawback, however, is that you may try to follow too many new leads, and the original goal and purpose get lost.

### Logical-Rational
Your interest is captured by ideas that trigger your thoughts. You may be reserved and cautious when someone tries to engage your feelings or connect to you on a personal level before you have time to think things through. You like to see logical progressions and patterns, and can be very analytical. You try to make sense of your experiences by thought and logic.

Your reserve at the beginning of your groups can lead members to feel that you are detached, do not care about them, and lack interest. Although it makes perfect sense to you to begin groups by spelling out the task and rationale, some members can feel that you are being demanding, and insensitive to their needs. You will have to take care to incorporate interpersonal connections at the beginning of your groups and to learn how to reach out to others in a way that they can feel connected to you.

### Creative-Imaginative

You tend to become interested when your imagination is triggered. Yours is a world of possibilities, and you want to explore them. You are not intrigued by relationships, routine, cautiousness, and the like, although you do see their value. You just do not want them as your guide or first priority.

You will be energetic in planning imaginative and creative activities for your group, but you may get so caught up in these that you neglect the structure and details that help groups to be successful. Because you are energized by exercises, you may tend to overuse them, and neglect the cognitive component.

### Factual-Realistic

You tend to be very much the opposite of the creative-imaginative person. You are grounded in facts and reality, and may not see the need or value of flights of fantasy. You tend to like a reality check and are very aware of what needs to be done.

You may get impatient with people who seem to be unrealistic and dismissive of facts when they insist on being imaginative. You want an orderly progression for your groups and can be dissatisfied when things do not go according to plan. You may tend to overrely on structure, guidelines, and lectures, and to minimize discussion, exercises, and flexibility.

### Reflective-Thoughtful

Your inner world is very important to you and is the source of your energy. You value contemplation over action and can be patient with the unfolding process for learning and growing. You prefer to think things through and can take time to do this.

Groups can be difficult for you as there is a lot of activity, talking, and other distractions from your reflection. When you are the leader, you may notice that members become restless and you do not think they understand the value of thought and reflection. You may forget that people learn in different ways and that you need to provide a variety of learning experiences.

### Energetic-Distractible

Your energy and enthusiasm can be contagious and group members can respond in kind. There is an excitement that can make group interesting for members and get them quickly engaged. You carry the group along with your personality.

The other side is that you may be easily distracted and keep things on a superficial level because of your need to keep things energized. You may conduct the group skipping from one thing to another without allowing sufficient time for understanding to develop. You will need to learn how to contain and manage your anxiety so that you do not become impatient with members who need time to reflect and think.

## BASIC PRINCIPLES OF LEARNING

There are several factors that affect the process of learning, including individual factors, methods, meaningfulness of material, transfer of learning, and retention. In the sections that follow, we look at each of these factors in turn. Intelligence, age, previous learning, motivation, and anxiety are some primary individual factors that influence the learning process.

Intelligence level is a combination of innate and acquired competencies. Worchel and Shebilske (1992) defined intelligence as "the capacity to learn and use information." There are many theories of intelligence, and I encourage you to explore them further.

Age and maturation also play a role in learning. Individuals cannot learn before they are ready to do so, and the interaction of age and maturation contribute to readiness. Learning is hierarchical in nature—that is, knowledge builds upon previous learning and is interrelated. Some readiness for learning relates to motivation, but some (especially for children) is dependent on age and maturation.

Education level contributes much to learning. How much a person has already learned relates significantly to his or her ease and speed in learning new material, particularly if the new material relates in some way to the material previously learned. For example, learning applications is easier if principles have already been learned.

Motivation to learn is a complex and abstract concept. Maslow (1943) and Murray (1938) proposed needs as motivating influences. For Murray, needs were psychological in nature, such as the need for achievement. Maslow organized needs into a hierarchical system, beginning with basic physiological needs (such as food, water, sleep, and oxygen) and progressing to self-actualization needs (the desire for self-fulfillment). Other motivators include drive determinants, goal seeking, interests, incentives, and reinforcements.

The level of anxiety experienced by an individual also influences his or her learning. Fear of failure, lack of self-confidence, degree of self-efficacy, and their reversed counterparts (e.g., anticipation of success, self-confidence, etc.) affect the ability of the individual to learn. It is not always possible to determine which response will be elicited by anxiety. For example, fear of failure may elicit a response of hopelessness, resulting in an unwillingness to try to learn new material. Or, people who fear failure may have a reverse response where they try harder so that they will not fail. Previous experiences of success or failure can be projected onto new situations, which influences how the individual responds and is able to learn. Emotions experienced during a particular learning experience also are important determinants of outcomes.

## Methods

The presentation of material is important in learning. Even with the large variations in individual ability and willingness to learn, there are optimum methods that enhance the effectiveness and efficiency of learning for most people. These methods also influence retention, recall, and transfer. Among the major methods are active participation, distribution of practice, knowledge of results, and whole versus part.

Active participation enhances people's ability to learn. This appears to be true for cognitive as well as psychomotor tasks. Taking an active role promotes better understanding, retention, skill development, and applications. Paying attention, thinking about presented material, searching for patterns and relationships, asking questions, making comments, and practicing skills are examples of active participation.

Distribution of practice is another important factor. Learning, particularly learning a skill, is more effective if practice time is sufficiently long and is arranged so that there is continuity between cue and response and between response and reinforcement. Sequencing tasks, frequent practice sessions, and an emphasis on speed over accuracy are important when teaching skills.

Knowledge of results (i.e., feedback) is an important component of learning. The learner is encouraged when he or she receives input. The input can be either to affirm correctness or to identify and correct errors. Knowing how someone is doing can increase his or her time on-task, thereby increasing learning.

Whole versus part refers to seeing how the part fits into the whole. Although people must learn discrete units in order to know the whole (as the keyboard and commands must be learned in order to use a software program), learners do better when they are presented with the whole before dealing with the discrete units. Orienting and reviewing the entire task allows them to better understand how each discrete unit fits and its utility. Breaking a task down into manageable units allows learners to focus, to avoid feeling overwhelmed, and to deal with one thing at a time.

## Meaningfulness of Material

Learners are motivated to learn and participate if the material has meaning for them. Students retain and understand material better when the material has significant associations for them. Associations with previously learned material, with internal needs or drives, or with emotional content contribute to meaningfulness.

Organizing material into conceptual categories can help the learner to see significant associations, particularly with previously learned materials. Humans appear to favor patterns and relationships, so it is helpful for their learning if the presenter takes time to ensure the meaningfulness of the material.

## Transfer of Learning

Gagné (1965) described two types of learning transfer: horizontal and vertical. *Horizontal transfer* occurs when the learner can perform a new task at about the same level of difficulty as an old task. *Vertical transfer* takes place when old concepts or learning are used to learn or understand more complex concepts. There are four major theories on transfer: formal discipline, identical elements, generalization, and transposition.

### Formal Discipline Theory

The classical curriculum of the 19th century was built on the idea that people should study Latin, Greek, logic, and mathematics because of their value in training the mind—for example, scholars held that the study of mathematics quickens the mental faculties so that they can meet any and all mental tasks. The real value of a subject, according to this theory, is that it is difficult: The study of difficult subjects strengthens the mind just as exercise strengthens the body. However, James (1890) demonstrated that practice in memorizing did not improve memory.

### Theory of Identical Elements

According to this theory, transfer can occur from one learning to another only so far as the two functions have elements in common. As the similarity decreases, there usually is a falling off in the amount of transfer. An application in psychoeducational groups is to highlight similarities between what is known (or previous experiences) and the new material.

### Generalization Theory

Judd (1908) emphasized that learning principles and meanings led to superior applications—that is, the principle learned in one situation could be applied to the performance of a task in a different situation. Leaders of psychoeducational groups can make use of this theory by providing numerous examples of applications for material and by soliciting possible examples from group members.

### Transposition Theory (Gestalt)

Also called *patterns of experience* (Wertheimer, 1959), this is the process of using the understanding of the inner structure of a problem to help deal with variations of the problem. According to this theory, the learner responds as a unified and integrated organism to the total stimulus using the following process:

1. A new problem is perceived as a whole with parts, as is the previous situation, which is deemed to have similarities to the new problem.
2. Similarities between the old and new subparts are considered without losing sight of the whole.
3. The inner structures of the old and the new are examined to determine how they are interrelated.

4. An understanding of the similarities and inner structure emerges, which aids in dealing with other variations of the situation that may present in the future.
5. The entire process is a consistent line of thinking with constant reference to the whole.

## Retention

Material must not only be learned but retained if it is to be of use to the learner. Retention is influenced by several factors and can best be understood by looking at what and why people forget.

Studies conducted by Ebbinhaus (1885, as cited in Garrison & Magoon, 1972) provided considerable information on forgetting and retention, and those findings are still relevant today. The most important of Ebbinhaus's findings was that there is a tendency to quickly forget material that has little or no meaning for the learner. Material with high meaningfulness may be retained indefinitely with little or no forgetting.

There are two primary theories of forgetting: trace decay and interference. *Trace decay theory* proposes that unused traces of memory will gradually fade away, while traces of memory that are used will be strengthened and retained.

*Interference theory* posits two causes of forgetting: proactive and retroactive inhibition. Proactive inhibition occurs when previous learning gets in the way of learning new material. Retroactive inhibition occurs when new information gets in the way of retrieving old information.

The *rate of forgetting* is a function of the degree to which the material was learned in the first place, the relevance of learning to the learner's needs, intervening influences, actions connected to the material following the learning, and the physical and psychological state of the individual both at learning and at recall. These factors interact and are interrelated, and the degree and extent to which they do so may differ between individuals. Material is more likely to be retained if these conditions are met:

1. It was thoroughly learned in the first place.
2. It has meaning for the learner.
3. Intervening situations, circumstances, or actions are not strong or traumatic enough to interfere.
4. The material is used in some way after being learned.
5. The learner is physically and psychologically able to learn and to retrieve the material.

The extent of forgetting is called the *curve of forgetting* (Ebbinhaus, 1885, as cited in Garrison & Magoon, 1972), describing how much of newly learned material is forgotten immediately after learning and how the part that is remembered is retained over time. The following five factors influence the curve of forgetting:

1. The principle of use it or lose it appears to hold true for retaining learned material. Use of material can refer to practice or to review.
2. Retroactive inhibition (new information interfering with old) does not just refer to new information about the subject under discussion, such as learning new theories of counseling. It also refers to moving from topic to topic when there is little or no relationship between topics (e.g., learning new material in mathematics, then learning new material in history). Some of both is retained, but much of both is forgotten.
3. Proactive inhibition can be seen in those not willing or not able to let new information in. Unlearning of and modifications to what has been learned before appear to be difficult.
4. Humans are attracted to patterns and relationships. Even when these are not apparent, the human mind seeks them or reorganizes material so that they appear. Newly learned material is reorganized to fit with familiar concepts or objects. When new material cannot be reorganized to fit, it is less easily retained. If patterns or relationships are not apparent to the individual, little may be retained.
5. Resistances and defenses also play a role in forgetting. People may have unconscious defense mechanisms against threatening or uncomfortable material. For example, individuals who lack confidence in their mathematics ability or who have a lot of anxiety about mathematics may unconsciously block mathematics material, either not learning it or easily forgetting it.

## PRINCIPLES OF INSTRUCTION
## FOR PSYCHOEDUCATIONAL GROUPS

Learning theories provide a framework for determining principles to guide instruction for psychoeducational groups. The same principles relate to instruction in more formal settings, but they are used somewhat differently for psychoeducational groups. Knowing how people learn, retain, and transfer material can help the leader develop strategies for presenting information in a group.

The educational component for most psychoeducational groups is significant; in fact, it is typically emphasized the most. Teaching participants specific information, strategies, and skills is a primary goal in most groups, so developing instructional strategies to maximize learning is a major task for the leader. Table 3.2 presents the primary principles and leader tasks in psychoeducational groups.

TABLE 3.2

Principles and Tasks

| Principle of Instruction | Leader Task(s) |
| --- | --- |
| Clear goals | Develop reasonable goals; review goals with participants; obtain commitment to goals from participants. |
| Readiness | Understand educational, maturity, and age levels of participants; develop goals, etc., based on participants' levels. |
| Motivation | Understand the role of personal needs, etc., in motivation; plan activities to meet needs; review activities with participants and incorporate suggestions. |
| Active vs. passive involvement | Provide for participants' active involvement; use experiential activities, games, simulations, etc.; encourage questions and discussion. |
| Organization | Plan for new material to be associated with previously learned material; present whole before part; organize presentation to be hierarchical; material should be meaningful. |
| Comprehension | Make significant connections of materials to participants; illustrate significance, meanings, implications, and applications. |
| Practice | Provide opportunities for repetition, review, etc. |

## Goals

The leader of a psychoeducational group usually develops the goals for the group, particularly for the educational component. These goals should be specific, clear, direct, and unambiguous. They should be developed with the needs, readiness, and motivations of participants in mind. This may be somewhat difficult, as the leader may know little or nothing of the participants as individuals prior to the first group meeting. However, the leader will know some general things that can provide suggestions about the learners' characteristics. For example, if the group is focused on time management for engineers, the participants are most likely to be college educated, and over 21.

In addition to developing clear goals, the leader must review these goals with participants and get agreement to work toward them. The leader should review the goals with participants at the beginning of the session and ask if they seem appropriate, what changes they might suggest, and if they can agree to work toward them. For groups with involuntary members, the leader may decide to have participants sign a contract to work on the goals. This has been shown to be particularly effective with children and adolescents.

## Readiness

The lack of knowledge about participants makes this factor difficult for the leader. Members usually are not prescreened, and the leader typically is not provided with records or background data for most groups. Exceptions may be involuntary participants for some groups (such as those focused on anger control).

However, the leader usually knows some general characteristics of members from which he or she can draw inferences about the readiness of participants for certain activities—for example, in preparing an adolescent social skills training group for boys, the leader can reasonably infer that the members lack certain skills, will likely be either silent or very active because of embarrassment or anxiety, may not have volunteered for the group, may be wary and suspicious of authority figures, and may lack maturity for their age. The leader of such a group might need to address safety and trust issues, "sell" members on participating, and present material more slowly.

## Motivation

Motivation may be external (i.e., in the form of a reward) or internal (i.e., by satisfying a need). Generally, the leader can expect that members will have or need both kinds of motivation. If the psychoeducational group does not provide mechanisms for achieving both or either, the leader will find the group difficult, and little or no learning will take place.

Since there usually is no pregroup interviewing, the leader typically does not have the opportunity to get input on participants' motivators. Some may be evident, such as the wish to avoid incarceration. Others, such as a need for achievement, are internal processes that must be inferred from behavior over time or by self-report.

The leader can make accommodations to provide motivators or to encourage group members' self-motivation. Planning activities to encourage participation by motivating is the first step. Younger participants typically respond to tangible rewards (e.g., candy). Older participants like tangible rewards as well, but they also want to know what participation will do for them. A motivator may be provided by outside forces, such as an employer. Accessing internal motivators is somewhat more difficult. Leaders can review the proposed schedule and activities and obtain input from participants on how well the planned activities meet their individual needs, request additional suggestions and incorporate them, or allow participants to help set the agenda.

The most important step a leader can take is to understand the developmental levels of participants, the background of the condition (such as anger and violence), strategies generally found to be successful, and the role of motivation in learning. Reading the literature can provide some needed information.

## Active Versus Passive Involvement

Active involvement enhances learning. Hands-on activities promote learning by doing. Active participation includes group members responding in a discussion, role-playing, drawing, writing, talking, and engaging in movement. Less learning takes place with passive participation—for example, by listening to a lecture.

The leader has more control over this factor than over most others. He or she is responsible for planning and designing the learning experiences, which provides the opportunity to ensure that the activities encourage active participation.

Another responsibility of the leader is to encourage questions and discussion. The "Questioning Skill Development" section in Chapter 2 gives more information on how to use questioning effectively and on how to respond to questions from participants.

## Organization

It is essential that the material being presented is organized in such a way that it is meaningful, can be associated with previous learning, is hierarchical, and is appropriate for the allotted time. Careful thought and planning promote good organization.

Organizing materials for a largely unknown audience is not easy. Even when the leader has relevant information about participants, organizing is a challenge. Most leaders overprepare and have more materials and activities than can be covered in the available time. This is preferred to underpreparing, however, because it is much easier to discard material than to stretch material out. There also are groups that will explore topics or activities in more depth for unknown or unanticipated reasons. A leader is well advised not to truncate the extended exploration if it is beneficial. If members appear to be getting more out of the in-depth exploration than they would be out of the next planned topic or activity, this is reason enough to stick with it.

Transition from one activity to the next should occur before boredom and disinterest appear. There must be adequate time to process activities, but you should not linger over a topic too long. A good sequence to follow in a group session is a short lecture or presentation; questions and discussion; exercise, role-play, game, or simulation; processing of activity; and summarization. Even a short one-time session can use this sequence. For additional information, see the section on "Taxonomy" below.

## Comprehension

The leader should provide many examples, illustrations, and descriptions for concepts and other significant material. These help participants learn through association and repetition. Often, the leader does not know participants' comprehension needs and levels. Giving examples helps increase the probability of making significant connections for most participants.

When applications are important, it is helpful to have several illustrations or examples. It also is helpful if participants can provide additional examples or make suggestions. The most important thing to remember is that meaningfulness of material promotes and enhances learning.

## Taxonomy

Bloom, Krathwohl, and Masia (1956) developed the cognitive domain for the *Taxonomy of Educational Objectives*, which is useful for establishing instructional goals. These are hierarchical and provide a framework for sequencing and organizing material. The cognitive domain has six levels that call for thinking to move from simple to complex:

1. *Knowledge.* The first level includes thinking activity focused on recall of specifics, universals, methods, processes, patterns, facts, terminology, trends, principles, and generalizations. Some implications for the leader of a psychoeducational group include the following: Be sure to define terms even if you believe that participants are familiar with them. Be specific about principles, concepts, and so on that are part of the presentation. Be cautious in making assumptions about what participants already know.
2. *Understanding.* The second level incorporates and extends knowledge to include interpretation, translation, and extrapolation. Leaders can use this level to get feedback from participants about their levels of understanding. This also gives an opportunity to fill in missing information and to correct misunderstandings and faulty knowledge.
3. *Application.* Level 3 provides for selective use of abstractions (formed from knowledge and understandings) in particular situations. The leader presents applications after presenting facts and giving feedback on the participants' understanding of the facts. Participants who can suggest appropriate applications demonstrate successful completion of levels 1 and 2.
4. *Analysis.* Level 4 cognitive processes include the ability to see discrete elements as well as the whole. Analyzing relationships, patterns, and organizing principles are examples. Analysis involves a relatively high degree of knowledge and experience with the topic, so the leader may be the only one at this level.
5. *Synthesis.* Level 5 incorporates the previous four levels with the creation of a different or new perspective, product, or process. This level of learning would be somewhat unusual for the purposes or goals of most psychoeducational groups. Groups that have a problem-solving focus may achieve this level. Groups that have personal issue involvement as a pri-

mary component may see some members reach this level, especially if the group runs for several sessions.
6. *Evaluation.* Although this is considered the highest level for cognitive processes, evaluation can interact with all of the other levels. It is defined as making judgments about strengths and weaknesses, positive and negative points, adequacies and inadequacies. The interaction with other levels can help increase accomplishments at those levels—for example, evaluating the adequacy of knowledge on a particular topic can lead to more in-depth information being sought or given.

## TECHNIQUES

Psychoeducational groups employ a variety of formats, making it difficult to name a specific set of techniques applicable to all. The variety of participants and their characteristics and the range of educational emphases provide additional confounding variables. Therefore, the techniques described here are not necessarily the preferred methods, but they give a sense of the variety of techniques that can be used.

The leader of psychoeducational groups can use several different techniques that will be effective. Experience promotes understanding of when to use what with whom and expected outcomes. Using these techniques to their best effect is a major thrust of this book, but the most effective group leaders also learn from their own experiences.

### Lectures

To be effective, lectures should be well-organized presentations that lead the listener from point to point to provide an integrated knowledge and understanding of the material. Lectures are efficient ways of getting across a large amount of information in a short amount of time. However, lectures have several drawbacks:

- Listeners tend to have short attention spans unless the topic and presentation grab and hold their interest.
- Listening to a lecture is a passive form of learning, which is less effective than active forms.
- Lecturing demands considerable planning, organizing, and presenting on the part of the leader.

If a leader plans to use lectures as part of a psychoeducational group, he or she should use minilectures lasting no more than 20 minutes. These are most effective if kept to 10 or 15 minutes. Members are more inclined to listen for that period than for a longer span. Further, having several minilectures interspersed with activities to reinforce the material will lead to more learning and retention. The leader also should restrict the amount of material to that which members can use.

## Discussion

This technique can be used to promote active involvement. Lively discussions contribute interest to the session and encourage participants to be involved. Discussion as a technique can be differentiated from discussion groups, where the main purpose is to engage in discussing. As a technique, discussion is not the goal of the group; it is typically kept short so that other activities can happen. Fewer members may be involved, and members tend to talk to the leader rather than to each other.

Leaders can initiate discussion by asking questions, calling for comments or questions, and encouraging exploration of points, issues, or concepts. The exchange of ideas, opinions, and experiences can be energizing to the group. Members feel their input is valued and that they have something to contribute.

## Exercises and Games

Exercises, games, simulations, and role-play are forms of experiential learning. They are designed to produce more active involvement on the part of participants, to focus on and emphasize a particular point, and to provide an opportunity for affective as well as cognitive learning.

Experiential groups constitute a major category of psychoeducational groups, and there is some overlap with skills training. When exercises or other forms of experiential learning are used, members can integrate affective and cognitive learning, which contributes to and intensifies retention.

Several specific strategies should be employed to ensure safety for group participants, since experiential learning can arouse unexpected and uncomfortable feelings. The leader must have the expertise to help members deal with these feelings, which can be intense, and to plan sessions so that the likelihood of these intense, uncomfortable feelings being aroused is minimized.

Exercises and games can be fun as well as educational. When learning is enjoyable, motivation is increased, comprehension is enhanced, and retention is promoted. Planning, conducting, and processing experiential group activities are discussed more fully in the "Planning Experiential Group Activities" section in Chapter 5.

## Media

Movies, audiotapes, and videotapes, computer presentations, and slides are examples of media. Media cover a large amount of material in a short time.

They tend to capture interest more easily, can provide visual illustrations of material, and have been demonstrated to be effective in learning. The primary disadvantage of media is that they do not actually involve the learner. (The exception may be computers, but that still depends on what is being presented via the computer and if the learner is expected to interact with the machine.)

The leader of psychoeducational groups should make judicious use of media. Used as accents or lead-ins, media presentations can be quite effective. Used too frequently or for too long a time, however, media presentations are ineffective. Timing is important as well: having participants passively watch a video immediately after lunch, for example, is more likely to induce sleep than to promote learning. Plan for media to be an enhancement, not the primary technique.

## Personal Development Exercise: Self-Description

**Objective:** To increase your awareness of how you perceive yourself.

**Materials:** Two sheets of paper, pen or pencil.

**Procedure:** Sit at a table in silence and reflect on a self-description of your abilities, personality, and character. Abilities are your potentials and accomplishments; personality is comprised of your strong tendencies and preferences for particular attitudes and behaviors, such as independence, autonomy, dependency, or reliability. Character refers to your inner core of being.

After reflecting on your self-description, write a list of descriptors for each of these three categories. You may wish to have three columns with labels at the top, and write your descriptors in these columns.

**Perceiving:** When you finish your self-description, again sit in silence and reflect on how your parents described you as a child. What did they say to you or others about your abilities, personality, and character? What actions seemed to please or displease them? Write these descriptors on the second sheet of paper.

Place the sheets side by side and note the similarities of how you describe yourself today and how your parents described you as a child and what pleased or displeased them about you. As you look at the two lists, try to decide if your present characteristics are how you really are—a conscious choice on your part—or if some are a carryover from childhood as a result of parental messages. You are not trying to evaluate or judge them as being right, wrong, good, or bad; that is not helpful at this point. You are only trying to better understand what some of your parental messages may be.

# Chapter 4

# The Group:
## *Process and Progress*

Major Topics and Concepts

*Science Factors*
    Group dynamics
    Group stages
    Helpful group factors

*Knowledge Factor*
    Developing the group

## INTRODUCTION

The previous chapter had a strong focus on the instructional part of psychoeducational groups. This chapter focuses on understanding what is taking place in the group as a whole and for individual members as the session unfolds. This understanding is critical for group leaders, as you have to be aware, understand, and respond as the session unfolds. It is easier to recognize what happened in retrospect, but the impact is lost when you miss it, fail to respond appropriately, do not identify the real or underlying issue(s), or remain blissfully unaware of what is taking place. It is also possible under these circumstances for members to be wounded, discounted, or ignored. Although these acts are unintentional on the group leader's part, they nevertheless can have a negative impact on group members and on the group.

Group leaders need to know the basics: group dynamics, group stages, and helpful group factors. These are relatively easy to define or describe in isolation, but they do not occur so clearly in the group. The difficulty is that many of these basics can be in effect at the same time, *and* they shift and change from moment to moment. An additional consideration is the nature of psychoeducational groups where group factors may be overlooked or minimized because of the instructional component. However, the process and progress for the group and for individual members are largely located in the group component. The instructional component is important, but the extent to which the material is incorporated and used relies heavily on the group component.

## GROUP DYNAMICS

Group dynamics refers to the ongoing process in the group. The shifting, changing, individual, and group-as-a-whole variables, including level of participation, resistance, communication patterns, relationships between members and between members and the leader, nonverbal behaviors, feeling tone, and feelings aroused and/or expressed.

Discussing individual dynamics does not allow you to understand the range and intensity, as the dynamics do not take place in the group one at a time. Group dynamics are continually and constantly interacting throughout the session, shifting emphasis, changing even as you observe them, and all are important in understanding what is happening in the group. However, the dynamics do have to be individually defined and described. Following are brief descriptions to help you observe group dynamics, along with a summary of focal dynamics for each stage of group development.

### Level of Participation

The extent to which participants cooperate, interact with each other and with the leader, contribute to the progress and functioning of the group, and seek to gain knowledge from the experiences determines their levels of participation. How do members participate? Are they active, passive, sullen, reluctant, or withdrawn? Does their involvement change significantly at some point? For example, do they become energized or fall silent after a discussion? Observing these kinds of behaviors helps you gauge the needs of participants, the intensity of emotions aroused, and the impact of the group and of particular experiences.

### Resistance

You should expect resistance, which will range from mild to intense. The presence of an observable resistance is a clear signal to move on to another person or topic. If the entire group is resisting, you may need to explore with members some of the reasons for the resistance—for example, if members do not want to do a particular exercise or activity, you can initiate a discussion on their perception of the usefulness of the activity. Simply asking what about the activity is a turnoff can produce some valuable information. The one thing you should *not* do however, is to try and breakdown the resistance.

## Communication Patterns

Members will communicate primarily to and through the leader, especially in the beginning. You can facilitate member-to-member communication by suggesting that members talk to each other directly rather than through you. Another pattern to observe is that some members talk to and support each other, while other members are excluded. You can help bring excluded members into the group by asking for their input.

How communications take place is an additional pattern to watch over time; you cannot judge it by one incident. Do group members communicate in a warm, caring, supportive way? Or are communications cold, hostile, or angry? Do members appear wary, aloof, or tentative when they communicate? Individual patterns as well as group patterns should be observed.

## Relationships

You should notice how members relate to each other and to you. Even groups whose members are not strangers to each other may be tentative at first and focus more on differences than similarities.

The leader usually is perceived as the expert at the beginning. Members will expect you to provide for all their unspoken needs and expectations. Sometimes members will seek and compete for your attention and approval. You can work on helping members establish relationships with each other and empower them to take charge and contribute to their own learning instead of looking to you to provide everything.

## Nonverbal Behaviors

Postures, gestures, voice tones, and other nonverbal behaviors provide significant clues to what members are experiencing; these nonverbal signals are called *metacommunication*. It is generally thought to be a more accurate reflection of a person's internal state than his or her verbal communication—for example, a person's words and voice may sound calm, but a tense posture, narrowed eyes, and clenched fists contradict the words.

## Feeling Tone

You can get a good idea of how well the group is progressing by tuning into the feeling tone of the group. This calls for a high level of self-awareness on your part, as you must listen to what you are feeling as a possible reflection of what the group is feeling. Chapter 2 addresses the development of self-awareness in leaders.

## Aroused/Expressed Feelings

Aroused feelings may be directly or indirectly expressed or they may be suppressed. A leader should be alert to feelings that are expressed in indirect ways, especially intense ones, as well as taking care to respond to directly expressed feelings. Suppressed feelings may be more troubling in some respects, but psychoeducational groups generally are not expected to deal with these. It is more appropriate that suppressed feelings be addressed in a counseling or therapy group.

## GROUP STAGES

While group stages are defined somewhat differently by the experts (Bion, 1961; Yalom, 1985), it is commonly accepted that groups do move through stages. Two of these stages are obvious: beginning and termination. Others are not as easy to identify. These tend to be labeled the conflict and working stages.

Counseling and therapy groups are structured in such a way (e.g., a number of sessions held over time) that all the expected stages usually occur and are important in determining what interventions to use. These stages also occur for psychoeducational groups, although the indices of group stages are manifested in different and less intense ways.

These stages are described, along with some primary issues for each, expected member behaviors that illustrate basic issues, and suggestions for the leader. The emphasis is on the psychoeducational group, whether it consists of one session or many. Longer-term groups—for example, skill development—also are addressed.

Table 4.1 presents behaviors representative of each dynamic for four different stages of a group. Table 4.2 presents examples of themes and behaviors for different stages of a group.

## Stage 1: Beginning

The first stage for psychoeducational groups can be characterized by a sense of anticipation, excitement, dread, confusion, and apprehension. Even if there is to be little or no personal disclosure in the group, participants are not sure what they can expect or what is expected of them. Members want to know if they will be valued and included, or if they will be devalued and excluded. There are several steps you can take to reduce some of the negative feelings

TABLE 4.1

Dynamics and Group Stages for Psychoeducational Groups

| Dynamics | Sample Expected Behaviors |
| --- | --- |
| **Stage 1** | |
| Level of participation | Tentative, cautious, anxious; may engage in storytelling. |
| Resistance | Usually high until safety is established. Ask many questions; appear or say they are confused. |
| Communication patterns | Most communication is to and through the leader. Members do not talk directly to each other but to the group, to the leader, or to no one in particular. Tend not to make *I* statements. |
| Member-to-member relationships | Tentative, polite, cautious. Fear of hurting others and of being hurt, fear of being different. Tend to focus on differences but search for similarities. Try to relate through advice giving. |
| Member-to-leader relationships | Respectful; see leader as the expert, the magician. Expect leader to anticipate and meet their personal needs. Want to be reassured that they are valued and accepted by the leader. Want to know they are safe and will be taken care of. |
| Nonverbal behaviors | Fluctuate for individual members from lots of movement (nervous) to little or no movement (tense). There may be little eye contact between members; closed gestures, such as arms folded across chest, backward lean; few attending behaviors. Speech may be rapid or slow and tentative. |
| Group feeling tone | The overall feeling tone from group members may range from apprehension to resentment, hostility, and despair. Usually, members leave with a sense of relief and hopefulness. Many feelings are experienced by members during these first sessions, but the overall feeling tone reflects the confusion, ambiguity, and frustration of group members as well as the changes induced by the leader's interventions. |
| Aroused/expressed feelings | Members will be somewhat reluctant to openly express feelings. Rather, they tend to try to suppress or deny them. This behavior affects the functioning of the group. Common feelings experienced are fear of rejection, fear of engulfment, fear of destruction, fear of shameful secrets, confusion, and frustration. The leader's behavior can contribute to feelings of hopefulness, being cared for and valued, and having something of value to contribute to the group. |
| **Stage 2** | |
| Level of participation | Increasing participation by members, a willingness to explore personal issues on a deeper but still superficial level, and more interaction between members. |

(*Continued*)

TABLE 4.1

Continued

| Dynamics | Sample Expected Behaviors |
|---|---|
| Resistance | There is still considerable resistance, especially to being present centered. Storytelling abounds with little or no recognition of commonalities between members. Members are also resistant to group-as-a-whole process commentary and may tend to personalize comments. |
| Communication patterns | Members begin to talk directly to each other. Communication through the leader to the group and speaking for the group are reduced behaviors. Members begin to make supportive statements to each other and to challenge each other. |
| Member-to-member relationships | Conflict emerges in the group. Members feel safe enough to challenge each other and to report their feelings of anger or irritation. Past experiences with each other are revisited; projections and transference become more apparent. |
| Member-to-leader relationships | The leader is attacked by members. He or she has failed to be the magician or expert and members feel the loss of that idealization. The members still expect the leader to take care of them but are more willing to make their needs and desires known. |
| Nonverbal behaviors | Members' postures and gestures are less studied and contrived. They appear to be willing to let their nonverbal communication be more consistent or congruent with their verbal behavior. The leader can tune into nonverbal communication because members are more genuine. |
| Group feeling tone | Members are combative and irritable, producing a group feeling tone that is uncomfortable. Some members may fear conflict because of past experiences; when conflict emerges, they may regress to old feelings associated with conflicts for them. If conflicts are worked through constructively, the feeling tone becomes one of relief, having a sense of accomplishment, and hopefulness. |
| Aroused/expressed feelings | Irritation, annoyance, anger, rage, fear, and guilt are common feelings that arise and are expressed in this stage. |
| **Stage 3** | |
| Level of participation | Members' levels of participation are high, and significant personal issues emerge and are worked through. |
| Resistance | Resistance is more openly acknowledged, worked through, and understood by members and the leader. Members are more accepting of comments about perceived resistance. |
| Communication patterns | Considerable member-to-member interaction. Cliques and subgroupings may be prevalent. The group functions more as a cohesive unit. |

TABLE 4.1

Continued

| Dynamics | Sample Expected Behaviors |
| --- | --- |
| Member-to-member relationships | Members are more willing to explore relationships with each other. They will work to develop and maintain relationships to the extent that conflicts may be minimized. When conflict does emerge, it can be worked on or through in constructive ways. |
| Member-to-leader relationships | The leader is perceived as a guide and consultant, not as a magician or expert. |
| Nonverbal behaviors | Members are much more congruent in nonverbal behaviors and verbal communications. |
| Group feeling tone | Warm, accepting, a spirit of cooperation and satisfaction, excitement. |
| Aroused/expressed feelings | Irritation, annoyance, caring, warmth, liking, excitement at accomplishments, anticipation of continued learning about self, shame, and guilt. |
| **Stage 4** | |
| Level of participation | Reduced or frantic participation. May withdraw or bring up new material; may end participating before the group ends (premature termination). |
| Resistance | Renewed resistance, this time to experiencing feelings around termination; either holding on or letting go. |
| Communication patterns | Members talk to each other, but communication may revert to occurring through the leader. |
| Member-to-member relationships | Members begin to pull back from investing in relationships that may be ending. The quality and quantity of member relationships will change after termination. |
| Member-to-leader relationships | May be a realization of the value of the leader, an awareness of what he or she contributed, or a feeling of deprivation at the loss of the person and relationship; can be experienced as anger, annoyance, or sadness. |
| Nonverbal behaviors | Failure to maintain eye contact; looking at the floor, ceiling, or away from the leader and members; shifting in seat; gathering possessions. |
| Group feeling tone | Sadness, relief. |
| Aroused/expressed feelings | Appreciation, pleasure, sadness, relief, abandonment, loss, grief. |

that members bring to the group; however, no matter what you do, you will not be able to eliminate negative feelings altogether. You can expect them every time you begin a group.

The most useful step to alleviate discomfort and uneasiness is to plan ahead carefully. Make sure that the facilities are adequate, materials and supplies are on hand, a schedule and an agenda are prepared, and you begin on time. Organized pscyhoeducational groups promote feelings of safety and trust.

TABLE 4.2

Stages of Group and Members' Behaviors

| Major Themes | Expected Behaviors |
| --- | --- |
| **Formative Stages** | |
| Orientation | Search for similarities |
| Hesitant participation | Giving and seeking advice |
| Search for meaning | Symptom description |
| Dependency | Questions about value of experience |
| Safety | Leader seen as all-knowing; desire for acceptance and approval, respect and domination; need for an omnipotent, omniscient, all-caring parent |
| Conflict | Conflicts between members |
| Dominance | Conflicts between members and leader |
| Rebellion | Negative comments; intermember criticism; one-way analyses and judgments; *shoulds* and *oughts*; jockeying for position; hostility toward the leader; discounting of leader's expertise |
| **Working Stages** | |
| Cohesiveness | Increased morale; mutual trust; self-disclosure; intimacy develops; may suppress negative affect |
| Working-through process | Subgrouping may appear; conflict expresses as (a) mutual contempt, (b) self-contempt, (c) transference, (d) mirroring, (e) projective identification, (f) rivalry |
| Working-through process | Self-disclosure: (a) appropriate, (b) inappropriate |
| **Terminating Stage** | |
| Termination | Ignoring the impending end of group; denying feelings around the ending of group; unresolved issues around separation |

The next step is to have an opening session that welcomes participants, introduces the personnel who will be working with the groups, and thoroughly reviews the objectives and schedule. Opening the dialogue to suggestions from participants also is useful. You should ask if the stated objectives meet the participants' expectations and needs, and if there are other topics or activities they want included.

The leader's listening, questioning, and facilitating skills make the difference in how the group gets off the ground. These topics are covered more completely in Chapter 2.

## Stage 2: Conflict and Controversy

The second stage usually begins with an attack on the leader. This attack generally is so indirect that you may miss it. It is not important for you to recognize the attack as such; it is important that you do not become defensive or retaliate. If you find yourself feeling defensive, explaining your rationale, reiterating something you thought was understood, or feeling that participants are being unfair, you probably are being attacked. There is no need to point this out, as it is unlikely that the group has moved to the level of development where members can accept your observation without feeling attacked themselves.

Another way the second stage is recognized is by the conflict that emerges between group members. If the group is on its way toward becoming more cohesive, then conflict will emerge; how you deal with such conflict will determine whether the group continues to grow. Strategies for managing conflict are discussed in Chapter 8.

### Stage 3: Working and Cohesion

The working stage is characterized by cooperation and cohesiveness. Members are interested in and supportive of one another. They also are willing to work on a task and not become sidetracked. Issues that emerge at this stage have more to do with working through misunderstandings and differences of opinion and maintaining relationships than with winning/losing, saving face, and avoiding conflict.

### Stage 4: Termination

Groups, especially psychoeducational groups, do come to an end. Members who are achieving their goals are reluctant to deal with ending and may refuse to discuss it at all. You should introduce the notion of termination before it happens—for example, in a one-day workshop, termination would be introduced after lunch, or before the afternoon break. Reminding participants of how much time is left and asking how they would like to use the time productively is one way of introducing the topic. The usual response is to change the subject or to move away from it in some way. Bring the topic up again when there is about an hour left in the workshop, and plan a summary or wrap-up session. Some groups may want to help plan how they will terminate.

One issue around termination is the leader's response. Leaders, too, deny and avoid dealing with termination. They may end the group or session, but they do not terminate. Termination is an opportunity to tie up loose ends, reveal suppressed feelings, and work out troubling relationships. A satisfactory termination allows participants and the leader to end and leave without residual feelings of unfinished business.

## DEVELOPING THE GROUP

### Pregroup Planning

Planning a psychoeducational group is a developmental process in which the leader's professional preparation and skill provide a basis on which the group is built. Knowledge of theory and techniques, skill in facilitation, and proficiency in the subject matter are all prerequisites for successful psychoeducational groups.

Several factors should be considered prior to developing strategies. The overall goals and objectives for the group should be established. Simply having a topic is not enough. The leader must have a clear goal for the group from which strategies will be developed. Participants' characteristics, such as age, educational level, maturity, readiness, and kind of participation (voluntary or involuntary), are significant in deciding on goals and objectives. Related to these variables are ethical issues and therapeutic factors, which are discussed more fully in Chapter 7.

Regardless of the topic, the group leader should research the latest literature in the field. Expertise is developed by constantly increasing knowledge and skill, not by sitting back and assuming you know all there is to know about a topic. There may not be significant new information, but this should be checked and not assumed.

## Setting Goals, Objectives, and Strategies

Reasonable goals and objectives contribute to feelings of accomplishment because they can be achieved. Try not to set goals that are so broad that there is little likelihood of achieving them. Both you and the participants will be frustrated if none of their goals are achieved in some measure. Generally, there is one goal for the group and several objectives. Objectives are manageable parts of the broader goal. They also point out steps needed to reach the goal.

You may use several strategies to attain an objective. For example, an objective for a time management seminar could be to increase awareness of personal time wasters. Strategies might include a minilecture identifying personal time wasters, a paper-and-pencil activity that reviews a day or the previous week, and brainstorming in small groups to develop suggestions for reducing personal time wasters.

## Participants' Characteristics

You probably will know a few characteristics about the potential participants in an upcoming group. The most significant are age range and educational levels. If the group is being held for a particular organization—for example, an agency—you also may know the occupations of the participants. One way you can obtain more information about participants is to write a description of the intended audience in the flyer or brochure announcing the group. It probably is safe to assume that those who choose to attend the group meet the description fairly well.

Just knowing the age range and educational levels will help you set goals and objectives and select strategies. Words and concepts chosen for minilectures and reading materials, the degree of complexity for directions, and the time frame for activities can be better determined knowing these two participant characteristics.

## Instructional Strategies

Learning theory, instructional principles, and participants' characteristics interact when selecting instructional strategies. Knowing what is effective for learning, retention, and transfer as well as the expected maturity and readiness levels will help you choose effective instructional strategies. Distribution of practice and learning, building on previous knowledge, and awareness of the most effective methods also contribute to successful strategy choices.

There are four general categories of instructional strategies: passive (e.g., lectures and use of media), active verbal (e.g., discussions, forms, and role-play), active combined verbal and nonverbal (e.g., exercises and games), and active nonverbal (e.g., movement). There is some overlap between categories, such as when discussion is used after an exercise. Your choice of instructional strategies for psychoeducational groups should emphasize active methods. Instructional strategies are discussed in more detail in Chapter 5.

## Helpful Group Factors

There are certain factors that have been found to enhance group counseling/ therapy. These have been termed curative factors (Corsini & Rosenberg, 1955); therapeutic factors (Yalom, 1995), helping factors (Schulz, 1993; Schwartzberg, 1993); positive group factors (Gladding, 1999); and change factors (Barbender, 2002). Regardless of the term used, these are generally thought to be enhancing for the group's functioning, and for individual members' growth.

- *Universality or Similarities:* Members recognize that others have similar problems, concerns, circumstances, and reactions as they do. This reduces the feelings of isolation and alienation.
- *Optimism and hope:* Members see that others get better, improve, and resolve their difficulties. This can promote hope and optimism which are shown to foster psychological and physical health. (Hafen, Karren, Frandsen, & Smith, 1996).
- *Altruism:* The unselfish giving of yourself without expecting recognition, rewards, or gratitude.
- *Modeling:* Members and the leader model effective and constructive behaviors.
- *Social skills development:* The opportunity to practice new ways to communicate and relate.
- *Guidance:* Learning new and unfamiliar material that relates to your growth and development.

- *Interpersonal feedback and learning:* Increasing your awareness of your personal issues through feedback obtained from others.
- *Mutual attraction and interaction of members:* When group members trust each other enough to engage in important and appropriate self-disclosure, care for each other, and to support and encourage each other. This happens when the group becomes cohesive.
- *Catharsis:* The release of pent up, suppressed, denied, and repressed emotions that produces relief, and leads to greater awareness and personal learning.
- *Family of origin:* Learning how your family of origin experiences contributes to your current functioning and relating. Developing new and more constructive ways to communicate and interact with others.
- *Existential factors:* The basic human concerns that are common to everyone, and continue to emerge at various times throughout your life. Concerns such as loneliness, despair, death, and the unfairness of the universe are some existential factors.

Many of these factors are present in psychoeducational groups and can be helpful, if not therapeutic. They manifest themselves in somewhat different ways than they do in counseling or therapy groups, and the group leader uses them in different ways. The purpose of the group makes a difference in the appearance or absence of a factor and how it may be used—for example, a discussion group may lead to exploration of existential factors, but a team development group is unlikely to explore these issues. Further, exploration of personal issues with in-depth self-disclosure is not expected in psychoeducational groups, and the appearance of these factors usually will be on a more superficial level.

However, the leader of any psychoeducational group can make effective use of these factors. The first step is to accept that they enhance the process and progress of the group. The second step is to recognize their value and to begin to identify their appearance. The third step is to openly bring attention to the factor in appropriate ways, paying attention to timing. The fourth step is promoting or introducing the factor. Factors and steps are discussed in the following sections. It is important to remember that group members may facilitate the emergence of a factor; it is not the sole responsibility of the leader.

## Factors Most Likely to Appear

### Universality or Similarities
This factor may be easy to identify in psychoeducational groups because members usually have several characteristics in common: they may be from the same organization, such as a school; have the same goal, such as anger management; be in the same age, racial/ethnic, or gender group; or have similar

interests, as evidenced by their choice to attend the group, such as parenting classes.

Most people can easily identify the surface similarities, but a leader's expertise is evident when he or she can identify important subtle similarities and bring them to the group's attention. For example, it may appear that the only things a group of adolescents in an anger management group have in common are their age, their need to learn anger management, and their presence in the group. What the group leader may identify as similar to all or most members is a feeling of helplessness when they do not see how to gain or manage control of a situation; feelings that others seek to control them; and an inability to focus on and be aware of milder forms of anger. These universalities promote bonding and reduce feelings of isolation and alienation.

It is the leader's responsibility to bring these commonalities to the attention of group members. Members seldom recognize deeper commonalities and tend to focus on differences, particularly on visible differences. The group bonds and becomes cohesive around similarities but fragments and dissolves around differences. Developing the skill of linking will help you identify and introduce the factor of universality.

## Altruism

Altruism often goes unrecognized, and often what is thought to be altruism is not, because the giver expects something in return. This factor can be helpful with members who are feeling helpless, hopeless, isolated, or useless. Children, in particular, benefit from knowing that they have something to give that is of value. They usually are on the receiving end, and few adults take the time and effort to help them understand that they have something to give that is valued by others.

Recognizing altruism is difficult because motives play a part, and this is an internal event that can only be inferred. The leader can model altruism, reinforce what appears to be altruism, and, in appropriate circumstances, describe altruism. An example of why altruism is difficult to identify can be illustrated in the following scenario: Group members are discussing a problem. One member tells the group that he or she addressed the problem in a particular way that is beneficial or gives suggestions for resolutions. Even an experienced leader will not always know if the suggestions are being offered get attention, garner admiration, show the teller's superiority, control or manipulate in some way, or out of altruism.

The leader can assume that there is not a hidden agenda until there is more evidence. If this is the only session or there are very few sessions, the leader should acknowledge the contribution as being useful and make no determination about the giver's motives. One of the nice things about this factor is that if it is present it can be beneficial in indirect ways, and the leader can simply allow it to emerge.

## Modeling

A major task for the group leader is to model appropriate behaviors. Many psychoeducational groups are designed to teach participants different ways of behaving, relating, or communicating. One way of learning is through observing and practicing. Modeling is a powerful technique for teaching new behaviors to those who may not have a clue how to behave, relate, or communicate differently than they do now. Telling someone how to do something is not as effective as showing him or her.

The leader may recognize when group members are imitating other group members. Members do learn from each other as well as from the leader. It is helpful if the leader can recognize and reinforce desired behaviors through praise.

## Guidance

Giving factual information is one of the primary tasks for a psychoeducational group. Some of the group leader's responsibilities are teaching new and unfamiliar material and guiding the learner. However, the leader may not be the only one who has relevant information. Group members also know important pieces and should be encouraged to share and participate in imparting information. Be alert to advice giving and *shoulds* and *oughts*. These behaviors are not helpful and must be blocked or reframed into more helpful behaviors.

Imparting of information may be the easiest factor to recognize, since it is so obvious. The leader usually does not need to openly identify it. It is useful, however, to reinforce when members impart information by saying things like, "That is important to know. Thank you for bringing it to our attention." Other members then become encouraged to share information. The primary thing to remember is that you must limit the amount of information to what participants can absorb and use—not what you think they need or what you want to give. Too much information can be overwhelming, frustrating, and confusing.

## Factors Likely to Appear

### Optimism and Hope

This factor is dependent on the type of group. It usually is associated with getting better, solving personal problems, and resolving personal issues. Many psychoeducational groups do not deal with these concerns; participants attend to learn more concrete and less personally related material. However, there are some groups for which personal issues, problems, or concerns are the focus; in such groups, this factor would be in the "most likely to appear" category. In these instances, the leader must take steps to introduce hope into the group.

Hope allows individuals to continue to work on and through their concerns. We have to hope that the distress or pain will end someday. Further, hope is one rationale for participating in the group in the first place. Why go through the experience if nothing will change?

Hope can be introduced by giving examples of how the group has helped others (personal experiences are particularly helpful), how group experiences are structured to address issues, and anticipated outcomes. Participants often ask, directly or indirectly, "How is this supposed to help me?" You can anticipate the question and provide the information before it is asked. By doing so, you increase participants' confidence that their problem will be adequately addressed in the group. It is helpful if there are group members who have resolved or constructively dealt with the problem or something similar. Seeing others who have come through it gives hope to members that they, too, can achieve. Effective leaders capitalize on these success stories. They can be found by asking the group if anyone has experienced something similar and allowing members to tell how they coped. These people are valuable resources to the group and to the leader.

## Social Skills Development

Socializing techniques may be relating, communicating, or social skills, but all are designed to produce better interpersonal relations, reduce feelings of isolation and alienation, and promote self-confidence. Some psychoeducational groups have this factor as a goal; others may focus on it or emphasize it without stating it as a goal. It may be incidental for other groups and for some it is unimportant. Where the factor is a goal or focus, the leader takes the responsibility for introducing the topic, attending to it, and recognizing it. When members learn a behavior and practice it in the group, the leader also provides reinforcement.

Even in groups for which development of socializing techniques is not a focus, or for which it is only incidental to the main goal, it still can be helpful. The leader needs to be alert to these opportunities and be prepared to capitalize on them. For example, the goal for the group or session may be on time management. Socializing techniques typically are not a part of the focus for this topic. However, telephone communication and manners may be on the agenda. It is then appropriate for you to introduce some socializing techniques and allow participants to discuss their problems or experiences. You may even build some awareness of transfer of learning to other situations.

## Interpersonal Feedback and Learning

Yalom (1985) described the interpersonal learning sequence. A behavior, usually a maladaptive or inappropriate behavior, is displayed. "Through feedback and self-observation, one (1) becomes a better observer of one's behavior; (2) appreciates the impact of that behavior upon (a) the feelings of others, (b) the opinions that others have of one, (c) the opinion one has of oneself."

Thus, it is through observation and constructive feedback that interpersonal learning takes place. For some members this may be the first time they have received constructive feedback. While this may not be enough to alter behavior significantly, it is the beginning of awareness that leads to significant change.

Interpersonal learning is not the focus for many psychoeducational groups, as it has an intense affective component that may not be appropriate for the group. Groups focused on study skills, time management, and meetings may not be suitable forums for interpersonal learning to occur. While it is not impossible for this factor to emerge for some members, it is not the goal or emphasis. Other groups, such as conflict management, anger control, parenting, and support groups, may have interpersonal learning as an expectation and provide appropriate means for it to emerge, be recognized, and be capitalized upon.

## Mutual Attraction and Interaction

It is not unusual for members of intact groups (e.g., a department) to be part of a psychoeducational group or to be the group. The group leader needs to be aware that some measure of cohesiveness may already be present. This may be both a plus and a minus.

Groups tend to become cohesive around perceived similarities. If group members already know their similarities, the leader does not need to point them out. The group has already moved toward cohesiveness. The negative sides are that others in the group (those not from that department) may feel excluded, and the unit may form a clique within the group. If there is tension or dissension in the unit, it also may impact the functioning of the larger group.

One major issue experienced by members of all types of groups is inclusion versus exclusion. Although not expressed openly or directly, members want to know if they will be accepted by other members and by the leader. When there is already a subgroup that knows and accepts each other, other members wonder if that subgroup will dominate, leaving them out, or if the group will be structured to include the subgroup *and* other group members. Leaders who do not actively attend to this concern will not be able to develop cohesiveness, and group members will not feel positive about the group experience.

An even worse possibility for the group and leader is if the unit forms a clique within the group. Not only do other members feel excluded but the leader may find that control of the group has been assumed by the clique. More time and attention may be given to dealing with the clique, which takes away time needed for the topic and for other members.

The most destructive situation is if the unit has tension or dissension among its members. Sometimes the suppression of intense negative affect will have an effect on participants, and the leader and other members will not understand why the group is not going well. Everyone will leave feeling churned up, without a clue as to why they feel this way. Or, worse still, conflict will break out into the open and the leader's lack of knowledge of history, people, or issues will prevent successful intervention. In this case, the entire purpose of the group will be lost.

What about groups in which members do not have working or personal relationships prior to joining the group? Can cohesiveness be developed in these groups? The answer is yes. Some level of cohesiveness can be established even if the group life is only 2 to 3 hours. While this cohesiveness may be minimal, shared experiences in an atmosphere in which members feel safe, respected, and valued does produce cohesiveness. This is where the personal characteristics and skills of the leader are needed most: you will use those skills and characteristics to produce a situation in which cohesiveness (albeit minimal) can emerge.

## Factors with Limited Appearance

Catharsis, corrective recapitulation of the family of origin, and existential factors are unlikely to appear in a manner that is useful to the goals of the psychoeducational group, except for support and therapy-related groups. The very experienced leader who has training in leading counseling/therapy groups may recognize the appearance of these factors. Leaders who do not have the training and experience are less likely to do so. These factors have their therapeutic value but probably cannot be successfully incorporated into psychoeducational groups.

### Catharsis

Emotional venting together with intrapersonal learning describes catharsis. Most psychoeducational groups are not conducted to promote this kind of response; if emotional venting occurs, it may be destructive to the goals of the group and safety concerns of the members. There are psychoeducational groups in which some level of catharsis may occur—for example, anger management or conflict mediation. In these instances, the group leader should be trained in these areas and able to use the catharsis constructively. These groups typically run for several sessions, which allows safety and trust to be developed before catharsis appears.

### Family of Origin

Recapitulation of the family of origin can be inferred from observation of group members' behavior over time. Most psychoeducational groups do not last long enough for the necessary observation, nor do most leaders have the necessary training and experience. Further, this factor does not apply to the goals of most psychoeducational groups.

An additional component necessary for this to be a therapeutic factor is for the group and leader to make the recapitulation of the family of origin a corrective experience—that is, to help the member recognize his or her transferences and projections so that they will not affect relationships outside the family of origin. For example, if a group member is in conflict with authority figures or with those perceived to be authority figures, being aware of the transference of feelings about a parent onto these figures can allow that member to understand his or her conflicts better and to make changes in behavior—seeing the person as he or she is, not in terms of past family relationships.

*Existential Factors*

Existential factors always seem to be present in some form; however, in order to be therapeutic, they must be dealt with on some level, and it is unlikely that they will occur in a manner relevant to the goals of psychoeducational groups. Further, a leader needs training and experience to recognize existential factors and to be confident of his or her ability to effectively deal with them.

Support and therapy-related groups are the only category of groups addressed in this book in which existential factors may be therapeutic. These groups tend to be long term, focused on a particular issue, and more personal than task oriented. They also tend not to have designated leaders, but a leader knowledgeable about existential factors can help the group make therapeutic use of such factors when they do appear.

Personal Development Exercise: Self-Awareness

> **Objective:** To increase awareness of parts of oneself.
>
> **Materials:** A variety of catalogues and magazines from which to cut pictures, index card, glue sticks, felt markers, scissors, sheet of paper, pen or pencil.
>
> **Procedure:** Cut out a variety of pictures from the catalogues and magazines. Do not try to sort them at this point.
>
> Make a minicollage on the index card using the pictures and glue sticks. The collage should have a theme, such as my dreams and wishes, my values, or my deeper self. Use the markers to draw symbols for ideas you want to express if you do not have an appropriate picture.
>
> **Process:** Write a brief summary statement or paragraph on the sheet of paper about your minicollage, noting the feelings aroused as you completed the collage.

# Chapter 5

# Planning the Psychoeducational Group

Major Topics and Concepts

*Knowledge and Science Factors*
General guidelines for planning
Planning experiential activities
Environmental factors
Session planning

*Techniques and Skills Factors*
Minilectures
Instructional strategies
Techniques
Exercises and games
Simulation and role-play

## INTRODUCTION

There is an enormous amount of work that needs to be completed prior to the first session. The group leader's work begins long before the group starts to work, and much of the success for the group is dependent on the leader's attention to the planning phase. It may be helpful to think of planning as having the following phases and components:

*Phase 1:  Information Gathering*

- Condition, topic, audience/participants
- Research findings
- Demographics and other participant data
- Available materials

*Phase 2:  Decisions About Proposed Group*

- Membership selection
- Open versus closed group
- Framework for sessions, such as number, duration, and the like

*Phase 3:  Preparing*

- Establish goals and objectives
- Plan for evaluating
- Gather supplies
- Write lectures
- Pregroup screening for members

Planning should be an orderly developmental process and should not be truncated even after you gain experience in leading groups. Careful planning can help promote safety and trust, reduce and eliminate some potential problems, and provide you as the leader with confidence. This chapter presents material to help guide your planning.

## THE LEADER'S ROLE IN PLANNING

Psychoeducational groups come in many forms, but all are characterized by a body of knowledge to be communicated, intended and specific learning outcomes, structured sessions, and an emphasis on active participation, or learning by doing. Leadership also has some specific tasks and roles such as the following:

- Extensive planning
- Structuring and directing throughout the entire experience
- Swift attention to problem behaviors
- Attending to helpful or therapeutic factors
- Continual awareness of ethical issues

The leader of psychoeducational groups is much more active than leaders for counseling, therapy, and psychotherapy groups. Leaders for the latter groups have the time and intention of letting group process and progress unfold, whereas leaders of psychoeducational groups have more time limitations and must be more task oriented. The other kinds of groups also have tasks and goals, but these are deeper, less specific for the group as a whole, more individualized, and leaders spend more time developing the therapeutic alliance or relationship prior to focusing on tasks.

Planning psychoeducational groups is critical for their success, and this is a major task for the group leader. Consultation, research, and input from others can be a part of planning, but the leader has the ultimate responsibility for planning. General planning guidelines for psychoeducational groups and guidelines for adapting packaged psychoeducational group materials are covered in this chapter. Specific guidelines are presented for planning groups for children, adolescents, and adults.

### Planning Guidelines

The major concerns when planning any psychoeducational group are as follows:

• Purpose for the group
• Target audience—for example, children
• Goals and expected outcomes
• Review of literature
• Environmental factors
• Session planning
• Instructional strategies and materials
• Evaluation (this is presented in Chapter 6)

Almost everything that is needed for the group is contained in these components, except for the expertise of the group leader, which is discussed in Chapters 2 and 3.

### Purpose

Every group should have a purpose. This could also be termed the theme or focus for the group. The purpose is the overall framework within which the group will be constructed. Purposes for psychoeducational groups usually encompass education, training, or support. You should try to be clear about the primary purpose for the group you are planning, because this will help you develop all other components.

The emphasis on primary purpose arises because there can be some overlap between categories, and it becomes easy to lose the focus for the group— for example, skills training can involve education, and support groups can involve education and training. In addition, education groups can have parts that are skills training and support. These overlaps can contribute to loss of focus. It is important that you, as the leader, not lose the focus, since that can allow the group to flounder, go off on tangents, meander around and not accomplish what you set out to do, or even fail to progress.

When you first begin to conduct psychoeducational groups, it can be helpful to construct a comprehensive written plan for every group you create or facilitate. The plan should begin with a distinct purpose—for example, social skills training. Everything then flows from that purpose. Even when you become so skilled that you can reduce your written plan to a topical outline, you will need to write down the purpose for the group as clearly as you can.

You can be tempted to have several purposes or a very general overall purpose that encompasses all categories of psychoeducational groups discussed in this book. Or, your agency, team, or supervisor may point out that the target audience needs all of these, and you feel a need to meet these expectations and client needs. Your own needs, wishes, and personality can lead you to becoming seduced into this mindset, as you want to help the clients, and if they need all these things, you want to try and provide them. After all, this is why you chose a career in mental health.

When you find yourself in the situation where there are competing purposes and each seems important, you can sort through the needs and prioritize the purposes so that one emerges at the top. The others can then be addressed in some form but will not be the guiding principle for the development of the group.

## Target Audience

You probably will know a few characteristics about the potential participants in an upcoming group. The most significant are age range and educational levels. If the group is being held for a particular organization—for example, an agency—you also may know the occupations of the participants. One way you can obtain more inferred information about participants is to write a description of the intended audience in the flyer or brochure announcing the group. It probably is safe to assume that those who choose to attend the group meet the description fairly well.

Just knowing the age range and educational levels will help you set goals and objectives and select strategies. Words and concepts chosen for minilectures and reading materials, the degree of complexity for directions, and the time frame for activities can be better determined knowing these two participant characteristics.

## Goals

Once you have established a purpose for the group, you can set goals. While it is helpful to have group member participation in choosing goals, you are unlikely to have this input, and, as the leader, you have a responsibility for these goals.

It may be helpful to think of the group you will lead as a class where you will teach members and/or facilitate their learning as you develop goals for the group. The focus here is on deciding what general knowledge, understanding, application, or skill you want members to learn. The goal is not what you present but what members will learn, understand, or be able to do as a result of participating in the group. Your goal will be somewhat idealistic, as it may not be entirely accomplished, but it does describe what the group is designed to achieve.

Restrict your goals to one or two at most. Any more and the focus for the group can get lost or diluted. You have only a limited time and you cannot expect to do everything in that time frame—for example, in a school setting you probably will not have the entire semester (14–16 weeks) for your group, and you will need to have realistic expectations for what can be accomplished in the time you do have. Examples for some goals for different groups and target audiences follow:

**Educational (children 8–10 years of age)**
    Goal: Gain an understanding of the world of work and various career paths.
**Social Skills Training (adolescents)**
    Goal: Increase confidence in social situations.
**Work/Task Group (adults)**
    Goal: Become more effective and efficient in assigned work.
**Support Group (adults)**
    Goal: Develop self-help and self-coping strategies.

## Expected Outcomes

The expected outcomes should be stated as behavioral objectives—that is, what do you expect group members to be able to articulate, apply, evaluate, or do as a result of their learning? Objectives should be written to include all of the following points:

- Focus on specific behaviors
- Objectives should be capable of being observed and assessed
- Provide structure and direction for chosen activities
- Identify techniques and strategies that will be used
- Contribute to additional planning

We use one of the educational goals that was previously stated to develop some specific objectives and expected outcomes:

Target Audience: Students 8–10 years of age
    *Goal: Gain an understanding of the world of work and various career paths.*
    *Objectives: As a result of participation in the group, members will be able to*

1. Define and describe work
2. List five different occupational categories
3. Describe one or more occupations or careers for each of the categories
4. Describe the education and training for one or more occupations or careers for each category
5. Understand how to research information on careers
6. Apply personal characteristics and interests to begin career exploration

These specific objectives can be observed, measured, and evaluated, and also provide guidance for structuring group sessions to fit within the framework of the overall goal. There is still considerable room for flexibility and creativity.

## Literature Review

This step cannot be overemphasized. Although you may be knowledgeable about the content for your psychoeducational group and/or have an understanding of the needs for your target audience, there is always more to be learned. There is new information, techniques, and other understandings emerging constantly, and you cannot really be confident that you know all there is to know. It is very helpful to conduct a literature review to accomplish the following:

• Refresh your knowledge and understanding.
• Gain new information about the topic and your target audience.
• Trigger new ideas, strategies, and techniques.
• Increase your depth of knowledge.

The literature review need not be extensive, and after you have done a few, you will have a good idea of which resources to consult and be better able to evaluate the findings. Just because something is published or is on the Internet does not mean that it is sound, valuable, or useful. You will have to make those determinations. Your training and education in all your courses should prepare you to critically read the literature.

## Environmental Factors

Environmental factors are specific and form the framework for the group. These factors are number of sessions, length of each session, frequency of sessions, physical meeting space, and any other concerns that impact the group and the setting—for example, the agency, school, or hotel. It is important to have these clearly defined and disseminated in advance to all who are involved.

Your setting and the type of group will factor into the number of sessions. For example, in an agency setting with court-ordered group attendance, you may plan for 8 to 12 sessions. A task/work group, on the other hand, has a business or corporate setting, and you may be limited to 1 day. Granted, that could be an 8-hour day, but it is still just one day. A support group could be open-ended, with new members being added and members leaving. It may mean there is no ending time for that group and no definite number of sessions.

Sessions can range from 20 minutes for very young children to a full day for work/task groups, with many variations in between. Some guidelines for making this decision include the following:

• Do not plan to hold marathon group sessions.
• Consider the emotional state of group members when planning the length of sessions.
• Decide what is a reasonable accomplishment or goal for each session, and allow sufficient time to achieve it.
• Each session should be self-contained so that important and/or emotional work is completed in that session.
• Allow sufficient time for every member to participate and have input.

How often the group will meet will vary considerably depending on the topic, purpose for the group, setting, and group participants. Groups can lose their focus and momentum if they meet less than once a week. The important thing is that group members know when the group begins and when it will end. Support groups are the only exception to the last statement.

The physical meeting space should be conducive to fostering interactions among members and should have facilities—for example, tables or desks—for completing the exercises. Ideally, there should be enough space so that these interacting and completing exercises are separate. It is essential that groups not meet around a table or that members sit at desks. There should be no barriers between members. The atmosphere is very different when groups have barriers, such as tables, and when they do not. If the space is not ideal for group meetings, move the barriers while the group is meeting and replace them after the meeting. Try to locate chairs if only attached desks are available.

Other physical space considerations are comfort, freedom from distractions, and privacy. It is not always possible to provide comfortable seating, but every effort should be made to do so. Heating and air conditioning are also a part of comfort and should not be neglected. Group meetings have a self-focus and should be free from outside distractions, such as interruptions by others entering the room, telephone, and so on. You cannot prevent all outside distractions, but planning can prevent some of them. Privacy is of the utmost importance. Safety and trust cannot be developed if members have reason to believe that people outside the group can overhear what members discuss, disclose, and reveal. Thus, the leader should take steps to ensure that sessions will not be heard by others—for example, people walking by the room, those in the outer office or waiting room, or through the duct heating and air-conditioning system. The leader needs to do all this prior to beginning the group, because you will find it extremely difficult to regain trust and safety if members have any reason to believe they were overheard.

## Session Planning

Groups are unpredictable in many ways, and even with considerable knowledge, understanding, and experience, group leaders can be constantly surprised by what emerges in a group. The ambiguity and uncertainty contribute to the difficulty for planning group sessions. However, you must have a tentative plan that presents when and how you intend to accomplish your goals and objectives. Sequencing information can also be important.

It is recommended that you write a session-by-session plan and revise it when needed. You will be more confident when you have a plan, and this confidence will be unconsciously communicated to your group members, leading to building their feelings of trust and safety. You will be less likely to flounder, become frustrated or confused, and can prevent potential problems when you have some sense of what you intend to do, when you will do it, and how you will accomplish your goals. Each session plan should at least have the following components:

• Objectives for the session
• A list of needed materials
• An outline or full text for the minilecture or information you intend to present
• A tentative schedule and sequence for activities—for example, an exercise

The session should be flexible and allow sufficient time for adequate discussion, exploration, and input from each member. Material loses its intensity and impact when carried over to the next session. Thus, it is extremely important to select learning activities and other exercises that can be completed in the session.

You may want to give homework assignments, which can be a valuable learning strategy. If you do plan for homework, be aware that many group members may not complete it, and the expected learning and discussion may not happen. It is not effective to have some members participate—for example, discuss their homework—while others are not able to participate. It can be frustrating for members who complete the homework if the material does not get discussed and explored because other members do not complete the assignment. Understand the pros and cons for homework before incorporating it into your group plan.

## Minilectures

Minilectures are relatively short. They have the same purpose as a full-length lecture: presenting a body of information. It can be more difficult to develop a minilecture, as you cannot have a sole focus on the material or information; you have to also consider the group members. The following discussion is intended to guide your planning and developing minilectures for your psychoeducational groups. Discussed are:

* the necessity for a narrow focus,
* why to write the minilecture before presenting it,
* the value of practice,
* how and why to prioritize information,
* sequencing

### Have a Focus

Your minilecture should have a focus and a purpose. It is not helpful to present a general or unfocused lecture, as you will lose members' interest and attention. Clearly and directly state the focus at the very beginning. For example, for a relapse prevention group, the focus of a particular lecture could be common triggers for relapse. The leader could begin the lecture with something like, "While each of you will differ in what can trigger the craving to drink, there are some common situations, events, and attitudes that have been shown to promote this craving for many people. These triggers are the focus for the lecture today."

### Write Your Lecture

When you become experienced and knowledgeable about the topic, you can lecture from an outline. However, it is not advisable to lecture without any notes or outline, as you may omit needed information, go off on a tangent, forget material, and so on. The best plan is to write your lectures and to read and time them to make sure that there is enough time for what you want to present. Beginning group leaders can make the mistake of either having too much material or not enough. The best plan is that the lecture will take 10 to 20 minutes. As a beginner, write every word, consult your notes frequently, and do not deviate from the lecture. Stick with what you have planned.

### Sufficient Information

The only way to know if you have sufficient information is to write it down. Thinking about it can be misleading as you do not know exactly what to say, how to say it, what examples to give nor, do you have any notion about the amount of time all that will take.

It is a balancing act to have sufficient information and to not have too much or too little. Experience will help you make this decision. The needs and abilities of the target audience are important. A good rule of thumb is to present less information than you think they need, but more than the basics.

*Prioritize Information*

All information you present is not of equal value. Thus, it becomes important for you to prioritize the information and to present it in order of importance. That way, the essentials are given, and if you do not have time to give all the information or must end the lecture unexpectedly, members will have the most important information. It is necessary to try and plan for unexpected events.

*Organize and Sequence*

It is helpful to have each session build on the previous one, but you also have to plan for each session to be self-contained. That planning includes the lecture. It builds on previous knowledge but has to be capable of standing alone. Leaders who organize and sequence the information will find that members learn and retain more of the material.

Planning includes the whole duration of the group no matter how many weeks or sessions it will meet. The best way is to write the basic plan for every session to include minilectures and activities so that you can organize and sequence to promote optimum learning.


## INSTRUCTIONAL STRATEGIES AND MATERIALS

The major factors to consider when deciding on strategies, and selecting materials are

- members' readiness for learning, maturity level, and their ability to participate and use the materials;
- pacing and scheduling of experiences to effectively use the available time;
- amount of material to be covered;
- the number of participants.

Members' characteristics and maturity are important as these can limit what can reasonably be done in the amount of time for sessions, and/or for the life of the group. Consider participants' ages, educational levels, possible resistance, and emotional involvement when deciding on instructional strategies. It is helpful to judiciously use lectures and media as these are passive events for participants, and this can be especially important when working with participants who have limited attention spans, such as children.

Select strategies and materials that keep the sessions moving, promote interactions among members, encourage interest and emotional involvement, and which keep the sessions moving. Do not put two passive strategies together, and do not have too many sequential active ones. This is another reason why it can be helpful to write out your schedule and lectures. That helps you to better see the pacing you will need.

The amount of material to be covered is difficult to gauge. You know what you think needs to be presented, but you don't know how much participants will be able to take in and use, so you have to use your judgment. Experience will make this easier. One suggestion is to have too much material, as you can discard some if needed. It is much more difficult when you finish early because you did not have enough material. You may wish to develop more examples, descriptions, and applications for a limited amount of material rather than presenting additional material. Know your audience and keep it simple.

The number of participants is a crucial factor as it plays a major role in determining how much processing, and attention to individuals you will be able to manage. You will not want to use strategies and/or materials that will evoke intense emotions, unless there will be adequate time to effectively process them. On the other hand, when there are few participants, you can use strategies and materials that will broaden and deepen the experience because you can give each person enough time to think through their experiences, and you can provide more guidance for participants.

## Forming Small Groups

Many psychoeducational groups include large numbers of participants. Active participation is enhanced when the participants can interact in small groups. Forming small groups can be accomplished in several ways. The most simple and efficient way is preassigning members to small groups: The leader simply decides how many members will be in each group, divides the participants by that number, and assigns them to groups by colors, numbers, or some other designation. Group designations can then be put on participants' name tags or on the folders given to them when they first arrive at the session.

Another way to make small group assignments is to decide on the number of small groups you want, then have participants count off by that number. This is more time-consuming, however, and can be confusing for participants if the group numbers more than 35.

The most inefficient method is to let participants choose their own small groups. This usually results in friends choosing the same group and perhaps forming a clique. This procedure can result in uneven numbers for groups as well.

## Materials

Gather all materials prior to the group session. There should be enough materials for every member. If art materials are being used for an exercise, it is possible to share things such as crayons, but it is preferable that there be sufficient materials so that members do not have to share. Prepare handouts and other materials so that they can be easily read and handled. Have extra copies of everything in case additional materials are needed.

It is more time-consuming to hand out materials in a large group, even when assistance is available. Try to place materials for small groups in the rooms or at the tables where groups will be working. Be sure to allow time in your schedule for distributing materials.

If participants are expected to write or draw, tables are essential. The best room layout provides tables for five to seven participants each. Individual desks are inefficient and provide barriers to small-group discussion.

Break-out rooms for small groups provide privacy and minimize the impact of environmental disruptions. When facilities do not allow for break-out rooms, the room must be large enough to allow for separation of small groups. Facilities should be clean, with adequate lighting and climate control. Rest rooms and water fountains should be easily accessible.

## Techniques

Psychoeducational groups employ a variety of formats, making it difficult to name a specific set of techniques applicable to all. The variety of participants, their characteristics, and the range of educational backgrounds provide additional confounding variables. Therefore, the techniques described here are not necessarily the preferred methods, but they give a sense of the variety that can be used. Included in techniques are lectures, discussions, exercises and games, media, simulations, and role-playing.

### Lectures

Effective lectures are well-organized presentations that lead the listener from point to point to provide an integrated knowledge and understanding of the material. Lectures are efficient ways of getting across a large amount of information in a short time. However, lectures have several drawbacks:

- Listeners tend to have short attention spans unless the topic and presentation grab and hold their interest.
- Listening to a lecture is a passive form of learning, which is less effective than active forms.
- Lecturing demands considerable planning, organizing, and presenting on the part of the leader.

If you plan to use lectures as part of a psychoeducational group, you should use minilectures that last no more than 20 minutes, restricting the amount of material to that which members can use. These are most effective if kept to 10 or 15 minutes, because members will be more inclined to listen. Further, having several minilectures over the life of the group interspersed with activities to reinforce the material will lead to more learning and retention.

## Discussions

Discussions can be used to promote active involvement. Lively discussions contribute interest to the session and encourage participants to be involved. Used as a technique, discussion is not the goal of the group, and it is typically kept short so that other activities can take place. Fewer members may be involved, and members tend to talk to the leader rather than to each other.

Leaders can initiate discussion by asking questions, calling for comments or questions, and encouraging exploration of points, issues, or concepts. The exchange of ideas, opinions, and experiences can be energizing to the group. Members feel their input is valued and that they have something to contribute.

## Exercises and Games

Exercises, games, simulations, and role-play are all forms of experiential learning. They are designed to produce more active involvement on the part of participants, to focus on and emphasize a particular point, and to provide an opportunity for affective as well as cognitive learning. When exercises or other forms of experiential learning are used, members can integrate affective and cognitive learning, which contributes to and intensifies retention.

Several specific strategies should be employed to ensure safety for group participants, since experiential learning can arouse unexpected and uncomfortable feelings. The leader must have the expertise to help members deal with these feelings, which can be intense, and to plan sessions so that the likelihood of arousing these intense, uncomfortable feelings is minimized.

Exercises and games can be fun as well as educational. When learning is enjoyable, motivation is increased, comprehension is enhanced, and retention is promoted. Exercises and games share some purposes, such as serving as warm-ups and ice-breakers, promoting active involvement, illustrating a point or concept, and helping to terminate a session. Exercises have a few additional purposes: promoting self-reflection, self-awareness, self-knowledge, and self-understanding.

- Participants in psychoeducational groups usually are strangers to one another. Even when members work together, they are somewhat strangers in the group setting. An ice-breaker/warm-up gets their attention, allows them to meet some other members, and gets the session started. Even in small groups (i.e., five to eight members), an ice-breaker/warm-up facilitates the beginning of the group, reduces tension, and relieves some anxiety.
- Active involvement supports learning, retention, and motivation. Exercises and games call for observable responses, such as oral, movement, drawing, and writing. These usually are easy to do, enjoyable, and have a discernible point, all of which contributes to motivation. Participants are encouraged by success, and exercises and games provide opportunities for success.

- Exercises and games provide alternative ways of presenting material. Whereas lectures and media presentations hold attention for a relatively short time (e.g., 15 to 20 minutes), even a short exercise or game can keep participants involved and learning for a considerably longer time. It is not unusual for an exercise or game to consume an hour or more, and the leader has to call time.
- Exercises and games are useful for termination of the group, which is as important as beginning the group. Leaders need to plan for termination and closing. It is important not to just stop. If the group has several sessions, each should be ended constructively, not simply stopped. There are exercises and games to effectively terminate and end groups or sessions.

Newstrom and Scannell (1991) described games as incorporating several classical principles of learning, including repetition, reinforcement, association, and use of the senses. The same can be said of exercises, with the addition of personal meaningfulness.

Repetition increases retention of material or skills. Exercises and games allow for repeating or use of concepts, information, skills, and applications. Reinforcement also contributes to the likelihood of the learned behavior being repeated. Success and other pleasurable consequences are positive reinforcers. Exercises and games are designed to be easily achieved and to be enjoyable, thereby promoting reinforcement.

Association of new material with previously learned material builds learning and understanding. Exercises and games help make gradual transitions and connections between the old and the new. This process promotes learning in a way that reduces anxieties around learning new things.

Increasing use of the senses contributes to more effective learning as well. Exercises and games provide opportunities for participants to use sight, sound, speech, and touch in learning. Further, exercises and games involve the cognitive, affective, and psychomotor domains of learning, making for a more rounded experience.

Meaningfulness of material promotes interest and retention. Exercises are designed to focus on personal involvement issues, leading to participants' having a personal investment in the presented material, which leads to more retention and motivation.

### Media

Movies, audiotapes, videotapes, computer presentations, and slides are examples of media. Media cover a large amount of material in a short time. They also have an advantage, as they tend to capture interest more easily, can provide visual illustrations of material, and have been demonstrated to be effective in learning.

The leader of psychoeducational groups should make judicious use of media. Used as accents or lead-ins, media presentations can be quite effective.

Used too frequently or for too long a time, however, media presentations are ineffective. Timing is important as well: having participants passively watch a video immediately after lunch, for example, is more likely to induce sleep than to promote learning. Plan for media to be an enhancement, not the primary technique.

Media can enrich your psychoeducational group when used in a way that promotes learning but does not distract from the main goal and purpose, overwhelm participants with information, promote passivity, or detract from interactions among members. Murray (2002) describes fours myths about the growing use of computerized slide presentations (e.g., Powerpoint). The following myths also apply to other forms of media such as video:

1. Your presentation is better the more media you use or the more you can manipulate the media.
2. More information can be presented and learned.
3. Media promotes active learning.
4. Structure for lectures is enhanced.

More is not better and manipulating media to get attention can detract from your real message. Some presentation via media can be interesting and stimulating and may be able to present your message concisely and very well. However, your intent with psychoeducational groups is to promote interaction and involvement among group members as well as to present information. Time spent looking at media alone does not promote interaction and lessens involvement or active participation. In fact, members can become detached and bored with too much media.

Can more information be conveyed via media? This is debatable. If your intent is to have members learn and retain information, you do not want to overwhelm them with too much information at one time. Your groups are not academic classes where students will be tested on the material. It is better to restrict the amount of information presented and to use what theories of learning teach us about how people learn and retain material, such as distributed practice and association.

A very important expectation for psychoeducational groups is active participation, and most media do not allow for active interaction and participation. Media tends to promote passivity. It can be used to stimulate thoughts and ideas, which can then be discussed among members. In this way, it can be helpful to the group, but the media stimulus should be short, there should be enough time for discussion in the session, and members should have sufficient time to make their personal associations with the material.

There are times when you may want to lecture, and media (e.g., Powerpoint) can help organize the material. Even for psychoeducational groups, this could be enhancing, although minilectures are usually so short that you can probably do just as well with a printed outline. Talking from the printed outline that you also give to group members could be all the organizing you need.

The final point about using media is that you may not be able to rely on working equipment. This is a personal issue for me in that I have frequently experienced equipment failure, so I am always prepared to present without having the use of media. I have found that it is less frustrating and upsetting to have an alternate mode for presenting that does not rely on equipment. That is my recommendation to you. Never have your presentation, or lecture rely totally on the availability of working equipment. Be prepared to adjust and use an alternate mode.

### Simulations

Simulations are designed to create a significant part or event applicable to a complex organization. They focus on developing solutions to a problem. Simulations present a range of interrelated factors that impact the individual, the problem, the setting, and the organization. Problems are not presented in isolation but in a simulated context.

Simulations are used in a variety of settings to present a wide range of problems. For example, they are used in educational settings to teach complex problem-solving skills related to economics; in business to address manufacturing production; in public agencies (e.g., city, state, or federal governmental agencies) to address issues such as global conflicts or transportation problems. Group members work together to define the problem, understand interrelated and complex restraining forces and supporting factors, collect relevant data, analyze the data, and suggest solutions. The war games in the Pentagon are an example of simulation on a global scale.

Simulations are usually long term—that is, they require more than one session; are complex to set up; are intricate to operate; and require ongoing as well as summative processing. It is possible to design minisimulations that focus on a smaller portion or a significant aspect of the problem. These can be accomplished in a shorter time period and are useful for teaching problem-solving skills. Minisimulations are not as useful for understanding complex problems because they are too narrowly focused and time-bound. There also needs to be a learning period during which participants learn to function in groups, a process for problem solving, and sources of data. Complex and interrelated situations are not grasped easily or immediately; they need time to be understood.

### Role-Play

Role-play attempts to create complex situations with interrelated factors focused on suggesting solutions to problems. Role-play concentrates on the individual and his or her personal issues and can be used to recreate a situation to obtain a better understanding of contributing behaviors and other factors, practice new skills, extend present knowledge to logical consequences, and highlight feelings experienced around a circumstance or situation.

Role-play has participants acting as if they were someone else; as if they were different in some way (e.g., younger); as if circumstances were different; as a part of a future, unknown circumstance or relationship. It may be structured or unstructured. In structured role-play, participants follow a prescribed script; in unstructured, they are free to develop their own script as the action unfolds.

Processing for role-play is critical, as both players and observers may experience intense feelings. A group leader needs to attend to all participants in some way and to allow for expression of aroused feelings after the role-play is finished. Role-play can be used effectively in psychoeducational groups, but leaders should be aware of the potential for deepening and intensifying the experience and feelings.

## Planning Experiential Group Activities

Experiential group activities can be effective parts of psychoeducational groups. They complement and enhance cognitive material, provide for more active involvement for participants, are enjoyable, and facilitate the movement of the group. Experiential group activities must be planned, however. This initial step is critical if the activity is to be successful (Brown, 1996). Planning incorporates goals, the participants, and environmental concerns.

### Goals
Specific experiential activities are selected only after goals and objectives have been established. The activities are strategies to help accomplish the goals and objectives, so they should have clear and direct connections.

For example, the goal for a group may be to learn time management strategies. An objective would be for each participant to become aware of his or her peak energy time so as to plan the most complex tasks of the day for that time. The experiential activity would be to have each participant recreate on paper the previous day's activities, emotions experienced during the activities, and the degree of difficulty of the activities. Participants could then divide into time period subgroups to discuss possible strategies for capitalizing on their peak energy periods.

### Participants
Experiential activities should be selected with the participants' age, maturity, and other readiness factors in mind. Although it generally is possible to use almost any activity with any group after suitable modifications, some activities are most suitable for adults in a particular setting (e.g., work). For example, an in-basket exercise would not be appropriate for children who have no knowledge or understanding of how an office functions.

On the other hand, some exercises work for almost any group, such as "Draw a Conflict." This exercise can be easily adapted for children or adults, personal or work situations, and various educational levels. Through experience, you will learn which experiential activities should be restricted to certain participants and which can be adapted and modified for differing groups.

### Time and Group Size
A variety of factors are incorporated under environmental concerns: time, setting, group size, materials, and staffing. Structural variables and details have a significant impact on the functioning of the group, participant learning, and effectiveness of experiential activities.

You must consider the time available for the group, the entire the session, and the particular activity in planning. An activity may meet many requirements, but it may take too long to complete and process. That time may be needed to accomplish other group objectives. Some flexibility should be built into the schedule to allow time to complete activities. It is not possible to accurately and precisely plan the exact time frame. All groups differ, and even when an activity is the same, each group will respond somewhat differently. However, you can approximate the time needed and you should be willing to either move on if it take less time than anticipated or allow enough time to complete the activity.

Activities appropriate for small groups are those that

• provide sufficient time for each member to have adequate input,
• use your expertise for processing to extend and enhance members' personal understanding,
• promote interactions among members,
• use the emotional involvement of members as springboard to learning.

Activities appropriate for large groups

• should be short,
• can be quickly completed by participants,
• limit the amount of emotional intensity that will be aroused,
• do not need the leader's personal attention to each member for processing.

An important point to remember is that activities should be completed, not stopped or truncated. You can never know for sure if there is some personal involvement issue that has been touched on for participants. These people should not be left dangling, and they are unlikely to speak up or to ask for guidance.

Controversial topics should be reserved for smaller groups, where the leader can block inappropriate input, help work through differences, and provide safety. The focus for most psychoeducational groups is on learning, not on working through personal issues or problems.

## Materials

All materials needed to complete an activity should be gathered in advance. Participants should not have to share materials. You should even have extras. Materials should be selected carefully. If preprinted forms or questionnaires are used, the font should allow for easy reading. Purchased tests or other materials should have reading levels appropriate for the educational level of participants. Some suggestions follow for selecting materials for drawing-related exercises:

• Provide extra paper in case group members make mistakes. The sheets should be large enough for expression, about 18 by 24 inches. Newsprint is adequate and has the advantage of being less costly than other kinds of paper. Paper should be neutral in color; colored construction paper is not recommended for drawing activities.

The art exercise should be selected for a particular purpose, and the same is true for your choice of media. Most drawing exercises can be accomplished with graphite pencils, charcoal, chalk pastels, oil pastels, felt-tip watercolors, or crayons. Each has specific qualities that contribute to the pleasure derived from doing art.

• Pencils have the advantage of being readily available and come with degrees of soft to hard lead. Soft lead does not take much physical pressure to make marks, but it smears easily. Children are very sensitive to messing up and may get upset if their drawing is smudged.
• Charcoal is easy to grasp, makes marks easily, can be smudged for shading effects, and can be used as a stick or with fingers to make designs. It is very messy, however, and cleanup materials should be kept at hand.
• Chalk pastels come in colors that are easily transferred to paper. Color can be layered, mixed, or smudged. As with charcoal, cleanup materials are necessary.
• Oil pastels glide easily on paper and have easy applicability, like chalk pastels, but they have the added advantage of being less messy. Colors are brilliant and can be mixed, overlaid, rubbed, or smudged.
• Felt-tip watercolors are available at very little cost in a vast array of colors. They can be secured in either fine-line or broad tips, clean up easily, and are easily applied to paper. Some are even scented.
• Crayons are also available in a vast array of colors. They are not messy, but there is some resistance when applied to paper. They do not glide as easily as felt-tips, chalk pastels, and oil pastels. Use crayons if other materials are not available in supplies sufficient for each member to have what he or she needs.

There are other media that can provide a satisfying experience. However, be careful that the emphasis is on the experience, not on the end product.

If you are leading a large psychoeducational group, you will find it helpful to have an assistant who can help distribute and take up materials, secure additional materials if needed, help answer questions, coordinate breaks, and run media machines. This assistance frees you to concentrate on the group and activities.

Some groups have coleaders. It is essential that coleaders be familiar with each other's working style. It is easy for conflict to emerge between coleaders, which can affect the functioning of the group, even when it goes unexpressed. Coleaders have a lot of personal work to do before trying to lead a group together.

If there are assistants involved in addition to the group leader, it is important that pregroup meetings be held. People who are expected to work together need time to understand their roles and functions, expectations, and goals of the group. They can help set the agenda and work out specific duties. Pregroup meetings facilitate the process of working together and help minimize misunderstandings and conflicts.

### Exercise: How Satisfied Am I With My Life

Objectives:  To identify aspects of your life that are satisfying, and those that need work.

   To start to understand what life changes you may want to make.

Materials:  Several sheets of paper, pen or pencil, a set of crayons or felt markers.

Procedure

1. Write the following at the top of separate sheet of paper, using one topic for each sheet of paper.
   a.  My interpersonal relations.
   b.  My work or career.
   c.  My family life.
   d.  My emotional life.
   e.  My physical self.
   f.  My spiritual life.
2. Complete the following procedure for each topic.
   a.  Close your eyes and allow an image to emerge for that concept, such as for your emotional life.
   b.  Draw that image under the title.
   c.  Write all associations that come to mind about that image, and that part of your life.
3. Review what you created, and write a summary statement about the extent of your satisfaction, or dissatisfaction with that aspect of your life.
4. List possible changes you can make to increase your satisfaction.

# Chapter 6

# Evaluating
# Psychoeducational Groups

Major Topics and Concepts

*Knowledge and Science Factors*
    Evaluation
    Instruments
    Assessment
    Questionnaires
    Rating Scales
    Semantic Differential

## INTRODUCTION

This chapter presents information to guide you in evaluating the components of the group program. Information about program evaluation is much too extensive to be included here, and you are encouraged to learn more. A general discussion about evaluation and suggestions for gathering data about participants' opinions, attitudes, and satisfaction with the group experience are presented. This can be applied to both a program and to individual sessions.

Evaluation is too often neglected or overlooked but is essential for improvement and serves several important purposes. It provides data to judge the following:

- How well the participants learned the material
- Behavior and attitude changes

- Lacks or weaknesses in the material presented and/or instructional strategies
- Efficacy of planning
- Participants' satisfaction
- Unanticipated results and effects

## RATIONALE FOR EVALUATION

Since learning is one of your primary goals when using psychoeducational groups, it seems feasible to evaluate how successful the group experience was for participants in increasing knowledge and understanding of the material. The question to be investigated is simply, Do participants know more about X than they did before the group? However, determining the answer is not as simple as it seems. The section on assessing learning gives more information about this topic.

Many psychoeducational groups will have behavior and/or attitude changes as goals. Assessing these goals depends primarily on participants' self-report. If planning includes a research component, these goals can be assessed by other means, such as objective tests and observers' reports, and can be compared with one or more control groups. This approach can provide results that more clearly associate group experiences with outcomes. It may be unrealistic to expect extensive changes in behavior and/or attitudes after one or even a multisession psychoeducational group, but any progress in the desired direction is helpful. It is also useful to determine if there was no change or if there was regression. The evaluator must be open to all possibilities. It is not possible to adequately cover the research component in this book, and readers are encouraged to consult appropriate materials and other resources to use research as part of evaluation.

No matter how well you plan, there are times when you may have some weaknesses or lack in the material. It could be that additional or different information is needed and you did not anticipate this. For example, you could find that material on diversity would enhance a group focused on building self-esteem. This material could be added to the next group you lead. Or, you could find that some material was not of interest and seemed to be off-target. This feedback allows you to make needed changes.

An additional piece of information that is helpful is the feedback you can get about your instructional strategies. You have probably used a variety of strategies with your group, and you will want to get participants' reactions to each one to assist in future planning. You may have used strategies appropriate for your group's needs and characteristics, and this information lets you know how successful you were. Or, your choice of strategies may require some fine-tuning, and evaluation can provide you with this information.

Evaluation results provide data on the efficacy of your planning. This can be reinforcing for spending so much time and effort on this task or can point out where more attention is needed. This continuous feedback regarding your efforts and refinement of your planning lead to better group experiences and success. Although all participants may not benefit as much as you desire, it may not be due to your planning but could point to a need to better understand participants' needs and characteristics.

Assessing participants' satisfaction with the group, your leadership, their learning, and their achievements is basic to understanding the success or failure of the experience. Although satisfaction does not equate to learning or other changes, it is a valuable measure for evaluating all aspects of the group experience and participants' interest and attachment to the group. This lets you know the extent to which members were interested, pleased, and valued the group.

You can seldom, if ever, predict what will happen with a group. There are always unanticipated events and/or results. Evaluation can give you insight on what to plan or try to prevent the next time. Unanticipated events have an impact on members' functioning, and these can be of a global nature, such as 9/11, or can be more group specific, such as the unexpected illness or death of a member. An example of an unanticipated event is having someone in the group who has a destructive narcissistic pattern. You cannot know this in advance; nor are you able to immediately recognize it. However, this person will have a tremendous negative effect on the group and on members.

## DEFINITION OF TERMS

There are several terms used in this chapter that may need to be defined: evaluation, assessment, measurement, formative evaluation, summative evaluation, and instruments (McMillan & Schumacher, 1997):

- Evaluation determines the worth and/or use of a program, product, procedure, objective, or process. It is the framework for making judgments and decisions.
- Assessment measures a variable such as attitudes or satisfaction.
- Measurement involves assigning numbers to variables or characteristics so that they can be aggregated, analyzed, or differentiated. The mode for measurement uses one of four scales: nominal, ordinal, interval, or ration.
- Formative evaluation continuously collects and analyzes data in order to make immediate changes or adjustments while the event, such as a group, is underway.
- Summative evaluation collects and analyzes data after the event is completed.
- Instruments are data-gathering devices and processes such as tests, questionnaires, self-reports, rating scales, observation systems, and interview schedules.

Evaluation is the total process that incorporates all the other topics: assessment, measurement, formative and summative evaluations, and instruments. Planning for evaluation begins before the group ever meets. Deciding what information you want, planning for when and how to collect it, and selecting suitable instruments will help you prepare for effective evaluation. There are several steps in evaluation planning:

- Start with the goals and objectives, and decide how to assess them.
- Identify the various strategies you will use, such as exercises and lectures, and how they will be assessed.
- Identify expected outcomes, such as behavior changes, and determine if or how they can be assessed.
- Plan to assess participants' satisfaction.
- Select or develop needed instruments.

## EVALUATING GOALS, OBJECTIVES, AND STRATEGIES

One way to begin the process is to list the group's objectives and strategies, then tie them to the method of evaluation. For example, one objective may be to have participants learn a body of material. The strategy to be used is a minilecture. Evaluation of learning might include having participants take a test, brainstorm or write applications of the material, rate the presentation, or judge their impression of how much they learned. You could also use pre- and posttesting to determine gains in learning.

Listing objectives and strategies allows for prioritizing so that you evaluate what is most important and do not waste time overevaluating. It is not necessary or desirable to evaluate everything in-depth. Instead, focus on the important elements and plan a short evaluation. Sometimes all you need is feedback on participants' perception of the major activities. A simple form listing these activities, a method for rating them, and space for written comments may suffice. For example, a half-day psychoeducational group on study skills that used an ice-breaker, handouts, a minilecture, and an exercise could use a form similar to the one in Table 6.1. (Note: More space would be provided for comments if used this way.)

The form in Table 6.1 provides for rating the major elements of the group, the leader, the quality of materials, the environment, and organizational components. It does not provide for evaluation of learning—that is, it does not ask how much participants learned about study skills. There are no items asking for feedback on specific leadership skills, only an overall rating for the leader. If one group objective were to improve leadership skills, the form would need items that specifically relate to leadership skills, such as reflected content and meaning.

TABLE 6.1

Sample Evaluation Form

Study Skills Group

I. **Directions:** Rate how useful you feel each of the following will be to you in improving your study skills. Write comments in the space provided:

    5 = extremely useful    2 = somewhat useful
    4 = very useful         1 = not useful to me
    3 = useful

    1. Handouts                                  5  4  3  2  1
       Comments:
    2. Lecture/discussion                   5  4  3  2  1
       Comments:
    3. Exercise (Setting goals)            5  4  3  2  1
       Comments:

II. **Directions:** Rate each of the items below using the following scale:

    5 = extremely useful    2 = somewhat useful
    4 = very useful         1 = not useful to me
    3 = useful

    4. Organization of the information and of the group    5  4  3  2  1
    5. Quality or interest of the presentation(s)    5  4  3  2  1
    6. The leader's preparation, enthusiasm, and delivery    5  4  3  2  1
    7. Opportunities for input or interaction    5  4  3  2  1
    8. Facilities    5  4  3  2  1
    9. Schedule: events, breaks, etc.    5  4  3  2  1
    10. Overall quality    5  4  3  2  1

## ASSESSING LEARNING

When you assess learning, it is helpful to know the baseline knowledge possessed by participants as a beginning point. What you really want to know is how much learning occurred because of group activities. So, just testing after the group is finished is not sufficient. You really need to do a pregroup test and a postgroup test. The ideal situation is to do these two tests and a follow-up test weeks, months, or years later to determine how much material was retained.

Learning focuses on specific material, such as definitions and facts. Thus, assessing learning will involve items that are directly related to the material presented. Assessment is similar to classroom tests, and there are considerable resources that describe how to construct valid and reliable tests. Only a brief summary is presented here.

Construct items that can be easily scored as right or wrong. It is seldom that psychoeducational groups will involve higher levels of thinking such as synthesis, which is best assessed in other ways. It is best to use objective items because of the group's short-term status, the briefness of material presented, and the highly focused nature of the presentation. Objective items such as multiple choice, true-false, and matching are suggested as appropriate. Be sure to ask for information that was presented to get a realistic picture of what was learned and understood.

## FORMATIVE AND SUMMATIVE EVALUATION

You can plan to gather and analyze data throughout the life of your psychoeducational group. This is formative evaluation that is used to make adjustments and adaptations for continual improvement. This approach allows you to have concrete justifications for changes, not just your subjective judgment. It provides for a more systematic process for making decisions. However, you do have to plan to gather and analyze information in advance for formative evaluation. It is not feasible to try to do this after the group has begun if it was not in the original plan, because you will be distracted and possibly cause disruption to the group.

Most groups that are evaluated use summative evaluation where data are gathered at the end of the experience and analyzed at some later time. These results are used for future planning. Summative evaluation can give you information about gains in learning, changes in behavior and attitudes, and the effectiveness of the various group components. The gains in learning and changes in behavior and attitudes are possible when you assess these at the beginning and end of the group. This procedure can allow for you to make some judgments that are supported with data about the extent of participants' learning and the efficacy of the group. However, unless you are doing this with a well-constructed research plan, these judgments can only be very tentative and general. You cannot make definitive conclusions; you can only consider possibilities suggested by the data.

## INSTRUMENTS

Instruments are the means by which you gather data. Only a general overview is presented here. Selecting the proper instrument involves knowledge of measurement, validity, reliability, and other psychometric concepts that are too complex to describe here.

Once you decide on the elements you want to evaluate, you must consider your instruments. Some groups lend themselves to standardized tests or rating scales. This is particularly true for social or life skills groups and for some educational groups, such as those that focus on career education. You will find many standardized tests and scales. In reviewing them, you should pay attention to the established validity for the kind of participants in the group, particularly with regard to age, gender, racial/ethnic group, and educational level. Reliability, usability, and cost are other factors in choosing a standardized test or rating scale.

Standardized tests and rating scales are useful when you want to determine or document changes that occur as a result of the group. For example, funding for career education groups may depend on how well learning is achieved in existing groups. Careful evaluation using valid standardized tests can give evidence to support continuation or may suggest that other avenues should be explored. Standardized tests and scales also allow you to make comparisons with previous groups.

Most often, however, leaders of psychoeducational groups do not use standardized instruments for evaluation because they are too expensive, they do not meet specific group needs, they are not designed around the group's topic, or the leader lacks the training to use them. If a standardized instrument is desirable and available, and cost is not a concern, a testing consultant may be used.

There is a detailed science and art to developing your own instruments that cannot be covered in this book. This chapter describes instruments that are generally used: questionnaires, rating scales, and the semantic differential.

## Questionnaires

Questionnaires are used to gather information about perceptions, needs, and reactions. They are very useful when constructed properly and with attention to detail. It is much more time-consuming to analyze the data, and responses cannot be easily aggregated. It takes time and skill to develop a questionnaire and to compile the results. When constructing a questionnaire, it is important to pay attention to the following:

- Make sure the items are stated clearly.
- Avoid using two or more ideas in the same item.
- Consider the respondents' abilities to read and understand the items.
- Make sure the items are relevant to the subject.
- Present ideas, concepts, and the like in as simple terms as possible.
- Avoid using general negative terms such as all, but, not, and except.

Items should be constructed to be direct, clear, and unambiguous. This takes skill and may require many revisions. It is helpful to avoid using two or more ideas in the same item separated by *and*. When you do this, one idea may be positive and the other negative, making it impossible for the person to respond yes or no to the item. For example, an item that asks, "Do you approve of the president's actions on the environment and on the economy?" could make it difficult for the person who favors one but not the other to respond.

It is just as important to consider participants' abilities to read and understand when constructing questionnaires as it is when planning the psychoeducational group. Eliminate items that are not directly relevant to the topic. It may be tempting to try to gather other information since you have a captive audience, but good questionnaires stay focused on the matter at hand. Making the questionnaire as simple as possible is crucial. Respondents are more likely to complete it, and to feel that their time has been well spent if the questionnaire is not too long, convoluted, and is easily understood and completed.

People can get easily confused when you construct items that call for them to remember exceptions. For example, try not to say, "The following are components of a psychoeducational group, EXCEPT (a) evaluation, (b) exercises, (c) games, or (d) interpretation."

## Assessing Opinions, Attitudes, and Affective Responses

There are several ways to obtain feedback on participants' opinions, attitudes, and affective responses. Commonly used methods include discussion, survey or rating forms, attitude and behavioral ratings. All have advantages and disadvantages:

- Discussion provides the most immediate feedback and promotes personal ownership of opinions. The primary disadvantages are that time typically permits only a few participants to give input, and many people are reluctant to openly verbalize their opinions.
- Survey or rating forms allow all participants to have input and to focus input on those parts of the group where feedback is desired. A disadvantage of survey or rating forms is that participants may limit their input to answering the form's questions.
- Attitude and behavioral scales usually are commercial in nature. In addition to the cost, they may have limited or questionable validity and reliability. Selecting appropriate instruments requires a knowledge of psychometry.

The best way to evaluate a psychoeducational group—and to receive information that can help you in making modifications, revisions, or a change of direction—is to use a form tailored for your specific group. I encourage you either to learn more about constructing evaluation materials or to consult with someone who is knowledgeable in the field and have him or her develop the form.

The majority of psychoeducational groups can get the data they need from carefully constructed instruments tailored to their groups. Designing and constructing such an instrument calls for expertise in the field and a knowledge qualitative evaluation and of various evaluation techniques. For the best possible evaluation, you should work with a consultant who has this expertise during the planning phase.

Despite these constraints, you can evaluate your group without paying an expert consultant, even if you are not an expert in the field yourself. The evaluation will be limited and the data will not be as extensive, but they can provide valuable information for designing and conducting future groups. The following guidelines are designed to help you develop a group-specific form, even if you are not an expert in evaluation.

### Constructing an Instrument

After deciding on which objectives and strategies you want to evaluate, you must choose which and how many areas to evaluate, decide how in-depth the items should be and the maximum number of items for each subarea, select what scale you will use, and decide whether you will ask for open-ended comments. The form may also contain items that evaluate participants' interest in additional groups.

### Selecting Areas

Table 6.2 lists three primary areas for evaluation: structure, program or content, and leadership. Each area has several subareas, under which one or more items could be constructed. Altogether there are 21 subareas listed. If only an overall rating is used for each, this produces 21 items. Most participants are

TABLE 6.2

Areas for Evaluation

| Areas | Topics |
| --- | --- |
| Structure | Organization |
| | Facilities |
| | Materials |
| | Media |
| | Providing for input, interaction |
| | Scheduling for events, breaks |
| | Objectives |
| Program or Content | Minilectures |
| | Games (e.g., ice-breakers) |
| | Exercises |
| | Handouts |
| | Meeting of personal needs or objectives |
| | Discussion |
| | Directions |
| Leadership | Keeping to schedule |
| | Responding to participants |
| | Interest, warmth, enthusiasm showed |
| | Able to clarify |
| | Respect for offering opinions and ideas |
| | Able to keep sessions focused |
| | Knowledge and understanding of topic |

more inclined to evaluate the experience when there are a moderate number of items, such as 10 to 15. Therefore, it is useful to select 3 or 4 subareas, write 2 or 3 items about each, and use overall ratings for the remainder.

Use of several items instead of one global or overall rating for a subarea allows for better definition of strengths and weaknesses. For example, the subarea "facilities" could contain items such as these:

5 = excellent; 4 = good; 3 = adequate; 2 = fair; 1 = poor

| | | | | | |
|---|---|---|---|---|---|
| Comfort of seating | 5 | 4 | 3 | 2 | 1 |
| Temperature control | 5 | 4 | 3 | 2 | 1 |
| Free of outside distractions | 5 | 4 | 3 | 2 | 1 |
| Availability, cost, and convenience of parking | 5 | 4 | 3 | 2 | 1 |
| Convenience of access | 5 | 4 | 3 | 2 | 1 |
| Proximity of rest rooms, restaurants, telephones, etc. | 5 | 4 | 3 | 2 | 1 |

## Item Content

After you have chosen the areas and subareas, the total number of items for the form, and the subareas where attention will be focused, you must decide on the content for items under those subareas. The overriding question to address is, What is most important to know about this subarea?

Even this short question may produce more topics than can be accommodated. Prioritizing is helpful at this point, with the more important topics receiving separate items and others combined into more global items. For example, assume that the subarea "games" was selected. Some topics would include number of games, timing, objectives, materials, interest, and usefulness. Focusing on the number of games provides data on whether too few or too many were used. It would be helpful for participants to name the games so that there is no confusion as to what you meant by "games." The item on timing tells you how accurately you anticipated the need for games. Asking for ratings of achievement of the objectives shows whether the intended objectives were met. Adequacy of materials used provides information that leads to improvements in the games. The degree of interest participants had in the games is an indicator for further use. This would not be the deciding factor, however, since each group is different. But if you continued to get ratings indicating little or no interest, the game may need to be retired. Using all of these items clarifies the strengths and weaknesses of the game better than a global rating would.

## Provision for Rating

When ratings are used, they are usually in a Likert scale format. This format uses five labeled categories, each of which has a numerical rating of 1 to 5, with 5 being the most positive. Numerical ratings allow summation, and, while they are not entirely psychometrically appropriate, some compilers of the data also compute mean ratings. It is useful to have ratings such as the following:

5 = excellent; 4 = good; 3 = adequate; 2 = fair; 1 = poor.

Provision also can be made for not applicable (NA).

## Form Format

Place the title of the group, the dates of the sessions, and directions at the top of the page. Directions should be specific, brief, and clear. If a rating scale is used, the designations or definitions belong in the directions. It may be helpful to underline directions or put them in bold type so that they stand out from the rest of the form. Participants will want to know whether the evaluations are anonymous and how they will be used.

Format the items so that the ratings are in rows and columns on the right side of the page. Double-space between items, and provide space between items or at the end for comments. If you are soliciting suggestions for improvements, say so in the directions.

If necessary, reduce the font, so that the entire form is no more than two pages. One page is preferable, but participants tend not to answer more than two pages.

## The Semantic Differential

A good procedure for assessing attitudes and perceptions is the semantic differential. This procedure uses paired bipolar adjectives placed on a continuum. Respondents check the number or space that corresponds to their perception, attitude, or feeling about the concept that is being assessed. For example, if the concept is exercises, then respondents would select one number for each of the following pairs of adjectives:

| warm | 9 | 8 | <u>7</u> | 6 | 5 | 4 | 3 | 2 | 1 | cold |
|------|---|---|---|---|---|---|---|---|---|------|
| boring | 1 | 2 | 3 | 4 | 5 | <u>6</u> | 7 | 8 | 9 | interesting |

This procedure was developed by Osgood, Tannenbaum, and Suci (1957), and has established validity and reliability. Studies have shown its applicability to all age groups and in differing cultures and languages. The semantic differential has a strong factoral structure and constancy, and can be analyzed using sophisticated statistical techniques, such as multiple regression analyses and factor analysis.

There are three dimensions that can be assessed: evaluation, potency, and activity. The evaluation dimension assesses adjective contrasts, such as good and bad. The potency dimension assesses the efficacy or strength, such as brave or cowardly. The activity dimension assesses movement or passivity, such as nap or play.

Heise (1970) recommends that you use four sets of bipolar adjectives for each dimension for every concept assessed. The same adjectives do not have to be used for each concept. Osgood and others (1957) provide 76 pairs of adjectives, but many people use the dictionary and thesaurus to develop their adjective pairs. Following is an example of a semantic differential for the group component "lectures." You can assess each component separately: exercises, lectures, media, discussions, and so on.

## ASSESSMENT OF ATTITUDES

DIRECTIONS: The purpose of this form is to determine how you feel about the group experiences. Each component is presented and followed by a set of bipolar adjectives. Check the number between each set of adjectives that best reflects how you feel about the particular component listed at the top of the set. For example, if the concept was book, and the set of adjective were as follows, you could check the underlined number:

Book

| like | 9 | <u>8</u> | 7 | 6 | 5 | 4 | 3 | 2 | 1 | dislike |
|------|---|---|---|---|---|---|---|---|---|---------|
| down | 1 | 2 | 3 | 4 | 5 | <u>6</u> | 7 | 8 | 9 | up |

Work as quickly as possible, and choose a number for *each* set of adjectives.

Lectures

| | | | | | | | | | | |
|---|---|---|---|---|---|---|---|---|---|---|
| *(E) good | 9 | 8 | 7 | 6 | 5 | 4 | 3 | 2 | 1 | bad |
| (A) slow | 1 | 2 | 3 | 4 | 5 | 6 | 7 | 8 | 9 | fast |
| (E) unhelpful | 1 | 2 | 3 | 4 | 5 | 6 | 7 | 8 | 9 | helpful |
| (A) active | 9 | 8 | 7 | 6 | 5 | 4 | 3 | 2 | 1 | passive |
| (P) powerful | 9 | 8 | 7 | 6 | 5 | 4 | 3 | 2 | 1 | weak |
| (E) boring | 1 | 2 | 3 | 4 | 5 | 6 | 7 | 8 | 9 | dull |
| (E) important | 9 | 8 | 7 | 6 | 5 | 4 | 3 | 2 | 1 | unimportant |
| (P) hard | 9 | 8 | 7 | 6 | 5 | 4 | 3 | 2 | 1 | easy |
| (P) shallow | 1 | 2 | 3 | 4 | 5 | 6 | 7 | 8 | 9 | deep |
| (A) calm | 1 | 2 | 3 | 4 | 5 | 6 | 7 | 8 | 9 | exciting |
| (P) sensitive | 9 | 8 | 7 | 6 | 5 | 4 | 3 | 2 | 1 | rough |
| (A) involved | 9 | 8 | 7 | 6 | 5 | 4 | 3 | 2 | 1 | uninvolved |

*(dimension)

Scoring

Following are two methods for scoring. Select one.

1. Add the rating for each dimension separately: evaluation, potency, and activity for the entire group. Compute the means for each dimension.
2. Add the ratings and compute the mean rating for each concept.

# Chapter 7

# Membership Problems, Concerns, and Skills

Major Topics and Concepts

*Knowledge, Science, and Skills Factors*
Involuntary members
The leader's role
Ethical guidelines
Problem behaviors, such as socializing
Teaching membership skills

*Art Factor*
Specific leader strategies
Resistance
Feeling Responses
Advice

## INTRODUCTION

No amount of planning and prepreparation will eliminate all problems, especially those provided by members. Most participants will not know good group membership behavior and skills. They will act in the group as they act in other situations. Some will view the group as another social event, others will recall their school days and act as they think you should in class, some will let current events influence their behavior, and some will have emotional intensity that makes it difficult for them to respond positively or appropriately to a new situation. A group leader has to psychologically and emotionally be prepared to deal with all of these circumstances.

It would be helpful for you to have experience as a group member as part of your education and training as a group leader. I've taught the graduate course in group counseling for over 15 years and find that students have difficulty as group members with expressing immediate feelings, staying present-centered, making reflective or empathic responses, and making personal statements. These membership skills enhance the group, and leaders who expect members to use them must also use them.

## MEMBER VARIETY

Groups are composed of a variety of individuals who are all unique but also similar in many ways. It can be surprising to a beginning group leader to be faced with group members who do not want to be in the group—members whose behavior is distracting, disruptive, or worse—and to realize that trying to address problems presented by one or two members leaves the other group members to flounder. There are other constraints when trying to deal with problem behaviors, such as the following:

- Other members can become fearful and resistant if the feel they leader will be punitive.
- The members whose behavior is addressed can feel criticized and blamed, so they stop participating.
- Old family-of-origin issues can get triggered along with emotional baggage.
- Group members can feel that the leader is unfair and collude on an unconscious level to let their displeasure be known in even more problematic ways.
- Feelings of safety in the group can be compromised.
- Trust becomes harder, or impossible, to establish.
- Taking care of members' behavior becomes more of a priority than does accomplishing the tasks and goals for the group.

There will always be some problem behaviors in groups, but the leader can understand the goal(s) for the behaviors; institute procedures to prevent, reduce, or eliminate them; learn to use these as relevant material for group consideration and exploration; and not assume a defensive, attacking, or ignoring stance.

This chapter addresses some of these issues and concerns with a discussion about involuntary members and the ethics that play a part in their participation. Also discussed are some problem behaviors with suggested strategies for constructive resolution. The final topic is on teaching group members behaviors and attitudes that will help them maximize their group experiences.

## Involuntary Members

A major factor in deciding on appropriate leadership strategies is if members are voluntary or involuntary participants. This can have a significant impact on participant level, expected behavior, and group development.

There are many instances in which members of a group are involuntary participants. Members may attend because they were ordered to do so by an authority (such as a court or school principal), as a condition for continued participation in a job or school, as part of a program for contained or incarcerated people (such as inpatients, felons, or juvenile group home residents), or as part of their educational training (such as groups for mental health professionals). The reasons for involuntary attendance may vary, but many of the same characteristics are shared and must be taken into account by the group leader.

Some involuntary participants will view group as an opportunity to learn, grow, and develop more effective ways of relating. Others will be defiant, resistant, or resentful about having to participate. Some will be openly hostile and others passive-aggressive. You can expect that involuntary participation will result in more barriers than voluntary participation.

It is useful to acknowledge the involuntary nature of their participation early on and give members an opportunity to express their feelings about it. This can be done during the screening interview or during the first session. You may also need to be more specific about what will be done in group and what is expected of group members. These members may be more fearful, as they usually can expect unpleasant consequences for failure.

## Constraints to Active Participation

Resistance and defenses are more intense for involuntary participants because they lack power and control: they do not freely choose to be in the group. Another reason for resistance is fear of the unknown. All group members share some of this fear, but it may be more intense for involuntary participants because they have been thrust into an ambiguous situation not of their choosing, and they often do not know what to expect or what is expected of them.

Fear of harm plays an important role for involuntary participants as well. They may fear that disclosed information will be given to others and used against them, or that other group members will use it to further their own personal ends. They may fear they will be evaluated and found inadequate.

Resentment at being forced to participate may also be a part of resistance. Such resentment may be focused on the authority ordering attendance, but it is more likely to be generalized and widespread. Everyone but them is at fault for their having to be in the group. Resentment may be more openly expressed and demonstrated by some members, such as court-ordered participants, than by others; but it is present, in some degree, in all involuntary participants. Some simply mask the resentment better than others.

## The Leader's Role

As the leader of a group with involuntary participants, you must be prepared to deal with their fears, resistance, defenses, and resentments. Knowing that these are not only likely but are certain to be manifested in some way allows you to better plan to address them. Your primary tasks are to:

- adequately address safety and trust issues
- diffuse hostility and resentment
- empower members to decide their own level of participation and disclosure
- have clear goals and objectives
- to understand boundary issues and respect them
- to refrain from power struggles

The first task of the group leader is to directly respond to unspoken or indirectly communicated safety and trust issues. You should provide specific guidelines for expected participation. If confidentiality can be maintained, you should say so. If, on the other hand, agency guidelines or legal constraints prevent you from maintaining confidentiality, you must notify the participants at the beginning of the group.

You can take steps to diffuse hostility, resentment, or defensiveness that may be directly or indirectly expressed. This, of course, is much easier to do in a small group, as you can make eye contact with each member and use some nonverbal behaviors to promote trust. One way to diffuse these feelings is to acknowledge that you know and appreciate that members dislike being forced to attend. If the group size is manageable, have a session in which each member responds to this question: "What do you like or dislike most about having to attend this group?" Or, "What would make this group experience worthwhile for you?"

Empower members to take charge of their group experience by giving them permission to decide how much they can or will participate. Assure them you will not push or demand responses, but you will provide opportunities and give encouragement. Give them some measure of control, and follow through on it to help promote feelings of safety and trust.

Another beginning step is to have clear goals and objectives and to review them with members. Develop attainable goals and be willing to modify them if necessary. Ask if there are any goals or objectives the members wish to include, or if there are any about which they have reservations. If you can be open and flexible, members can buy into the goals and objectives, which will lead to more personal involvement in the group and in achieving the task.

It is very helpful to delineate firm and permeable boundaries for involuntary participants. Take some time to discuss boundary issues such as the following:

- What topics members and the leader can discuss with people not in the group and under what conditions
- What material should not be discussed with people not in the group
- What group content can be talked about between members in the group when they are outside the group (e.g., socializing)
- What data the leader has to share with other professionals and in what form (i.e., with or without personal identifying data)
- What use will be made of the information shared by the members

Talking over these issues helps members to better judge what is appropriate participation for them.

One boundary that is under the leader's control is time. Adhering to the specified schedule provides support for consistency. Many involuntary participants have not had clear and unambiguous boundaries before. Ambiguity promotes feelings of insecurity and wariness. You cannot be expected to address and allay all insecurities, but you can provide firm time boundaries so that at least one thing is consistent.

Do not engage in power struggles with members. Many members will attempt to engage you in them either to test you or because it is their characteristic way of behaving or relating. Walton (1987) noted that, "when power is unequally distributed, the low-power person will automatically distrust the high-power person because she (he) knows that those with power have a tendency to use it for their own interests." As the group leader, you are seen as the high-power person, and members may fear your use of such power because of past experiences.

You are not engaging in a power struggle when you develop guidelines for expected behaviors, do not permit physical or verbal violence, or protect a member from emotional abuse or a barrage of questions. These are legitimate leader behaviors designed to protect group members and provide for effective group functioning.

### Ethical Guidelines for Involuntary Participants

These ethical issues are the most important when you are dealing with involuntary participants.

#### Freedom of Exit

With the exception of students and professionals, most involuntary participants do not feel they have the freedom to exit. While it may be possible for members to physically exit or to refuse to participate, the alternatives (e.g., jail) are often worse. This promotes feelings of being trapped and forced to do things against their will. For many involuntary participants, this increases defiance and passive-aggressiveness, while others are more open in their hostility.

As the group leader, you will receive the brunt of participants' feelings about lack of freedom to exit. Many participants are not able to accept personal responsibility, cannot or will not express their negative feelings to the official(s) who sent them to group, and are fearful of what will happen if they stay or if they leave.

## Confidentiality

Typically, there are more limits on what can be kept confidential with involuntary clients. Legal, moral, and training issues often prevent confidentiality from being complete—for example, case notes sometimes must be kept and can be read by others; consultation with supervisors may be mandated or encouraged; certain crimes (e.g., incest) must be reported to the proper officials; and participants who might harm themselves or others must be screened. Further, in a closed setting, such as a group home, hospital, or jail, there is no way to fully ensure that the content of sessions can be kept confidential.

Members must be informed at the beginning of group what cannot be kept confidential. Ideally, the issue of confidentiality and constraints should be discussed in screening or pregroup sessions as well as in the first session. However, if it is not possible to do so prior to the first session, you must initiate the discussion early in the first group.

## Screening

Screening of potential group members is desirable. Even if you are not able to reject members because of policies or rules, it is still desirable to have an individual pregroup interview session. It may also be possible to reject those who would be disruptive to the group if officials making decisions about participants can be shown sufficient reasons. The screening interview could provide you with the rationale for your judgment.

## Orienting and Providing Information

If you cannot schedule pregroup orienting sessions, you can use the first session for this purpose. Group work is scary for many participants, and when involuntary participation with possible negative consequences is added to the usual fears about participation, the situation is greatly exacerbated. An important thing to remember is that group business—goals, process, and so on—gets accomplished during orienting sessions. Your time will not be wasted in helping members understand what is expected of them, how they should behave, and what will be done in the group. Group participation is enhanced if you do adequate orientation.

## Coercion and Pressure

Although there is an element of coercion implicit for involuntary participants, you must take care to ensure that neither identification with the aggressor nor displacement of feelings around the coercion has a negative impact on the group. It is not possible to prevent either of these from happening, but if you realize that they are possible and take steps to neutralize their impact, you can help both individual members and the functioning of the group.

Identification with the aggressor produces behavior similar to that perceived by the authorities. Examples of such behavior are giving orders and expecting to be obeyed, expecting deference from others and becoming angry or enraged if it is not given, sadistic acts that are passive, and so on. While these behaviors may be characteristic for some members, others may assume them as a defense mechanism.

Displacement is a common defense mechanism used by many people for various situations. Under these circumstances it may be manifested in the group and become a barrier to progress. This is one reason it is so important to get the issue of coercion on the table early and the feelings around it expressed. You usually can expect to be the target of displaced feelings, but other members may also be targets.

### Dual Relationships

Dual relationships involve a power differential, and effects on the leader's objectivity. It is difficult to avoid dual relationships with involuntary group participants. Even if you have only arm's-length input into an evaluation or decision, you cannot avoid it altogether; you probably will be perceived by group members as having an evaluative role and function. For example, in training groups for professionals the leader may also be the clinical supervisor. It may not be possible to separate the impact of group participation and disclosure on the perceptions of clinical behavior/expertise. The group leader/supervisor typically makes every effort to do so, but as these effects and interactions are not clearly understood, you cannot be sure that the roles and functions are kept separate.

When the group leader also has an evaluative function, no matter how slight, there is an increase in the power differential between the leader and members. Members may perceive the power differential as being greater than it actually is and relate to the leader in terms of their perception. This perception can increase mistrust, inhibit disclosure, intensify resistance and defenses, promote deference, or prevent honest participation.

Having more than one role and function has an impact on the leader. His or her objectivity can be impaired because of interactions, behaviors, and relationships resulting from group participation. Countertransference, projection, and projective identification are all possible for the leader and can lead to impaired objectivity. The leader's objectivity is subject to manipulation by group members and can carry over into other leader roles and functions.

## PROBLEM BEHAVIORS AND THEIR GOALS

Most problem behaviors in psychoeducational groups can be categorized as overparticipation, underparticipation, or socializing. Overparticipating members monopolize, tell stories, interrupt when others are speaking, and use other distracting behaviors. Underparticipating members withdraw, are silent, make few responses even when directly addressed, and may do the minimum required for an activity.

The socializer engages in side conversations when others are talking, interacts repeatedly with the same person(s), introduces topics at variance with what is being discussed under the guise of being friendly, starts conversations instead of participating in the activity, is late coming back from breaks, and so on. The socializer does not act alone; you are likely to have two or more in the group.

The disengaged member is present in body but not in any other aspects of his or her being. Nonparticipation is due to being emotionally or psychologically somewhere else other than in the group.

## Overparticipation

The overparticipating member wants attention from the leader and from other members. At first, you may appreciate the input. Having a group member respond or initiate questions can energize the group, which helps the process move along. It does not take long, however, for one member's overinvolvement to become a real problem. The dilemma for the leader is how to block overparticipating behavior without squelching the member or discounting him or her in some way.

Remember that other members will assume that how you treat this person is how you will treat them, whether or not they engage in the same type of behavior. Sometimes the group will handle the behavior by confronting the member with its impact on them. For example, if one member interrupts others frequently, at some point another member may ask the interrupter if he or she would let the speaker finish.

### Storytelling and Monopolizing

The task of blocking monopolizing and storytelling behavior can be a difficult one. Most often, the group has not progressed to the point where members feel safe handling the leader's intervention. One rule of thumb is to let the storytelling or monopolizing behavior occur the first time without comment. Try to link what the person is talking about to the goals of the group. Express appreciation for the member's input to encourage others to participate. After that, try to intervene before the storyteller gets started.

If several members want to speak, let others talk before the monopolizer. Call on reticent members by asking if they have comments. Do not ignore the storyteller; just try to limit the time he or she has the floor. If necessary, you can break into a story with, "I am sorry to interrupt you, but it is time for a break (or the next scheduled activity, or to move on if we are to stay on schedule). I would like to get back to you on that."

## Physically Distracting Behaviors

Children and adolescents are more apt than adults to engage in physically distracting behaviors, such as pushing, getting out of their seats, and walking around. You should clearly articulate guidelines for expected group behaviors. These may be somewhat flexible but are developed to ensure smooth running of the group and focus on the task. Members who engage in distracting behaviors can be gently and tentatively confronted. You might say, for example, "I am interested in what Joe is saying, but I find it hard to pay attention when you are making noise kicking the chair." If the group has developed to a point where members can handle being reminded of the rules without feeling criticized or put down, a simple reminder of agreed-upon behavior may be adequate.

## Attention Seeking

Basically, you must decide to either ignore or attend to attention-getting behavior. Sometimes ignoring the behavior causes it to stop because it is not reinforced. Sometimes the behavior will cease or be modified if attention is received, because the goal is attained. At other times, attention simply escalates the behavior. You must judge the appropriate response.

## Under- or Nonparticipation

The goals for under- or nonparticipation typically are rebellion, self-protection, or revenge. Rebellion ("You cannot make me participate") usually occurs with involuntary group participants. They did not choose to be in group, and because they were forced or coerced in some way to attend, they will refuse to participate. The refusal may not be open and direct, but their lack of participation speaks volumes. The leader needs to go slow and not try to force participation, acknowledging that they, indeed, cannot be forced to participate.

For some, such as court-ordered participants, you may want to address the issue of involuntary participation openly and make the topic a part of the group process. Asking participants for their thoughts and feelings about the proposed group and its activities, and acknowledging that you can only encourage participation and cannot force it, will allow some members to express their resistances. Generally, many will then cooperate, if only on a superficial level. You must model genuineness by not insisting that the under- or nonparticipant become more involved. Offer opportunities to become involved in the group, but do not push.

When under- or nonparticipation has the goal of protecting the self, you are wise to let the member alone. Even in a counseling/therapy group, the member would be allowed to determine the level and extent of his or her participation. Safety and trust are critical issues, and it is unlikely that these issues can be sufficiently addressed in a psychoeducational group because of the limited time frame. You can encourage input by asking members directly from time to time if they have any comments. Acknowledge comments with a response to reinforce the positive behavior of participation. Ask nonthreatening questions that do not require self-disclosure or opinions.

The revenge goal is similar to the rebellion goal but with the added component that members are getting back at those who hurt them by trying to hurt others. These members are the sullen, hostile, silent ones. There is a kind of threat about their silence, whereas the rebellious member is not necessarily sullen and hostile. The best strategy is to leave these members alone but block attacking behavior. Extend an invitation to participate, but openly acknowledge that you cannot make them participate and that you will respect their decision. If they must be present—that is, they do not have the freedom to leave—you can try asking them what the group can do to make the experience more meaningful for them.

## Socializing

The socializer is having a grand old time. He or she is talkative, enjoys interacting with others, may giggle or laugh a lot, and wants to be involved with others and have them involved with him or her. In counseling/therapy groups, other members often will confront the socializer. But in short-term groups, the group usually does not take responsibility. Further, the task function of psychoeducational groups makes it less likely that personal development is a significant goal, and the group is not likely to confront the socializer.

Strategies you can use in dealing with socializers include physically moving toward them and standing near them, making sure they are in different groups, speaking to them during break about their behavior and its impact on the group, and directly soliciting their input by calling on them by name. Table 7.1 describes levels of participation, and suggested leadership strategies.

## Disengaged Group Members

Group members are, or become, disengaged from the group in a variety of ways and for a variety of reasons. Disengagement can be physical, mental, emotional, or any combination of these. Physical disengagement is seen in the following behaviors:

- Absence
- Tardiness
- Putting or having one's chair less than completely in the group
- Lack of body orientation to speakers
- Eyes focused elsewhere—for example, ceiling, floor, window
- Back turned to the group or speaker
- Leaning back in chair
- Turning chair around and sitting with the back of the chair facing the group
- Temporarily leaving the group
- Premature termination

TABLE 7.1

Levels for Participants and Leadership Strategies

| Participants' Level | Characterization | Leadership Strategy |
| --- | --- | --- |
| **Low** | | |
| Little understanding, unclear goals, ambiguous | Confusion, resistance, questioning, seeks clarification | Directing, structuring |
| **Low to Moderate** | | |
| Lacks clarity of task, personal involvement, wait-and-see attitude | Insecure, less confusion, less resistance | Motivating, encouraging |
| **Moderate** | | |
| Understanding of task, self-motivation, and personal involvement | Responsible, participating, initiating | Involving, mutuality |
| **High** | | |
| Understanding and appreciation of tasks, very motivated, eager to proceed | Works independently and as a member of the team | Empowering, delegating |

All these behaviors can be disruptive to the group's process and progress, and are especially of concern when they appear as a change from a member's usual behavior. Some of these behaviors are subtle, nonverbal ones that can trigger leaders' and members' concern just below the level of consciousness— that is, you sense something but are not consciously aware of just what you are sensing or why. Other physical disengagement behaviors are more overt (e.g., absence) and can be openly explored.

Mental disengagement cannot be observed and must be inferred, unless a member reports it. Examples for mental disengagement include:

- Thinking about outside-the-group concerns
- Daydreaming
- Wondering how and what to talk about, or how to respond
- Planning what to say or do (e.g., questions)
- Mental rehearsals
- Free association, stream of consciousness
- Analyzing

It can be relatively easy to use mental disengagement because thinking speed is very fast, especially when compared to speaking or acting speed. This differential can make it easy to mask or deny being disengaged. Thus, someone can pretend to be attentive if challenged, because you generally say or do something, such as using the member's name, prior to challenging him or her. This allows for just enough time for the member to snap back into the present.

Free association and analysis can be tied to self-exploration—that is, the member has something triggered by an event or comment in the group and begins to follow where that leads; hence the disengagement. Sometimes new learning and understanding can emerge for that person.

However, most mental disengagement is an attempt to flee the group, get away from uncomfortable triggered feelings, and/or deny personal associations to what is taking place in the group. Leaders will want to know what the stimulus was that triggered the mental disengagement.

Emotional disengagement can be less difficult to observe for some group members than mental disengagement, because the leader has become familiar with this nonverbal attending behavior and is aware when it changes to withdrawal. The person can physically alter his or her posture, eye contact, limb positioning such as crossing arms across chest, and tone of voice. Emotional disengagement is generally the basis for the following behaviors:

- Changing the topic
- Moving back from the group or turning away from the speaker
- Refusing to initiate or maintain eye contact
- Starting side conversations
- Fiddling with possessions, or self, such as hair
- Trying to soothe or reassure someone by giving advice, or making comments to lessen emotional intensity
- Asking questions, especially rhetorical questions
- Intellectualizing
- Becoming numb or confused
- Monopolizing group time by telling a personal story in detail
- Becoming aggressive

These behaviors and others are used to keep the person from awareness and from experiencing personal and uncomfortable feelings. The fear and dread of this personal discomfort motivates the disengagement, not the other person's emotions. Other people's emotions may trigger emotional detachment, but the person who uses it is trying to get away from something that is personally threatening.

The short-term nature of psychoeducational groups makes it difficult for group leaders to effectively challenge, manage, and explore these disengagements. Rather than working through the causes for the disengagement, leaders may have to be content with noting it, reflecting on what may have triggered it, and encouraging members to speak more often about their feelings, ideas, and thoughts in the here and now. In-depth exploration requires a strong therapeutic alliance and more time than is available for most psychoeducational groups.

## TEACHING MEMBERSHIP SKILLS

It may be helpful to plan one session that teaches group members how to be productive and constructive. Their learning, personal development, the group's progress, and the group's process are all facilitated when members have and use certain skills. You cannot teach all of these at one time, nor do you want to lose the primary focus or purpose for the group. It can be effective to choose a few skills you want to teach, present them in writing to members in the first meeting, and remind members to use these skills throughout the life of the group.

Do not try to teach all group membership skills at one time. These skills have to be internalized, practiced, and fed back in order for members to learn and use them. This takes time, and you do not want to give members too much new material at one time. The major group membership skills are as follows:

- Speak your feelings, thoughts, and ideas out loud.
- Make personal statements using *I, me,* and *my.*
- Do not use the universal or general designation of *we* or *us.*
- Members and the leader cannot read your mind; you must verbalize what you experience.
- Do not expect your nonverbal communication to be accurately understood.
- Make an effort to not suppress your feelings, and allow yourself to experience and explore them
- When you find yourself resisting, do not try to deny or repress it; accept it and let it protect you until you are ready to explore it.
- Respond by sharing your feelings instead of asking questions.
- Refrain from giving advice. However, providing information is different and is encouraged.

### Feelings, Thoughts, and Ideas

Members will have to be encouraged and reminded to speak about their thoughts, feelings, and ideas in the here and now. A major constraint for members is social convention—that is, many people are taught that speaking openly about these feelings is rude or inappropriate. However, speaking openly and directly facilitates personal development and group process. Leaders can more accurately and easily judge and evaluate members' experiences when thought disclosure takes place. Further, the process and theme of the group is more visible.

When an extended silence becomes uncomfortable, leaders can invite members to speak of what they are experiencing at that time. This intervention also can be useful when a member makes an emotionally intense remark or disclosure. Members may be uncertain how they should respond and this reminder can direct them.

## Personal Statements

The group is the one place where it is appropriate and expected that members will use personal pronouns such as *I, me,* and *my* in their comments. Culture again may work against members' willingness and comfort with making personal statements. The one group of people that this does not apply to is the narcissist. Indeed, you may have difficulty getting narcissists to recognize that there are other people in the world, much less in the group.

Making personal statements is one form of taking personal responsibility and forces people to acknowledge that they are in charge and have some power. These are all desirable states for group members and should be encouraged.

Leaders must be judicious in reminding members to use personal statements and not remind them every time they fail to do so. It may be better to wait until you are more confident about the strength of the relationship before interjecting a reminder, as some members may take offense or be embarrassed when reminded in front of other members. After a connection is made and a therapeutic relationship is established, it becomes less threatening to remind individual members to make personal statements. It could be effective and helpful to remind the group as a whole at the beginning of each session to try to use personal statements. That way, no one is put on the spot.

## General Designations Are Not Helpful

This skill is closely aligned with the previous one of making personal statements. When general designations are used (e.g., *we*, *us*, or *they*), it diffuses responsibility, and it is inaccurate to speak for other people. While it can be less threatening to speak as if others were in agreement or involved, it may not be reflective of others' attitudes, thoughts, opinions, and so on. Members need to become aware of their reluctance to accept personal responsibility when they use general or universal designations.

## Mind Reading Is Not Possible

It is not unusual for group members to have an unconscious expectation or need for the leader to be a fully empathic nurturer and to be able to immediately know what members want, need, mean, and desire without their having to verbalize it. This ability is called mind reading. However, it is very unlikely that leaders have this ability or are adept enough to "read" group members' inner self. Nor should group leaders have this unrealistic expectation for themselves.

It could be helpful to tell members at the very beginning of the group about the expectation that their thoughts, feelings, ideas, wants, and so on must be spoken aloud, and that they should ask for what they want or need from each other as well as from the leader. You may need to give gentle reminders.

This expectation for mind reading may be deeply ingrained for some members because they grew up in families where this was expected. They could have had one or more parents with a destructive narcissistic pattern (Brown, 2001) who expected their children to read their minds and give them what was needed or wanted. Other members may have a deep longing for an empathic nurturer, since they did not receive this at crucial periods in their lives. Whatever the reason, this unconscious desire and expectation can lead to considerable misunderstandings, disappointments, and even resentment. Leaders need to be aware of their own needs and behaviors that are reflective of the expectation of mind reading and to stay aware of members' expectations for it.

## Identifying Feelings

Members may have a very narrow vocabulary for identifying and expressing their feelings, be reluctant or embarrassed to identify them, and/or not have much experience at doing this. It is very helpful to the group's progress and process when members are able to identify and express what they are feeling, especially what they are feeling in the moment.

Ask members to name or label what they feel, even if they can only describe body sensations. Encourage them to use metaphors—for example, lower than a snake's belly, free as a bird, jumpy as a long-tailed cat in a room full of rocking chairs, cool as a cucumber, shy as a fawn, or uplifting as a hot-air balloon. Leaders may also want to use some exercises that expand members' vocabulary of words to identify and express feelings.

## Nonverbal Communication

Clusters of nonverbal gestures and postures form metacommunication, which carries over 90 percent of the message being sent. Attending to this metacommunication can contribute to understand the *real* message, which can be different from the spoken one. Some people are very adept at reading these nonverbal messages and base their responses on them rather than on the overt spoken message—for example, you may have a parent or sibling who is able to read and respond to your nonverbal message.

Group members may have an unrealistic expectation that others should be able to understand their nonverbal communication. Group leaders should make it clear from the very beginning that understanding each other's feelings, intents, and so forth will be based more on spoken messages, because trying to read and interpret nonverbal messages is risky and subject to error. Leaders can become more experienced at understanding a member's nonverbal communication over time, but still need to verify their perception rather than accepting their experience as valid and acting as if it were true rather than considering it a hypothesis or possibility.

Group members are often surprised when they realize that their nonverbal communication is not congruent with their verbal communication. They become aware of this through other members and the leader's feedback and responses to them. This can be important learning for these members as the incongruence they display in the group could be reflective of their interactions outside the group that are negatively impacted because they are sending mixed messages.

## Expressing and Exploring Feelings

Encourage members to express and explore their feelings that emerge during group sessions. The group is intended to be a safe place where feelings are acceptable and new understandings and associations for these feelings are possible.

Members may fear some of their feelings, as they can be threatening to the self, uncomfortable and painful, or very shaming. These reasons for suppressing feelings are common and understandable. However, it is much more beneficial to express and/or explore these feelings in order to promote resolution for underlying issues, problems, and concerns. It is the group leader's job to help members with this task. Willingness to express and explore feelings is facilitated by building safety and trust in the group.

Leaders can find ways to help members express feelings other than constantly asking, "How does that make you feel?" or "What are you feeling?" Members will tire of this questioning quickly and begin to resist, thus putting another barrier in front of exploration.

When leaders use empathy, or active listening and responding, they can help members express important and difficult feelings. These responses are much more helpful than asking questions about what the person is feeling because these responses convey that the leader understands what the member is experiencing.

## SPECIFIC LEADERSHIP STRATEGIES

There are three common traps that beginning and ineffective group leaders can encounter, and fall into: trying to overcome resistance; asking questions as a way of showing interest, or in an attempt to guide the client down a particular road of thought; and wanting to fix the problem by giving advice. Effective group leaders, on the other hand, understand resistance and are not threatened by it; use their active listening and responding skills to connect to and encourage the client in self-exploration; and deeply understand that the client is in the best position to fix his/her problem, and does not give advice. These traps are continually present at all times, and in all groups.

## Resistance

Leaders have to be patient with resistance. It is not wrong; it is there to protect the person from threatening material. Members have to be taught the following:

- They need to become aware of their personal resistance.
- Defenses are ways by which resistance is manifested.
- When the leader recognizes resistance and highlights it, he or she is not pointing a finger of blame or shame at the member.
- Members do not have to stop resisting.
- It can be helpful for growth and development to analyze the roots of the resistance and what triggered it.
- Members can choose to continue to resist.
- The leader will not attack resistance.

Beginning group leaders can confuse active participation with lack of resistance and think that there is not resistance because members are pleasant, verbally active, and cooperative. However, resistance is always present and is manifested in a variety of ways. Sometimes the resistance is direct and overt, such as when a member is sullen and silent. Most often resistance is indirect and covert, such as a verbally active member who is actually directing attention away from a sensitive topic. Further, considerable resistance remains on the unconscious and nonconscious levels, and group members employ their defenses to resist without being aware of what they are doing.

Leaders of short-term psychoeducational groups need to become aware of resistant behaviors, as these are clues to the members' sensitive material. This awareness does not translate into acts to reduce, break through, or attack the resistance. It is best to leave the resistance alone. If the therapeutic relationship is developed to the point where members can tolerate being told of the resistance or defense, leaders can gently do so in a manner that does not blame or shame. It can take a long time for members to accept that resistance is not wrong, that it can be helpful to analyze it, and that the leader is not accusatory when pointing out resistant behaviors.

## Feeling Responses, Not Questions

Members can be helpful to other members and to the group process when their responses focus on their personal feelings and they do not ask questions to elicit more detail or as a way of showing interest. This practice can be difficult. Social convention and cultural expectations work against open expressions of feelings as responses.

When questions are asked, it moves the interaction to the cognitive level, decreases or moderates emotional intensity, and deflects attention. Worse is when questions arc askcd to guide thoughts and feelings in the direction the questioner thinks they should go. These are not helpful questions at all.

Members will know how others perceive them or their situation when responses are feeling focused—for example, when a member tells of a distressing situation and members respond with their feelings that reflect the speaker's feelings (e.g., hurt, resentment, or fear), that person may feel validated and supported. On the other hand, if members were to respond with questions, the speaker might feel misunderstood or unsupported, thus becoming resistant.

Leaders can block this questioning behavior by interjecting and telling responding members that it would be helpful to the speaker if they could verbalize their feelings that emerged as they listened. Leaders can also model this behavior and speak of their feelings as they listen to members.

## Advice Giving Is Not Helpful

Advice is seldom helpful, since it is given on the basis of personal understanding and status, conveys what the advice giver thinks the other person should or ought to do, seldom fits the receiver's situation or personality, and can be wrong. Many people are aware of the risks and dangers of giving advice, but that does not deter them from doing so. Stage 1 in group development is characterized by advice giving by members who are trying to be helpful.

There can be a strong desire or a life's expectation for some members that leads them to rush to give others the benefit of their experiences. There are many different reasons for advice giving, but they are all for the benefit of the giver, not the receiver.

It is much more helpful for members to find their own answers and to fix things their way. This does not mean that the leader and members should refrain from giving needed information. Whenever it is evident that a member lacks essential information, is misinformed, or is not aware of changes that can affect him or her, withholding facts is inadvisable. Giving information is not the same as giving advice.

## Personal Development Exercise: My Life

> **Objective:** To increase awareness of the important events in your life.
> **Materials:** Two or more sheets of paper; pen or pencil; sheet of paper 18 by 24 inches or larger; colored pencils, crayons, or felt markers.
> **Procedure:** Spread the large sheet of paper on a table and sit in silence,

reflecting on one of the following periods in your life: early childhood, middle–late childhood, early adolescence, late adolescence, early adulthood, or now.

As you reflect on your chosen period, try to remember what it was like from its beginning to its end. Draw a lifeline on the large sheet of paper that reflects the course of that period. The line may wander, turn around, or present in any way you choose. Use the markers to denote special events along the line—for example, moving, getting an award, birth of a sibling, death of a grandparent, divorce. Try to have 8 to 10 of these special events.

List the events on one sheet of paper. Look at both the drawing and the list. On another sheet of paper, write a response to "It was a period in my life when . . ." Pay special attention to feelings associated with the events, other people involved, and so forth. Use as many sheets of paper as you need.

# Chapter 8

# Managing Conflict and Guidelines for Confrontation

Major Topics and Concepts

*Knowledge, Skills, and Technique Factors*
Characteristic conflict behavior
Variable conflict management model
Variable conflict management strategies
Confrontation
Types of confrontation
Guidelines for confrontation

## INTRODUCTION

Do not be afraid of conflict emerging in your group and do not seek to squash it, unless there is potential physical or psychological harm to members. Attaining this psychological and emotional perspective of conflict is not easy, and for some of you who have had negative outcomes for conflict in their past, it may be extremely difficult for you to accept that conflict can be constructive. Your groups will take their cues from your actions, words, and nonverbal communication, and will either suppress conflict if you are fearful of it, or try to work through it if you are accepting of it as a potential for strengthening relationships. Your verbal and nonverbal communication about conflict can teach members new ways to perceive and behave in conflict, how to recognize mild forms of conflict, to constructively resolve conflicts, a positive approach for confronting, when and how to confront, the positive and negative outcomes for various kinds of behavior in conflict, how to not fear conflict, and that constructive resolution of conflict strengthens relationships.

Conflict can emerge in a group at any time between members, between a member and the leader, or between the group and the leader. Conflict with others outside the group may be brought into the group and displaced onto members or the leader. There may be differences of opinion, personal animosities, defiance or rebellion against authority figures, or a general hostile attitude. Whatever the cause of the conflict, the leader must be prepared to handle it in ways that benefit members and facilitate the progress of the group.

Variable conflict management uses a multifaceted approach, taking into account the stage of group development and the maturity level of group members. This strategy can be used for most of the conflicts that commonly emerge. Probably the most important components in managing conflict are the leader's abilities to tolerate ambiguity and anxiety, anticipate and plan for managing conflicts, and use blocking and confrontation constructively. The leader is in control and has the responsibility for constructively managing conflicts.

## CHARACTERISTIC CONFLICT BEHAVIOR

Most discussions of conflict management list five characteristic ways people behave in conflicts: withdrawing, forcing, soothing, compromising, and confronting. The discussion that follows describes these behaviors and advantages and disadvantages of each. Leaders can and should use more than one conflict management strategy, but they also need to be aware of members' needs, outside forces, and the stage of group development.

*Withdrawing* is defined as a physical or emotional retreat, a refusal to engage. The advantage of withdrawing is that the conflict ceases. The disadvantage is that the underlying issue, problem, or concern does not get addressed, and this strategy may leave residual uncomfortable feelings.

*Forcing* is characteristic of individuals who must win at all costs. They attack, intimidate, and generally behave in a way that forces their point of view on others. Again, conflicts do not get worked out; the conflict also may escalate if others fight back or may be suppressed if others withdraw.

As a management strategy, *soothing* may keep the conflict from escalating or becoming more intense. The attempt to produce harmony can sometimes work if there are intensely uncomfortable feelings involved. However, this strategy can be manipulative if the soother is meeting his or her own needs to reduce tension and not taking into account the needs of others to work through the conflict. For some, even a slight hint of conflict produces strong feelings based on childhood experiences, usually in the family, which leads to soothing behavior. There are other times when soothing is appropriate—for example, when a conflict cannot be worked through because intense feelings are involved or out of control. Participants may be able to work through the conflict if they are soothed to the point where they can each hear what each other is saying.

*Compromising* takes place when both sides give up something to arrive at a resolution or solution. Negotiating takes skill and a willingness to meet the other person at least halfway. However, compromising assumes that both parties are willing to be involved in reaching a solution or resolution. One person in a conflict cannot compromise without the other. Some individuals perceive compromising as losing.

*Confronting* is a skill that can be learned. It is not easy, especially since it has come to be synonymous with attack. Confrontation is an invitation to the other person to examine his or her behavior and its impact on you. It assumes there is a relationship to be preserved and that you want to preserve it. It is not an opportunity to dump on the other person all the negative thoughts and feelings you have experienced about him or her. Further, the other person does not have to accept the invitation. Confrontations are not forced; they must be accepted. All of these characteristics limit the usefulness of confrontation as a conflict management strategy in psychoeducational groups.

## VARIABLE CONFLICT MANAGEMENT STRATEGIES

Variable conflict management strategies (VCMS) include the five listed above plus four other skills: distracting, ignoring, delaying, and holding firm. *Distracting* involves introducing a new topic, reframing, or refocusing on some other aspect of the conflict. Distracting may be useful if the leader does not want to withdraw or ignore the conflict but, instead, redirects it to focus on something more useful. For example, the conflict may be a flare-up over some small event that does not have much to do with the task of the group. The leader can intervene and block an escalation of the conflict by introducing another topic.

Just as with children, it sometimes is better to *ignore* conflicts. Some people use conflict as an attention-getting mechanism, and the leader can get sucked into dealing with the conflict instead of focusing on the task at hand. Learning to recognize when to ignore it comes with experience.

*Delaying* intervention to manage the conflict gives participants time to cool off. There may be times when the leader wants to teach positive conflict management skills or model them, but the intensity of feelings involved in the conflict makes it unwise at this time. Some reasons for delaying include the group may choose sides, the differences may escalate, physical violence may ensue, or the emotional fragility of members may be such that working through the conflict at that moment would produce more disturbance. Delaying does not mean withdrawing from the conflict; it is a temporary disengagement.

*Holding firm* is a conflict management strategy that is somewhat authoritarian in nature. The leader takes the responsibility for blocking behaviors that contribute to the conflict, stating rules and guidelines for participation by reminding participants of them and enforcing them.

Variable conflict management strategies (VCMS) use the status of group members on two dimensions: responsibility and expertise. The assumption behind VCMS is that the group leader needs to respond differently to conflicts in the group depending on the responsibility levels and expertise of the group members. These dimensions may be more important than age, gender, and education. A single conflict management strategy may not fit the abilities of the group members. The expert group leader will be able to use the full range of strategies and judge when and where to use each.

An individual group member's conflict with the leader, the group's conflict with the leader, conflicts among members, and conflicts between groups or cliques of members all require different management strategies. The leader must deal with each of these conflicts in different ways at different stages of the group, and take into consideration the status of the members involved.

## Levels of Responsibility and Expertise

Members will vary greatly in their degrees of responsibility and levels of expertise. These dimensions may be more important in terms of conflict management than age, gender, and education.

### Responsibility

Responsibility is defined from the description of class II scales for the *California Psychological Inventory* (Gough, 1975). The scales measure socialization, maturity, responsibility, and intrapersonal structuring of values. The functions of the scales are "to identify persons of conscientious, responsible, and dependable disposition and temperament; to indicate the degree of social maturity, integrity, and rectitude the individual has attained; to assess the degree and adequacy of self-regulation and self-control and freedom from impulsivity and self-centeredness; to identify personal with permissive, accepting, and nonjudgmental social beliefs; and to identify persons capable of creating a favorable impression, and who are concerned about how others react to them" (p. 10).

While age plays a role in the degree of responsibility and maturity, this dimension is not totally age related. The expectation for exhibition of responsibility is age related in that you do not expect the same manifestation of responsibility from a child or adolescent as from an adult. Instead, it is reasonable to expect children and adolescents to manifest responsible behavior appropriate for their age level.

High-responsibility descriptors include cooperative, outgoing, sociable, warm, planning, capable, conscientious, and dependable. Low-responsibility descriptors include undercontrolled and impulsive in behavior, defensive, opinionated, passive and overly judgmental in attitude, wary, and overemphasizing personal pleasure and self-gain.

## *Expertise*

The dimension of expertise is defined with descriptors of communication skills, such as attending, ability to suspend judgment and listen to the other, focusing on issues, ability to tolerate ambiguity, and personal ownership of feelings and attitudes. Expertise is the dimension that can more easily be developed and forms the focus for some skill development groups. When dealing with conflict in the group, the leader can evaluate the participants' expertise by observing interactions.

## VCMS MODEL

The model in Table 8.1 categorizes participants' behavior into six categories using the dimensions of responsibility and expertise. A description of some behaviors illustrates each, and the nine management strategies are associated with each category of dimensions.

### Description of Categories

#### *Low Responsibility/Low Expertise*

Participants in this category can be very difficult, especially if they are also involuntary participants. They are unwilling to trust and cooperate and unable

TABLE 8.1

Model for Management Strategies Based on Member Status

| Status | Behavior | Strategy |
|---|---|---|
| Low responsibility/low expertise | Unwilling and unable (defiant, hostile) | Holding firm |
| Low responsibility/ moderate expertise | Tends to be unwilling but has some skills | Ignoring, distracting, delaying, or confronting |
| Moderate responsibility/ low expertise | Willing but not knowledgeable | Delaying (leader), soothing, or withdrawing |
| Moderate responsibility/ moderate expertise | Willing and able with sufficient support and encouragement | Compromising, confronting, or soothing |
| Moderate responsibility/ high expertise | Knows what and how to approach conflicts; may choose not to do so | Compromising or confronting |
| High responsibility/high expertise | Both willing and able | Withdrawing or confronting |

to adequately attend to the task. The group leader may experience them as being sullen and hostile. Conflicts involving these participants need to be handled with clear, firm directions that remind them what the expected behaviors are and just what will and will not be tolerated.

### Low Responsibility/Moderate Expertise
This category includes participants who are not as difficult to deal with as the previous category, since they have some skills and could attend to the task, but they appear to be unwilling to do so. They would be described as immature for their age. While these participants also profit from clear, firm guidelines, their conflicts can be managed with ignoring, distracting, and delaying.

### Moderate Responsibility/Low Expertise
These participants are willing to be cooperative and try to accomplish the task, but they lack the knowledge and skills that would enable them to do so. The group leader who assumes that because these participants are cooperating they can do what is required to meet the groups goals will be very disappointed when he or she realizes that the participants simply do not know how to accomplish what needs to be done. Conflict management strategies that are useful include confronting, delaying, and soothing.

### Moderate Responsibility/Moderate Expertise
These participants are willing and have the necessary knowledge and skills but need encouragement and support to carry out the task. They need reassurance that they are doing what is needed. The group leader can use withdrawing, compromising, confronting, and soothing as conflict management strategies.

### Moderate Responsibility/High Expertise
The participants in this category are very able to accomplish the task. They have the knowledge and skills, but for some reason they may choose not to use them constructively. The conflict management strategies that work best are compromising and confronting.

### High Responsibility/High Expertise
These ideal participants have both the sense of responsibility and the needed expertise. The group leader may need to withdraw and let them handle the conflict or confront if they do not seem to be on the right track.

### An Example

The following brief scenario shows behaviors representative of each category, along with a leader response that illustrates four of the suggested variable conflict management strategies: Two members get into a heated argument over a minor point. Their voices get louder, their fists clench, and their facial expressions are angry.

### Holding Firm Response

"I am going to break into the discussion here and remind members of the agreement we all made to maintain respect for differing points of view. We can continue to discuss this point if you like. However, all group members must take part in the discussion, and respect for one another must be demonstrated. Or, I can address the point in question and make a decision. Which do you prefer?"

### Distracting Response

"I wonder if you two can hold off presenting your points of view until the group deals with_____? I promise that we will get back to them."

### Soothing Response

"I can see that both of you feel strongly about this issue. It would be helpful if each of you would help me and the other members understand your point and its importance to you. If you agree, you can present your viewpoint one at a time. We'll go in alphabetical order by last name."

### Confronting Response

"Your argument is affecting group members, and I can see that they are uncomfortable. I feel somewhat uncomfortable as well, as you both seem ready to have a physical fight. I wonder if it is possible for us to discuss the disputed point with you."

This conflict is between group members. The specific responses would be different when dealing with other types of conflicts, such as member–leader conflict.

## CONFRONTATION

Confrontation can be negative and destructive or positive and constructive. Often it is perceived only as negative, destructive, and aggressive because the term is used improperly and the purpose is misunderstood. Confrontation is *not* synonymous with aggression, and it should not be used to accomplish these purposes: telling people off, attacking, browbeating others to get them to see your point or agree with you, criticizing, one-upmanship, for someone's "own good," to be perceived as right, or for vindication. These motives are harmful, and they will promote feelings of hostility and defensiveness in others. In order for relationships to grow, develop, and become strong, confrontation should be a positive and constructive interaction. "Confrontation is an invitation to an individual to examine his or her behavior and its consequences or impact on others" (Egan, 1975).

## Major Types of Confrontation

Berenson, Mitchell, and Laney (1968) identified five major types of confron tation: didactic, experiential, weakness, strength, and encouragement to ac- tion. Each approaches the invitation to examine behavior in a different way, and all are constructive when used appropriately.

### Didactic

*Didactic confrontation* assumes the receiver lacks important information or has misunderstood the information; in this case, the confrontation is used to remedy the condition. Didactic confrontation, however, involves more than simply giving information. The receiver is asked to examine his or her behav- ior and how it may be affecting the confronter because of faulty perceptions or ignorance. An example of didactic confrontation would be if a member in- sisted that the group end at 4 P.M. when the scheduled time for ending was 5 P.M. After correcting the misinformation, the leader could explore the impact of early termination on the process.

### Experiential

*Experiential confrontation* is so named because there is a significant differ- ence in how the receiver's self-perception and how you perceive him or her. This is particularly useful when the receiver has a distorted (either positive or negative) self-perception and does not see the impact of his or her behavior on others because of the misperception. The confronter shares how he or she ex- periences the receiver, and how this perception appears to differ from the receiver's self-perception. For example, a group member says that he finds it difficult to express anger. Other members confront by saying that this is not how they have experienced him. They note that he has been open in expressing irritation and annoyance, and the openness has been appreciated because they did not have to try to guess his feelings.

### Weakness

In *weakness confrontation*, the focus is on the receiver's deceits or inadequa- cies. A weakness confrontation is not an attack or a put-down but an invitation to the receiver to examine these weaknesses and how they influence his or her relationships. For example, asking a member to examine how she continually interrupts others and the impact this has on communications and relationships is a weakness confrontation.

### Strength
*Strength confrontations*, on the other hand, ask the receiver to look at underused or overlooked resources, assets, or strengths. This can be a particularly positive and powerful confrontation, as the receiver gains more awareness of previously hidden resources. For example, in a strength confrontation, the group might point out to a member that he has been persistent in the face of many obstacles and then list instances of that persistence.

### Encouragement to Action
The encouragement to action confrontation supports the receiver in taking an action instead of reacting passively. Many times, individuals know what would be beneficial for them but lack the resolve to take action. Confronting them with encouragement and support can give them the confidence to move forward.

Kurtz and Jones (1973) found that strength and encouragement to action confrontations are most positively received and acted on. The least effective confrontations are didactic and weakness. Didactic confrontations can easily become lectures, and weakness confrontations can be perceived as criticizing and fault finding. These should be used with caution.

## Guidelines for Confrontation

The group leader needs to consider several things before a confrontation: the purpose of the group, the extent of safety and trust developed in the group and with members, the type of conflict, the current psychological state of members and of the group as a whole, the expectation of change in behavior, personal motives for confronting, and the rationale for confronting.

### Purpose of the Group
In a skills learning group, the confrontation may be appropriate for modeling and learning. If, on the other hand, the group is more like a class, you may be better off not engaging in confrontation. The question you must ask yourself is: Will the confrontation help the group and its members? If the answer is not an unqualified yes, you should avoid confrontation.

### Established Safety and Trust
Confronting before adequate safety and trust have been established in the group produces a lot of anxiety. Other members may fear that they, too, will be confronted, so they may restrict their input. Confronting too early can put a damper on the group and cause more resistance.

### Type of Conflict
The type of conflict also plays a part in deciding when or whether to confront. Is the conflict between members? Should they be given a chance to work it out

before you intervene? Is the conflict between the group and you? This is expected at some point and may not require a confrontation; instead, it might call for another kind of response. Is the conflict one in which most of the group is in agreement and in conflict with one member? Is it scapegoating? Should it be blocked or confronted? Is the conflict between you and one member? Will a confrontation be perceived as a power struggle or as an attack on the member? These are not easy questions, but they should be considered before you engage in a confrontation.

### Psychological States of Group Members

You must consider the psychological state of the member and of the group before embarking on a confrontation. If there is a great deal of intense emotion involved, the confrontation should be delayed or discarded. If the member or the group is in a fragile state, the confrontation may not be appropriate. The receiver of the confrontation must be able to hear what is said and meant, and also be able to use it.

### Willingness to Consider Changing

Confrontations are invitations to examine behavior, and the receiver should be left free to decide whether to use the information. However, if you do not have a realistic expectation that a positive behavioral change will result, the confrontation is counterproductive. You must ask yourself if the receiver is willing to change. If the answer is no, you should not confront.

### Leader's Motives

Your motives for confronting also play a part in your decision. Indeed, they are crucial. You should never confront if your motive is to maintain control, to exert power or domination, to manipulate, to attack or take revenge, to punish, to show off your expertise, or as vindication.

### Rationale for Confronting

All positive purposes for confronting are related to promoting development of the individual or the group. Confrontation may be aimed at giving the receiver more direct awareness of his or her behavior and its consequences. Confrontation can provide additional perspectives if validated by other group members. It can provide an opportunity for safe self-examination, self-exploration, and behavior change. Positive confrontations can strengthen relationships.

## Confronter, Receiver, and Condition Variables

In every confrontation, there are three distinct, dynamic variables: the confronter, the receiver of the confrontation, and the conditions surrounding the confrontation. Each of these variables must be examined before the confrontation if it is to be a positive experience.

## Confronter Variables

- *Emotional state of the confronter:* Confrontations are most effective if the confronter is calm, empathic, accepting, and caring.
- *Motives or reasons for the confrontation:* The confronter must be aware of his or her rationale for the confrontation. If the confronter is unsure or confused about those reasons, the confrontation should be delayed or discarded.
- *Ability to distinguish clearly between facts and feelings:* Confrontations are most effective when the confronter can identify feelings as feelings and facts as facts. Awareness of and sensitivity to the relationship is also a component: What kind and level of relationship exists between the confronter and receiver? Are you seeking to strengthen the relationship? Do you care about the relationship? The confronter's feelings about and expectations for the relationship are vital components in the decision to confront.

## Receiver Variables

- *Receiver's emotional state:* Individuals under the influence of intense emotions are less likely to be open to confrontation. It is better to wait and confront when emotions are less intense.
- *Receiver's capacity for self-examination:* Individuals who are closed to self-examination or who deny the need for self-examination cannot be confronted with positive results.
- *Degree of trust the receiver has in the confronter:* If the person being confronted does not trust the confronter to be genuine or to have positive regard for him or her, the confrontation will not be perceived as justified, correct, or necessary.

## Condition Variables

The circumstances surrounding the confrontation are also important. The group leader has to remain aware of the potential impact of the confrontation on the entire group as well as for the particular group member. When leaders confront, there is some effect on other members, and that should not be minimized, or overlooked.

A further consideration is the group's stage of development. Sufficient safety and trust should be developed before using a confrontation as these are critical in determining how the confrontation will be received. It becomes an art to know when to use confrontation so that it benefits the individual and the group.

In addition to the stage of the group, it can be important to understand what the members may be internally processing. For example, if there was a heated exchange that just took place, or a member had made an emotionally intense disclosure, the leader would need to refrain from doing a confrontation because of the timing. In other words, do not do a confrontation just because you as the leader think it is needed, or would be helpful, do so when the group is ready and able to effectively use it.

Other considerations include the following:

- *Audience:* Who beside the confronter and the receiver is present? There are
  times when the support of others can be helpful, if they reinforce the confronting statements. If, however, the relationships are not trusting, accepting, or caring, then the presence of others can be perceived as ganging up.
- *Environmental conditions:* Social gatherings, meetings, or family reunions
  are not appropriate venues for positive confrontations. Being sensitive to
  the purpose of the setting can make a difference in whether the confrontation is successful.

## Fundamentals of Confronting

Once the decision to confront has been made, the confronter should keep some
communication fundamentals in mind, including the following:

1. Use a positive approach.
2. Choose words that suit the receiver's emotional state.
3. Be concrete; say what is on your mind.
4. Be aware of the impact you are having on the receiver.
5. Wait for a response or reaction.
6. Be sure of your facts.
7. Do not exaggerate or make broad generalizations.
8. Think before you speak.
9. Check to ensure that you are being understood accurately.
10. Stick to the topic; do not bring in other concerns or issues.
11. Try not to criticize.
12. Do not impose your views; just express them.
13. Be receptive to feedback.
14. Listen to the other person.
15. Do not interrupt.
16. Give people the time they need to absorb the information.

## Summary of Constructive Confrontation

You should approach confrontation as you would positive feedback. Use some
of the same criteria and assumptions to promote constructive reception of the
confrontation.

### Make Your Statements Descriptive, Not Evaluative

Describing the behavior is objective; making judgments about the behavior is
subjective. The more objective you can be, the more apt everyone is to agree
that this is, in fact, the observed behavior.

## Focus on a Specific Behavior Rather than Being
## General in Your Description

It is not helpful to use terms that are ambiguous and do not describe a specific behavior. For example, telling someone he or she is domineering is not concrete or helpful. However, telling someone that he or she has been interrupting the conversation often, then giving examples, is specific. In addition, do not infer motives for the behavior. This is speculative, making it subjective and part of one's personal experience. It also raises the possibility that others will not agree, as their experiences may have been different.

## Remember That the Needs of the Receiver Are More
## Important Than the Needs of the Confronter

This is a sensitive and risky undertaking that may be very threatening for the receiver. While you as the confronter may undergo some of the same feelings, you are the initiator. Be tentative and ready to stop at any time if the receiver appears overwhelmed.

## Wait for an Invitation to Confront

Confrontation is most useful and constructive if it is solicited rather than imposed. Asked-for confrontations generally mean that the receiver is willing and able to use the feedback and feels a need to get it. However, it takes a long time for relationships to develop to the point where confrontations are actively sought. You may wish to use moderate confrontations even if they are not solicited.

## Time Your Confrontations Well

Timing is critical. Feedback is most useful when given close to the time of the behavior. If it is not possible to give the feedback at that time, wait until the behavior occurs again, delay it, or discard it. If the receiver is in an emotional state that is not conducive to receiving the feedback, if other activities intervene, or if it is time to break or stop, the confrontation should be delayed or discarded.

## Be Prepared to Listen, as Confrontation Involves Sharing of Information

Confrontation is not *telling* the receiver; it is a *dialogue*. Listening also gives cues as to the emotional state of the receiver, which tells you when to back off and when to continue. As part of the listening, the feedback should be checked to ensure clear communication. Did the receiver hear what you said, or was it distorted in some way? Did you say what you intended to say, or was it different? It is easy for feedback under these conditions to be misunderstood.

Attend to the consequences of the feedback. Pay attention to the impact of your words on the receiver and on other group members. Remember that the confrontation will affect all group members in some way, not just the receiver.

Personal Development Exercise:
My Achievements and My Disappointments

> **Objective:** To stay in touch with both positive and negative life events.
> **Materials:** Paper and a pen or pencil.
> **Procedure:** Create a poem or write an essay about your greatest achievements and your deepest disappointments.
> **Processing:** After completing the exercise, write a summary statement about feelings that were aroused as you completed the exercise and awarenesses that emerged.

# Chapter 9

# Leading Psychoeducational Groups for Children

Major Topics and Concepts

*Knowledge Factors*
>  Types of children's groups
>  Research findings

*Science Factors*
>  How children groups are different
>  General guidelines for leading

*Skills Factor*
>  Sample procedures and structure for sessions

## INTRODUCTION

Psychoeducational groups for children are conducted in a variety of settings, but schools provide the most extensive use for these. Schools have counseling programs designed to help students with developmental issues, life transitions, behavior problems, social skills development, and as support for crises and other difficulties.

Mental health professionals in other settings also find children's groups to be helpful, and these have as much variety as do adult groups. Children are recognized as active participants in life events that are personal for them, and in events for others in their lives as these can have a major impact on them. This is a major shift from the time when children were viewed as passive recipients, and considerable efforts were expended to keep them from knowing what events were occurring to other family members. Much more is now known about the effect of these on children.

## TYPES OF CHILDREN'S PSYCHOEDUCATIONAL GROUPS

Thompson and Randolph (1983) provide a way to categorize groups for children that has implications for psychoeducational groups. They propose four categories: common problems, case centered, human potential, and skill development.

### Common Problems Groups

Common problem groups are focused on an identified or potential problem. The theme or purpose for the group is narrowly focused; there is commonality around the problem for members, and they may also have other unifying characteristics; the homogeneity of the group contributes positively to developing trust and safety; and planning can be easier.

Brown (1994) describes a model for creating groups for children that uses commonality of problem as the basis for the group. This is different from using common situations as the basis in that situations may differ, but the underlying problems are similar. For example, in a group focused on grief and loss, members could have a variety of losses, such as divorce, death, or incarceration. Members need not have the same loss—for example, death of a mother.

Sheckman (2001) describes another example of a common problem group. The group was for fourth-grade students in Israel, and the purpose for the group was members' tendencies to make aggressive responses to peers. Results indicated a positive increase in empathy and a decrease in aggressive responses for participants.

### Case-Centered Groups

These are groups where members are working on different problems. Each member receives the attention, feedback, and support from other members as well as from the group leader. This type of group recognizes individuality and differences, and uses the resources of the group to help members. The underlying theme that links members can emerge, although they appear to have very different problems or situations.

The heterogeneity of case-centered groups can be a drawback at first, because members will focus more on differences than commonalities. There are two helpful factors that leaders can foster in these groups that will promote safety and trust. The first is universality—that is, the leader uses linking skills to highlight similarities that may not be readily apparent. These similarities could be feelings such as fear of abandonment, or values such as the desire for achievement, or personality characteristics such as determination.

The second helpful factor is altruism. Children are seldom given opportunities to help others where that help is recognized. Peer interaction in these groups can be guided toward understanding of others and speaking of that understanding directly, pointing out each other's unrecognized strengths, and learning to give constructive feedback. There is a richness in heterogeneous groups that can be tapped to the benefit of all members.

## Human Potential Groups

Thompson and Randolph (1983) defined human potential groups as having a purpose to provide opportunities for developing members' positive traits and strengths. Developmental concerns are emphasized rather than remediation of existing problems. A good or extensive knowledge of human growth and development is the foundation for creating these groups. Also helpful is an understanding of life transitions and cultural factors. The two examples that follow illustrate this type of group.

Franklin and Pack-Brown (2001) conducted a group for elementary African-American boys that was designed around the seven principles of Kwanzaa. The group was held for 24 sessions, and focused on awareness and skills of conflict resolution, stress management, and problem solving. Pre- and posttest teacher ratings of classroom behavior showed an increase in positive ratings. There was also a 48 percent decrease in disciplinary actions.

Garrett and Crutchfield (1997) described a seven-session "talking circle" group that was based on Native American principles for developing self-esteem, self-determination, body awareness, and self-concept. The talking circle was the forum for each member to express thoughts and feelings, and a "talking stick" was used to signal that the holder was the speaker and was to receive attention, acceptance, and respect from other members.

## Skill Development Groups

Psychological groups play an important role in social skills training. Indeed, these groups are the primary mode of delivery for such training. The following is a selected overview of studies on the effectiveness of this training, with an emphasis on the group. Studies were selected as samples of social skills training models for children, adolescents, and adults with a variety of conditions.

In a meta-analysis of the effectiveness of cognitive-behavioral outcomes for children and adolescents, Durlak, Fuhrman, and Lampman (1991) found that 41 percent of studies employed group sessions, and approximately 75 percent used combinations of skills training with other techniques, such as role-play. The computed normative effect size (NES), an index of the comparison of the treatment group with a normative or nonclinical group, showed that participants improved significantly. Their scores on such measures as anxiety, depression, and self-esteem not only significantly improved but rose to levels similar to those of children in the normative group.

Goldstein and Glick (1987) surveyed studies on the effectiveness of interpersonal skills training for aggressive adolescent and preadolescent subjects. The subjects were adjudicated juvenile delinquents, status offenders, or high school students with a history of aggression. Study settings included psychiatric hospitals, residential institutions, schools, group homes, and clinics. Most studies used multiple groups, with members receiving instruction, modeling, role-play, and performance feedback. The groups focused on topics such as coping with criticism, negotiating, and problem solving. The results for acquiring skills were consistently positive.

## RESEARCH FINDINGS FOR CHILDREN GROUPS

Skills training in nonhospital settings has evidence to support its efficacy. Much of the training has targeted conflict resolution for schoolchildren. These skills training programs generally involve communication skills, negotiating skills, recognizing options for behavior, and interpersonal helping.

Moreau (1994) described a program for third-grade students that addressed development of social and conflict resolution skills. Teachers in a middle-class suburban school identified the problems and participated in a training program to prepare them to teach conflict resolution skills. These skills were taught for 30 minutes daily over a 6-week period. Results indicated that the children were better able to communicate with one another and to understand options available to them to solve their problems.

Kamps, Leonard, Vernon, and Dugan (1992) investigated the effect of social skills groups on three autistic boys and their classmates in an integrated first-grade classroom. Results indicated increases in the frequency and duration of social interactions. Shure (1993) found that low-income preschoolers who were trained to think of alternative solutions to conflicts performed significantly better than their untrained peers at controlling impulsive behaviors in the classroom.

Weist, Vannatta, and Wayland (1993) described the outcomes for a group training program for sexually abused girls, ages 8 through 11. Teachers reported improved perceived academic competence, peer functioning, appearance, and global self-concept following the training program.

## HOW CHILDREN GROUPS DIFFER

Psychoeducational groups for children differ from those for adolescents and adults in several important ways: size, length of sessions, management of content, and special facilitation skills needed by the leader. The ages and educational levels for participants are very important in groups for children, as developmental levels can make a significant difference in the amount of material presented, learned, and retained; and in the quantity and quality of participation—for example, younger children can feel intimidated by older children in the group.

## Size

The size of the group is important even when a large group is broken down into smaller groups. Because children's group sessions are generally of shorter duration than groups for adolescents and adults, it becomes important that each child has an opportunity to actively participate (i.e., talk). Too many members in the group can be a barrier to participation. Therefore, it is recommended that children groups be limited to five members. If the participants have significant behavior and impulse control problems, it may be necessary to limit the number of group members to three or four.

## Length of Sessions

When conducting a group for a class, or other large groups, you will probably have a 50-minute class period for the session. A considerable amount of this time will be for distributing materials, breaking the large group into smaller groups, and answering questions. Thus, any planned activity should be short enough to be completed and discussed in that time frame. You can probably count on 30 minutes for the tasks.

A good rule of thumb for smaller groups is to plan for 20- to 30-minute sessions. The younger the children, the shorter their attention span, and the shorter the session should be.

## Management of Content

Leaders will find it effective to plan extensively for presenting information and to prioritize what information is most important for members to learn. This is necessary because of time constraints, the limited number of sessions, and members' attention spans. It is not helpful to present more information than members can absorb.

Attention is also needed to how information is to be presented. It is wise to limit the length of minilectures, write important points for the lecture on the chalkboard, and use exercises and other activities to enhance and reinforce the learning.

Discussion and media can be helpful presentation tools when judiciously used. Do not overuse media, as this detracts from developing relationships and promoting interactions among group members. Allowing time for members to express thoughts, feelings, and ideas can be very supportive on intended learning, and this is encouraged.

## Special Facilitation Skills

The leader will need to be more of a hybrid of a teacher and a facilitator. Keeping control and maintaining focus is more of a concern when leading children's groups, as children can be impulsive, excited, and easily distracted. These states can produce behaviors that are detrimental to conducting a group. Therefore, the leader has to pay special attention to establishing a relationship with the group where each child receives some attention at every session. This is necessary even for large classroom groups. Other facilitation skills that are of special importance are

- Highlighting commonalities among members
- Encouraging and supporting
- Blocking negative comments by members
- Being patient when a member is trying to find the words to express thoughts or feelings
- Accepting negative feeling expressions
- Making empathic responses

## GENERAL GUIDELINES FOR CHILDREN'S PSYCHOEDUCATIONAL GROUPS

### Group Composition

Psychoeducational groups for children will be more effective if participants are in the same age/grade group or within 1 or 2 years of each other. The younger the participants, the more homogeneous the group needs to be in terms of age and grade level. It may be more effective, in some cases, for older children to be in gender-specific groups. Group sessions should be 20 minutes of working time for children ages 7 to 9, and 30 to 40 minutes for older children. Group management becomes the primary focus instead of the psychoeducational topic when children's attention span has been exceeded.

If there is to be more than one session around a particular topic, the number and duration of the sessions should be specified in advance—for example, there could be six 30-minute sessions held once a week over 6 weeks. Planning for each session should be done in advance.

### Setting Goals and Objectives

Develop realistic goals and objectives. Participants' time and attention will be limited, and what can be accomplished in the group will be limited. It is less frustrating to have a few goals and objectives that are met than to have many goals and objectives, few of which are met. For example, a series of six sessions around career education may have the overall goal of identifying personal interest related to careers. Objectives for each session would be focused around one of Holland's (1973) interest areas. It then becomes easier to select appropriate activities and strategies.

Too often, group leaders have too many goals and objectives—for example, feeling that they must address self-confidence, self-esteem, self-awareness, and so on. These topics are too complex and involved to be primary goals and objectives. While some parts of them may be addressed or developed through the group, they will be limited and indirect. They can be secondary goals and objectives, but not the main emphases for the group.

It may be helpful to include the participants in setting goals and objectives. Getting their input promotes involvement and commitment, both of which enhance group participation. Even if you do not get anything different from what is already planned, simply asking for input helps promote participants' feelings of being involved.

## Environmental Concerns

The major environmental concerns are adequate space, appropriate furniture, and freedom from intrusion. You should provide enough room for participants to be comfortably seated without being too close to one another. Children tend to push, shove, and kick at one another when they are too close together, particularly when they do not have enough room to move around in their seats.

Most psychoeducational groups for children use exercises, games, and other active processes. Appropriate furniture contributes to the success of the group. Most desirable are tables around which five to seven participants can sit, and chairs in which participants can sit comfortably with their feet resting on the floor and not dangling. If there are multiple tables, there should be sufficient space for the leader and helpers to move between them and to allow those at one table to talk to each other without overdue intrusion of noise from another table.

Freedom from intrusion also refers to intrusive noises and people. Outside noises and other distractions can be very disruptive to the group.

## Parental Consent

One of the most important considerations when planning a psychoeducational group for children is the need for parental consent. This is always necessary and must not be overlooked, as there are ethical and legal consequences. This holds true even when a school system has obtained global parental consent for the entire program, as it is prudent to keep parents fully informed. Make a practice of determining the agency, school, or site policy and procedures for obtaining parental consent prior to starting groups for children.

## Limits for Confidentiality

No matter where you work, there can be limits on what disclosures of group members can be kept confidential and what has to be reported to authorities. There are legal requirements for reporting some disclosures, such as abuse, molestation, and incest, and you are expected to report your suspicions and/or actual disclosures.

You are expected to know what limits there are on your ability to keep disclosures in the group as confidential and what you are required to report. Familiarize yourself with the policies and procedures for confidentiality wherever you work, and you should know what ethical guidelines are required by your professional organization.

## SAMPLE PROCEDURES AND STRUCTURE FOR SESSIONS

The following procedures and structure can be used for all types of psychoeducational groups for children: educational, social skills training, support, and therapeutic. These guidelines are presented with the following assumptions:

- Some screening of participants has been used or some demographic data are known.
- Goals and objectives were established in advance.
- Planning for sessions was completed.
- Exercises and other activities were selected with participants' characteristics and needs as guiding principles.
- Materials were developed and/or gathered prior to beginning the group.
- Environmental concerns were addressed.
- Rules for participation were created.
- Parental consent was received.
- Limits for confidentiality were established.

The following procedures and structure can be modified and adapted for your particular situation. For example, the first session calls for introducing yourself. However, if you are already known to participants, such as in a school setting, you may need to have only a minimal introduction. If you are not known to participants, you will need to give a more extensive introduction.

## Procedures for the First Session

Although the following procedure for the first session is very much the same as what would be used for adolescent and adult groups, there are some significant differences for implementation. The focus for this presentation is on groups for children.

As the leader, you can expect to have some personal anxiety, as you can never be sure what the group will do. Your planning and experience can help reduce some of this anxiety, but it may never be completely eliminated. How you manage and contain this anxiety will be evident to group members on both the conscious and subconscious levels and will serve as a model for members. The sequence for the first session is as follows:

• Welcome and introductions.
• Purpose, goals and objectives, and limits for confidentiality are explained.
• Review of rules and establishment of commitment to them.
• Plan of activities for session is reviewed.
• Questions and comments are solicited.
• First activity is introduced. This can be an exercise, a minilecture, a video, and so on.

Reducing members' anxiety and ambiguity is important, as these emotional states can interfere with the ability to participate. One step toward addressing them is the welcome you give members and the opportunity for introductions. Pay attention to how members enter the room and how they choose to introduce themselves. You, of course, start off by welcoming members, introducing yourself as the group leader. Get in the habit of making a professional disclosure statement as part of your introduction, even if you are confident that members know who you are. It can also be helpful to develop your own procedure for having members' introductions, such as names or nicknames by which members want to be called, an animal that expresses something about them, a favorite television show or favorite anything, and what they expect to get or learn from the group. You may want to write your responses to the items in your introduction on paper and post it where all members can see, or write them on the chalkboard. It is hard for children to remember all items for the introduction; posting or writing them serves as a reminder.

Introductions should not be rushed or skipped. The time you take will not only reduce anxiety but can help establish trust and safety, as well as start to form interpersonal connections in the group. Even when members think they know each other prior to the group, new information can emerge. Pay attention to how members introduce themselves, because many clues to their emotional states and functioning can be present in these introductory comments.

## Purpose, Goals, and Confidentiality

Prepare and make a short statement about the purpose for the group, the goals and objectives, and the limits on confidentiality. This should be relatively easy to do, since you made these items a part of your planning.

It could also be helpful to write the purpose, goals, and objectives on paper prior to the session and post them as you explain them. Take into account terminology and members' reading levels. This is your opportunity to sell the group experience as beneficial to members, encourage active participation, and motivate in an indirect way.

Members need to know from the very beginning of the group what the limits are on confidentiality, as self-disclosure is expected in the group. Further, although you will ask members to keep the personal material and disclosures confidential, you have no means to enforce this, and it is ethically responsible to inform members of the limitation. Likewise, you are bound by laws and policies to report certain disclosures and clinical judgments to your supervisor or other authorities. It is also your ethical responsibility to let group members know this in advance.

## Rules

Every group needs the structure provided by rules. These are the guidelines for expected member behaviors. Prepare the basic few you feel are needed for the group to be managed for the members' benefit. Do not have too many rules or ones that will be impossible to enforce. Limit your rules to expected behaviors, such as no physical aggressive acts; how to participate, such as raising your hand to be recognized, or the speaker holds the scarf and other members must listen; immediacy, such as speaking your present thoughts, feelings, and ideas; freedom to not disclose by just saying "pass"; and other such guidelines. Also convey expectations for attendance, arriving on time, and active participation.

It may be appropriate for you to ask group members what rules they want for the group. You need to be aware that children are likely to develop a long list of rules that are unenforceable. However, member participation does promote commitment to the group. You will be the best judge of whether to open the floor up to rule setting.

This is an opportunity for you to listen to what members want from you and from other group members. For example, group members may suggest a rule of no yelling. It could be a clue that these members become fearful when someone yells, and they expect negative actions because of past experiences. You now have some insight about safety and trust needs for these participants.

Obtain members' commitment by asking if they can abide by the rules. Tell them you will remind them of the rules at the beginning of each session. Children may have expectations of punishment for violating rules, and you must also have a suitable consequence for the violations—for example, if members miss a certain number of sessions, they are dropped from the group. Do not have punishments such as detention, writing assignments, loss of privilege, and so on. When rules are violated, much of the behavior is due to forgetting, excitement, and resistance. Learn ways to handle this in the group that are more constructive and beneficial for members.

## Plan for Activities

Describe what you plan to do at the beginning of each session, as this will help to reduce ambiguity and uncertainty. It does not take long to give a short description of planned activities. You can ask for comments and agreements to participate. You can determine if there are any objections and reluctance to become involved.

After the group has met for a few sessions, you may find that what you have planned does not meet members' needs. Your review can give members an opportunity to let you know this if you are open to change and are flexible. You may have done an excellent job of planning the group, but what you planned does not fit this particular group. You do not have to make major changes; you probably can make minor adjustments to what you have already planned. For example, you may have expected that members would grasp the material faster. You can break the material down into smaller units, eliminate some pieces, or make other modifications. If members are resisting what you have planned, it is time for you to reflect on possible causes and make some adjustments.

## Questions and Comments

Children like to be asked for their comments. Questions can reveal confusion, anxiety, and/or frustrations, and can reveal much hidden information. Take some time to listen to comments and questions, as this can encourage participation. For some children, this experience may be one of the few times where an adult conveys respect and interest.

Even a comment or question that seems unrelated to the group experience can be revealing for that member. Do not immediately assume that the question or comment does not relate to the group. It may relate in an indirect way. You will have to listen and understand group dynamics and group stage development in order to discern the relation of the comment or question.

Listen to each question and comment, and try to make your response a direct one. Do not infer motives or be dismissive about the importance of the question, although some may seem silly. Do not respond in a way that suggests the speaker is not valued. How you respond will be monitored by other group members who are in the process of deciding how they feel about the group.

## First Activity

The first activity begins to address the purpose and goals for the group. Although you may have used an ice-breaker exercise earlier, it was used to reduce anxiety and tension, and to start the process of developing interactions and connections among group members. It is unlikely that the ice-breaker was related to the purpose, goal, theme, or cognitive content of the group, which activity begins at this point.

The first activity could be a minilecture, discussion, exercise, or any other presentation. Regardless of the purpose for the group, it is strongly suggested that your first activity be an integration of members' goals with the goal for the group. It should determine members' apprehensions and expectations for the group. If the focus is on these two objectives, you will increase commitment to the group and the task, reduce expressed and unexpressed fears, start development of group norms for active participation, and encourage and support group members. Do not try to move too fast into the cognitive content for the group. One way to accomplish integration of goals and overt expressions of apprehension is through the use of the following two exercises.

## Exercise 9–1 My Goals

**Materials:** Your group goals written on paper and posted where members can see them or written on a chalkboard or other medium; a sheet of paper and a pencil for each member; a suitable writing surface for each member.

**Age level:** 8 years and older. If members are younger than 8, just use item 3 of the exercise.

**Procedure:** 1. Ask group members to write one or two goals they would like to accomplish in the group. For example, what would they like to learn? You can give them some suggestions—for example, my career when I grow up, or to make friends, or to learn how to control my anger. Be careful with your suggestions, as children may think you are telling them what their goals should be, and you want them to think about something that is meaningful for them.

2. Allow 3 to 5 minutes for them to write their goals. If a member seems stuck, reassure him or her that a goal could emerge as the other members discuss their goals.

**Processing:** 1. Ask each member to read and explain his or her goal. Respond to each goal and ask clarifying questions when needed. Help members who could not write a goal to verbally express one.

2. Refer back to your posted goals and try to link members' goals with the predetermined ones.

## Exercise 9–2 Apprehensions

**Materials:** A large sheet of paper and a marker, or a chalkboard and chalk.

**Age Level:** All ages.

**Procedure:** 1. Post the large sheet of paper on a flat surface where members can see it and you can write on it.

2. Introduce the exercise by saying, "It can be scary to try something new and many people, including adults, get scared and anxious about the unknown. This group is unknown to you, and may be scary or anxiety-producing for some members. Some may have some ideas about what to expect. I would like to hear what members think might happen, what members are scared will happen, and other thoughts you have about the group, the leader, and other members."

3. Write all ideas, thoughts, and feelings on the paper or chalkboard. Do not try to minimize, dismiss, judge, or evaluate them. It is also not helpful to try and reassure members that their fears are groundless at this time. Just note what they are.

**Processing:** Review the list and tell members what may keep these fears from being realized where possible. For example, someone may fear that other members will not listen to him or her. You could point to the rule about respectful listening and tell the group that you will listen.

## A Sample Psychoeducational Group Plan

A sample psychoeducational group plan follows. Presented are: the group's goals, objectives, and pre-group preparation; a schedule, exercises, and minilectures. The plan could be used for either a small group (six to nine members) or a large classroom group where members are divided into small groups for exercises and discussion.

## Program: Building Myself

**Focus**: Building strengths.

**Objectives:** To increase awareness of personal assets; to help participants perceive the positive aspects of characteristics that have been criticized by others; to develop an action plan for building on existing strengths.

**Materials:** Handouts; pens and pencils; index cards; glue sticks; sandwich bags; paper; large sheets of paper or newsprint; masking tape; medium-size boxes; felt-tip markers in a variety of colors; crayons or oil pastels in a variety of colors. Catalogues and magazines for cutting out pictures.

**Time:** One 50-minute session each week for 8 weeks.

**Age/education:** 9- to 11-years-olds; no more than a 2-year age difference between members.

**Number of participants:** Six to eight per group.

**Preparation:** Review literature on building self-esteem. Interview participants if possible; if not possible, try to find out as much as possible about participants from teachers and counselors. Secure a room with appropriate privacy with tables that can be used for group activities and that is free from outside noise and distractions.

**Sample Schedule for a Six-Session Program**

| Session | Activity |
| --- | --- |
| Session 1 | Introductions; Program Exercise 1. "Getting to Know You" Game; Overview of group (not included); Goal setting and review of rules (not included) |
| Session 2 | Summary of previous session; Program Exercise 2. I Want . . . , I Need . . . ; Minilecture: Personal Management Skills |
| Session 3 | Unfinished business from previous session; Program Exercise 3 Attitude Skills Survey; Minilecture: Effective Attitudes |
| Session 4 | Unfinished business from previous session; Program Exercise 4 The Positive Side of Criticism; Minilecture: Becoming More Effective |
| Session 5 | Unfinished business from previous session; Program Exercise 5 Developing Personal Affirmations; 15 Qualities of an Effective Person, plus discussion |
| Session 6 | Unfinished business from previous session; Program Exercise 6 Sketch of My Future; Termination issues (not included); Closing exercise (not included) |

Session 1
Program Exercise 1. "Getting to know you" Game

**Objectives:** To help group members get acquainted; to focus on important components of self, especially strengths.

**Materials:** Index cards for each member; glue sticks; a sandwich bag with 10 to 15 cut-out pictures; sample minicollage; tables or other hard surfaces for preparing the minicollages; chairs in a circle for processing.

**Time:** 30 minutes for construction and processing.

**Age/education:** 6 years old and above.

**Number of participants:** Unlimited.

**Preparation:** The group leader should prepare the bags and sample minicollage in advance of the session.

**Procedure:** Tell members that this is a get-acquainted activity. Since one objective for the group is to increase awareness of personal assets, you will ask each member some of his or her assets. Use the sample minicollage to illustrate. Instruct members to use the pictures in their bags to construct minicollages on their cards. The pictures should be symbolic of their strengths, assets, things they do well, and accomplishments. They are free to exchange pictures if they want. Allow approximately 10 minutes for construction.

**Processing:** Ask members to return to the circle and talk about the symbols in their minicollages. Allow only clarifying questions and positive comments. Try to highlight and emphasize strengths and commonalities.

## Session 2
## Program Exercise 2. I Want . . . , I Need . . .

**Objectives:** To increase awareness of the difference between wants and needs; to focus attention on personal wants and needs.

**Materials:** A sheet of paper with a line lengthwise down the middle for each participant; pencils or pens; large sheets of newsprint or a flip chart and masking tape.

**Time:** 30 minutes.

**Age/education:** Sixth-grade reading level and above.

**Number of participants:** 30 to 35.

**Preparation:** Gather materials.

**Procedure:** Ask participants to list all of their wants on the left side of their sheet of paper. Have them label that column "Wants." Allow 3 to 5 minutes for completion. Once lists have been generated, allow 10 minutes for members to read their lists aloud. You can tabulate the items on a sheet of newsprint posted on the wall. Tabulate the items into the following categories: relationships, objects, accomplishments, spiritual, emotional. Add other categories as they emerge. Discuss any commonalities that appear and the most frequently chosen categories. Have members list all their needs in the next column, labeled "Needs." Ask them to star (*) any wants that are also needs. Ask members to read their needs aloud, then tabulate these into the same categories as "Wants."

**Processing:** Discuss any commonalities and the most frequent categories. Ask members to summarize what they see as similar and as different in their personal wants and needs.

### *Minilecture: Personal Management Skills*

What kind of person are you right now? What kind of person do you want to be in 5 or 10 years? Beyond that? You can help yourself become the kind of person you want to be. While others can help and support you in this endeavor and life circumstances can have a significant impact, *you* are the most important part of the outcome.

There are five personal management skills you can use to help you become the person you want to be. These attitudes and behaviors can help you make decisions about practically everything, from what career to pursue to which activities to engage in. While I briefly describe each one, I want you to think of examples that are personal for you:

1. *Valuing* means investing in yourself. When you value someone, you take care of him or her and use whatever resources you have to make sure his or her needs are met. Make the same investment of time, energy, and resources in yourself. Take care of your physical, emotional, psychological, and spiritual needs. Others can help, but you must invest in yourself.
2. *Planning* is a critical life skill. Few activities are more important than this one. You should set both short-term (1–6 months) and long-term goals (these may be years in the future). Having goals gives you a sense of direction and can suggest strategies for getting where you want to go. Remember, if you don't know where you're going, you may end up somewhere else.
3. *Commitment* to yourself is important as well. Knowing your abilities, aptitudes, and goals—and valuing them—is crucial. However, you also must believe in yourself and have faith that you can and will succeed in becoming the person you want to be. Belief can be difficult to maintain sometimes, especially when you make mistakes or others criticize you. No matter how difficult it may be, keep faith in yourself.
4. *Priorities* are important in successful time management and in successful personal management. Prioritizing allows us to focus our time, energy, and resources on the most important things instead of allowing them to be wasted. Determine what is important for you and stay focused on it.
5. *Pacing* yourself is a valuable skill. Anything worth accomplishing takes time. Becoming the person you want to be is a process that will take time. Become comfortable working toward your goal. You will get there one step at a time if you remember what is important and work on that, believe in yourself, know your goals, and invest in yourself.

### Personal Management Skills

| | |
|---|---|
| **Valuing yourself** | Invest in you. |
| **Planning** | Set goals for now and for the future. |
| **Committing** | Believe in yourself. |
| **Setting priorities** | Stay focused on what is important. |
| **Pacing** | Take it one step at a time. |

**Program Handout A. Personal Management Skills.** Permission is granted to photocopy for group use.

Session 3
Program Exercise 3 Effective Attitudes

> **Objective:** To introduce members to the attitudes that promote and encourage a sense of well-being.
>
> **Materials:** A copy of the Attitude Skills Survey and a pencil for each participant.
>
> **Procedure:** Distribute materials and introduce the exercise by telling participants the following: "There are some personal qualities that effective people have, and one quality is their attitude or perception about some personal qualities they find important. Today, we are focusing on your perceptions of yourself and some qualities that you may need to develop. We will start with assessing these." Explain the rating scale and allow members to rate themselves.

### Attitude Skills Survey

**Directions:** Rate the degree to which you possess these attitude skills using the following scale:

| | |
|---|---|
| 5 = Always; a great deal | 2 = Seldom; on occasion |
| 4 = Usually; to a considerable extent | 1 = Never; almost never |
| 3 = Sometimes; to some extent | NA = Does not apply to me |

Ability to be honest with myself: ——

Creative: ——

Appreciative of beauty: ——

Willing to learn: ——

Present-centered: ——

Capacity for happiness and joy: ——

Courage to try new ways of being and behaving: ——

Spontaneous: ——

High self-regard: ——

Self-acceptance: ——

Score: ——

**Program Handout B. Attitude Skills Survey.** Permission is granted to photocopy for group use.
**Minilecture Effective Attitudes**

## Self-Honesty

Sometimes it can be hard to be honest with yourself, particularly when you have made a mistake, disobeyed, broken a rule, or failed to do something. Even some adults can find it hard to admit these errors. However, very effective people can be honest with themselves, even if they do not tell anyone else—for example, you may want to review how you rated yourself on the survey and see how honest you were.

## Creativity

Creativity does not mean you have to show artistic, musical, acting talent, or the like. These people do have special talents, but everyone has the capacity to be original, imaginative, and to do something novel, which is being creative. Using ordinary things in a new way is an example of creativity. You can be creative in many parts of your life. Some examples are a new way to fix your favorite food, decorating your room, putting your outfits together in a different way, presenting your thoughts and ideas, writing essays, poems, music, and so forth, inventing something, and finding a new way to do something. There are no limits to being creative, but you do have to think about what you are doing and figure out another way to do it.

## Appreciation of Beauty

It has been said that beauty is in the eye of the beholder. Each of you can determine for yourself what is beautiful to you. Beauty does not need consensus where everyone has to agree about something as being beautiful.

Do you see something beautiful every day? Do you take time to pause and look at something beautiful? How do you show that you appreciate beauty? Begin to notice what you consider to be beautiful, take time to enjoy its beauty, and carry this with you. In time, you will have many beautiful things to appreciate.

## Willingness to Learn

A big part of growing and developing is a willingness to learn new things. Learning is a lifelong process that keeps us energized, interested, and can promote creativity.

It is important for you to continue to learn, and how you feel about learning new things is extremely important. If you dread new learning, you will cut off your ability to learn. You need to be open to learning, willing to explore and learn new things, and not shut down when presented with new material.

### The Ability to be Present-Centered

You can be fully present wherever you are and not be thinking about the past or the future. You do not have to daydream, think about other things, or be preoccupied with your own concerns.

The ability to be present-centered is important in relationships. It means you are paying attention to the other person, listening to what he or she has to say, and you are not distracted by other things or people. Your entire attention is on that person.

### Capacity for Happiness and Joy

Do you know what it feels like to be happy and joyous? These are peak feelings that only occur once in a while. If you were to tell me right now if you are happy or unhappy, what would you say? Many people would say that they are not unhappy, but are unsure if they are actually happy.

Think of a time when you were happy. What did that feel like? How long did it last? Do your spirits rise when you recall that happiness? You do not have to be happy all of the time, but it does help to be happy some of the time.

### Courage to Try

New ways of being and behaving can make you anxious and are scary because they are unknown. It takes courage to be willing to face the unknown and the uncertain. Because the unknown is vague and ambiguous, it can be frightening, as you do not know what to expect or what to do. It takes courage to try under those conditions.

Do you demand certainty before you try something new? Everyone wants certainty, but some people do not want to try something new without knowing what to expect. This is unrealistic, as life will present us with new challenges constantly where little or nothing is known or certain. It is helpful when you can be courageous and willing to try new things.

### Spontaneity

Spontaneity can be exciting, energizing, and interesting. When you are spontaneous, you are acting on present-centered feelings and are tuned into your feelings without losing your ability to think things through and make good choices. Thus, being spontaneous is not the same as being impulsive, where you do not think things through and are unable to make good choices. Impulsivity is action without thought, whereas spontaneity is action with thought and reflection. An example of being spontaneous is giving a parent a hug just because you want to. There are many other constructive ways to be spontaneous.

## High Self-Regard

As you think about yourself, what feelings do you experience? Do you feel happy, satisfied, proud, secure, and/or loved? Or, do you feel the opposite? High self-regard means that you like and think well of yourself, even while recognizing that you have some faults.

When you like yourself, you can like other people and be more accepting of their faults. Faults do not mean violent or emotionally abusive actions—for example, bullying or harassment. Faults can mean that others do or say things that are irritating to you, but irritation is as far as it goes. You do not become angry, hurt, or resentful.

## Self-Acceptance

Accepting yourself as you are is a very important part of building self-esteem. Accepting yourself also means liking who you are and working to become the kind of person you want to be. It is not that you think you are perfect. You may be very aware of your imperfections. It only means that you are aware of the imperfections, and are working to change what can be changed about yourself.

## Session 4
## Program Exercise 4. The Positive Side of Criticism

   **Objectives:** To help participants perceive strengths; to increase awareness of personal strengths.

   **Materials:** Paper and pens or pencils for each participant.

   **Time:** 20 to 30 minutes.

   **Age/education:** Sixth grade reading level and above.

   **Number of participants:** 30 to 35.

   **Preparation:** Gather materials.

   **Procedure:** Tell participants that a strength is embedded in almost every criticism or perceived weakness. Each of us needs to capitalize on our strengths as well as seek to overcome any perceived weakness.

   On one side of the paper, have participants list 8 to 10 criticisms they have of themselves or that others have of them. They do not have to agree with the criticisms.

   After the lists have been generated, ask participants to look at each item and list on the other side of the page all strengths they see in that criticism. Post some examples of embedded strengths. For example:

| Criticism | Strength |
|---|---|
| Take things personally | Sensitive to others' perceptions |
| Lazy | Relaxed |
| Talk too much | Seek to connect and communicate with others |

If members have trouble perceiving a strength, you can make suggestions. Members may be able to help each other with suggestions.

**Processing:** After members have generated their lists, allow time to share them. If the group is too large for each member to share, divide into smaller groups.

Allow enough time for each member to share some part of his or her list. Process the experience by asking a few questions: What was difficult? What was easy? How hard was it to see a strength? How do you feel about the criticisms after doing the exercise?

### Minilecture: Becoming More Effective

We all have a tendency to focus more on weaknesses than strengths. Weaknesses are those things about which we feel shame: we think we are flawed, and there is little we can do to change things. We may feel that our time and energy should be spent on remediating those weaknesses.

Some of our perceptions of weaknesses are generated by others' criticisms and some arise from within us. Parents, siblings, and others we care about give us feedback on how they perceive us, and this is often in the form of criticism, which we take to heart. Consequently, we begin to feel ashamed and guilty. Worse are the criticisms we have of ourselves—those that arise from the notion that we should not make mistakes or that we should be perfect. Both forms of criticisms can be beneficial, but often they cause us much discomfort.

However, there are some things we can do to be more effective. In Program Exercise 4, we focused on seeing strengths in criticisms. Other strategies that can enhance a sense of self-efficacy and promote effectiveness are relabeling, surrendering, recognizing personal limitations, using your imagination, and practicing affirmations.

*Relabeling* is very much like seeing the positive side of criticisms. When you feel put down, unworthy, or ashamed, try to relabel the event and see the positive side or strength that is embedded in it. Try not to look only at what you did *not* do or what you do *not* have; instead, look at what is positive and good about the event or perception.

*Surrendering* refers to changing what you can and letting go of the rest. Few things are all-or-nothing events, but we often find ourselves thinking that there is nothing positive in a situation. Try to focus on what is possible to change, then *let go of the rest*. Do not obsess over those things you cannot change.

*Recognizing personal limitations* is a part of maturity. This does not mean you should sit back and avoid taking any risks or trying anything difficult. It does mean that you should judge yourself realistically and accept yourself for who you are. Knowing your limitations and accepting yourself in spite of or because of them is healthy and mature.

*Use your imagination* to visualize what could and can be. What if you were to work hard at becoming what you want to be? How would you see yourself? Imagine that you could be whatever you wanted to be, given your abilities and physical self. What then?

*Giving yourself affirmations* is another positive and important strategy. The difference between a winner and a loser is that the winner says, "I can do better," then goes out and works harder. The loser sulks and says, "I lost." Tell yourself you have strengths, you can do, you will try, and that whatever happens, you will continue to accept yourself.

## Session 5
## Program Exercise 5. Developing Personal Affirmations

**Objectives:** To develop a list of personal assets that can form the basis for self-affirming statements; to focus on strengths.

**Materials:** Paper and pen for each participant.

**Time:** 30 to 60 minutes.

**Age/education:** Third-grade reading level and above.

**Number of participants:** 30 to 35.

**Preparation:** Gather materials.

**Procedure:** Review 15 Qualities of an Effective Person. Ask participants to make a list of 10 to 12 phrases or words to complete the sentence, "I am . . ." Ask them to focus on their positive qualities—those things they do well or about which they feel a sense of accomplishment. Then allow time for each member to read aloud or to share with at least one other member.

Next, have members generate another list to finish the sentence, "I can . . ." This list should enumerate the abilities they possess and the steps they can take to enhance existing strengths, develop new ones, or overcome a perceived deficiency. Allow time for sharing.

**Processing:** Processing should focus on helping members highlight the positive parts of their lists. Have them rewrite their lists into self-affirming statements that they can refer back to whenever they need a pick-me-up.

## 15  Qualities of an Effective Person

1. An ability to be present-centered

2. A clear sense of purpose and direction

3. A caring and loving attitude

4. Well organized and able to accomplish much

5. Intellectually sharp and able to handle quantities of information

6. A sense of humor

7. Experiences and can express a wide range of emotions

8. Accepting of his or her limitations and mistakes

9. Practices self-care

10. Can be assertive when necessary

11. Assumes responsibility for his or her own life

12. Has a deep commitment to a cause outside of him- or herself

13. Willing to take psychological risks

14. Allows him- or herself to be creative

15. Is aware of personal values

---

**Program Handout C. 15 Qualities of an Effective Person.** *Permission is granted to photocopy for group use.*

Session 6
Program Exercise 6. Sketch of My Future
    **Objectives:** To help members formulate goals for their personal development; to summarize personal learning from group sessions.
    **Materials:** Large sheets of paper or newsprint; a set of felt-tip markers, crayons, or oil pastels for each pair of group members.
    **Time:** 40 minutes.
    **Age/education:** Third grade and above.
    **Number of participants:** 30 to 35 (works best with a small group of no more than 10 members).
    **Preparation:** Gather materials; ensure adequate drawing space for each participant.

**Procedure:** Distribute two sheets of paper or newsprint for each member and a set of markers for each two members. Introduce the exercise by briefly summarizing the material from the preceding exercises.

Direct members to close their eyes and to imagine they are 5 years older. What are they doing? How do they look and feel? What are they most proud of in terms of personal development? Allow a short period for reflection, then have members open their eyes and draw what they saw. Drawings can be realistic or symbolic. Have members title their drawings.

Ask members to close their eyes and fast forward 10 years. Go through the same process.

Post both drawings for each member and have each member describe both drawings.

**Processing:** Process the experience by having members focus on their identified strengths. If the group is larger than 10, ask for volunteers to share what emerged as strengths. In a smaller group, everyone can contribute.

**Note:** Some of the activities can be done with larger groups when used in isolation—that is, when they are not part of a program such as the one described here. When used in a larger group, opportunities for sharing are reduced and the time needed is increased.

# Chapter 10

# Leading Psychoeducational Groups for Adolescents

Major Topics and Concepts

*Knowledge Factors*
    Examples of adolescent groups
    Characteristics of adolescents

*Science Factors*
    Major considerations in planning
    General guidelines for leading
    Considerations for the group leader

## INTRODUCTION

The Carnegie Council on Adolescent Development (1995) states that the goals for adolescents are as follows:

- Become a valued member in a constructive group.
- Learn how to form and maintain long-term and satisfying relationships.
- Develop a sense of self-worth.
- Learn a process for making appropriate choices.
- Begin to tap into available support systems.
- Find ways to access constructive curiosity and exploratory behavior.
- Become altruistic.
- Believe in a promising future.

These tasks can be daunting for adolescents who are experiencing physical, emotional, and psychological changes in addition to uncontrollable societal, community, cultural, and familial events and changes. Malekoff (1997) states, "Group work has been, for the past century, a significant protective factor for youth" (p. 16). He further reports that group work has facilitated life transitions, developmental task accomplishments, addressing special needs, preparation for democratic participation in the community and in society, and help in finding ways to cope with the various forces that impact the lives of adolescents.

Psychoeducation groups can be effective ways to provide adolescents with skills, knowledge, understanding, guidance, and support. They are helpful for a variety of conditions and situations:

• Reducing isolation and alienation (Caluza, 2000)
• Stress prevention (Baker, 2001)
• Depression (Beeferman & Orvaschel, 1994; Fine, Forth, Gilbert, & Haley, 1991)
• Parental loss (Aronson, 1995)
• Psychiatric and substance abuse comorbidity (Pressman & Brook, 1999)
• Preparing adolescent males to be fathers (Kiselica, 1994)

## CHARACTERISTICS OF ADOLESCENTS

Hanna, Hanna, and Keys (1999) present the following common characteristics for adolescents that could be influential in how you plan and facilitate these groups:

• A need and insistence on immediate results and/or relief
• A desire for clear and unambiguous boundaries, rules, and limits that are uniformly enforced
• Intense feelings that are easily and readily accessed
• The need to shock, startle, and/or surprise adults
• A heightened awareness of sexuality and sexual power

Age-appropriate narcissism and underdeveloped narcissism can also be characteristics that will impact the group. Age-appropriate narcissism for adolescents can be seen in their degree of self-absorption, which can be less than what is expected for a child but more than would be characteristic of an adult with healthy adult narcissism (Brown, 1998). For example, the adult with healthy adult narcissism is able to delay gratification when needed without complaining, whining, or feeling put on. The adolescent with age-appropriate narcissism can delay gratification some of the time without complaining and so on. However, adolescents with underdeveloped narcissism and children are much less able or are unable to do this.

Underdeveloped narcissism refers to behaviors and attitudes reflective of a much younger person. These people exhibit much more self-absorption, and almost everything in their world is perceived in terms of self. There are many aspects of underdeveloped narcissism, and they will be reflected differently for each person—for example, one person may have underdeveloped narcissism in entitlement attitudes, while someone else may exhibit it in failure to recognize when he or she is violating someone's psychological boundaries.

Adolescents are in the process of moving toward or developing healthy adult narcissism, which is described as the ability to delay gratification, empathy, creativity, the ability to reach out and care for others, an appropriate sense of humor, and the capacity to form and maintain lasting and satisfying relationships (Brown, 1998, Kohut, 1977). Thus, most adolescents will show some areas where they are growing toward healthy adult narcissism—for example, flashes or instances where they are empathic—and all will demonstrate several areas of underdeveloped narcissism, such as an entitlement attitude, excessive attention needs, and admiration seeking.

All of the characteristics, including underdeveloped narcissism, have implications for your planning and facilitation of psychoeducational groups for adolescents. It is recommended that you learn more about adolescent growth and development and common issues faced by this population. Some influences of these characteristics are discussed here.

The tendency to want immediate results and/or relief means that group leaders need to plan for some focused and short-term outcomes. While the condition or situation may be complex, long term, and take time to unfold, the adolescent group members have to be motivated and convinced to stick around long enough for this to happen. Plan for some visible or readily identifiable result for each session. You may need to highlight and emphasize results so that members can be aware of their learning and progress.

Adolescents feel safer and more secure when some limits, rules, and boundaries are set for them. They can function better and understand what is expected of them. Further, they appreciate a firm, consistent, and fair enforcement of these limits.

Some leaders can make the mistake of not observing an appropriate boundary between them and members by seeking to be pals or friends with the group members. It is entirely appropriate to be friendly, but you are in a position of authority, not on their level, and they know it. You can arouse mistrust and insecurity when you fail to remember this.

A focus for many groups is on having members increase their awareness and expression of feelings. There can be considerable resistance and defenses around members' intense feelings, and leaders work hard to help members access these feelings and appropriately express them. However, this is usually *not* the case with adolescents, as they can readily access their intense feelings but do not always express them in the most appropriate way. Indeed, there can be a lot of acting out for this age group.

Therefore, the leader's tasks are to teach, guide, and model how to contain, manage, and appropriately express intense and/or uncomfortable feelings. Another task is to select activities and experiences that will not trigger intense reactions that cannot be contained and managed by the group, individual members, and you as the leader.

One major task for adolescents is to establish their self-identity, and many work toward this by dressing, acting, and talking in a way that is designed to shock, startle, and surprise adults. They are aided by the media, which helps to set trends and standards that seem to emphasize shock value.

It is important for the group leader to see beyond the mannerisms, language, apparel, and other means used by adolescents to express their differences, and self-identity. Beneath all this is still the person who is struggling to define himself or herself, connect to others in a meaningful way, and prepare for adulthood.

The awareness of sexuality and sexual power increases to new heights during adolescence. In today's world, this awareness is encouraged and supported wherever the adolescent turns. It is displayed in music, movies, television, clothing, and other ways, and it is the rare person who does not tune into it.

This can have implications for the group, as members can bring erotic material to the forefront at any time, there can be considerable flirting, and there can even be sexual acting out both in and out of the group. The group leader needs to prepare for members to attempt seduction and must always remember the ethics and legal ramifications as guides for your leader behavior.

## MAJOR PLANNING CONSIDERATIONS

One major consideration when planning groups for adolescents that is generally overlooked is to not form groups of adolescents with similar problems. At first glance, the idea of not grouping members around problems would seem to be wrong. Similarities can reduce isolation, promote cohesion, and have a number of other positive outcomes. However, for adolescents there is research that indicates this is counterproductive.

The Cambridge-Somerville Youth Study (McCord, 1992) found that the comprehensive program for high-risk male adolescents showed that the participants were more likely to have more problems with delinquency, substance abuse, and other things than the control participants who did not have access to the many constructive program activities. The activities for the program included summer camps, attention to academic problems, and groups that focused on academic or family problems.

Dishion, Reid, and Patterson (1988) researched the effectiveness of parent skills training for the participants' parents, peer psychoeducational groups, a volunteer self-directed change group, and combined activities for the adolescents and their families for 119 male and female high-risk adolescents. Short-term findings indicated that the combined group had positive results. However, findings at the 1-year follow-up showed that the peer group participation had negative effects—for example, increased use of tobacco, problem behaviors in school, and delinquency. These conditions persisted at the 3-year follow up.

Coie, Miller-Johnson, Terry, Maumary-Gremaud, and Lochman (1996) and Vitaro, Tremblay, Kerr, Pagani, and Bukowski (1997) found that early adolescents who had friends who were also deviant tended to engage in more serious forms of antisocial behavior, and this persisted. Catalano and Hawkins (1996) concluded that association with deviant peers was a major factor in adolescents' escalation of problem behaviors.

These are but a few of the studies that seem to support the idea that adolescent groups should be heterogeneous in terms of problems if "deviancy training" (Patterson, Dishion, & Yoerger (1999) is not to occur. Having a mix of problems in a group may not be possible in some situations—for example, group homes, inpatient facilities, and so on. The leader should be aware, however, that there may be unintended effects with heterogeneous problem groups for adolescents.

## GENERAL GUIDELINES FOR ADOLESCENT PSYCHOEDUCATIONAL GROUPS

Most adolescents have sufficient attention spans to benefit from an extended psychoeducational group. A 2- to 3-hour group provides more time to cover a topic in depth but is not usually so long as to produce boredom. A day-long (8 hours) group may be too long for younger adolescents, but a well-planned one may be effective for older ones. If the group is to be longer than 50 to 60 minutes, you should have a variety of activities that require active participation and provide for small-group interaction. It is also advisable to have a helper for more than 10 participants.

### Group Composition

Restrict the range of ages and grade levels to no more than 2 years or grades. For example, it would not be productive to have 13- and 17-year-olds in the same group. For some topics, such as health education, it may be advisable to have same-gender groups to reduce embarrassment and promote interaction on sensitive topics.

There may be little or no opportunity for you to screen group members, but simply knowing who has difficulty paying attention, who is inclined to be disruptive or aggressive, and who is shy can help in your planning. Consult with teachers, counselors, and others who work or interact frequently with proposed participants.

## Group Size

You should plan to divide larger groups into small ones of five to seven members, with a helper for every two to three small groups. The helper can move between the groups to distribute materials, answer questions, and manage behavior. The helper's presence is often enough to reduce disruptive behavior and keep arguments from escalating. Organizing the group in this way enables you to present to larger groups.

## Length/Duration/Number of Sessions

Adolescents can tolerate more in-depth sessions than children. They also remember more over time, even with intervening events. Therefore, psychoeducational groups for adolescents can be longer, greater in number, and held over a longer time period. Sometimes the setting, such as a school, church, or club, will dictate the length, duration, and number of sessions. The topic also plays a part, as some topics require more sessions than others—for example, career education covers more extensive material and requires more sessions than test-taking skills.

## Setting Goals and Objectives

As with children, it is useful to set limited, realistic goals and objectives for adolescent psychoeducational groups. There may be a need for extensive information on the part of the participants, but there also is a limit to how much they can absorb and learn. Some topics may have an extensive emotional component that also limits how much can be taken in. Give participants as much information as they can use but not so much that they tune it out.

It is useful to elicit participants' input into the goal and objectives of the group. Whenever possible, incorporate their suggestions and point out how you have done so. Share your developed goal and objectives and ask if these seem to meet their expectations and needs. Participants are likely to be more active when they have some personal interest.

## Environmental Concerns

The same concerns listed for groups with children (for adequate space, furniture, and freedom from intrusion) apply to adolescent groups. Physically, adolescents are much larger, and many (especially younger ones) have not adjusted to their bodies—for example, they may not realize that being 5 inches taller means they take up more space. Adequate space is important to provide comfort and sufficient personal space.

Tables and chairs should be adequate for all planned activities. When attached seats and desks must be used, they should be formed into a circle for the small groups.

Freedom from intrusion is important for adolescent groups. This is not so much to preserve confidentiality, but adolescents typically do not want adults to hear what they are saying. While they do not become as easily distracted, interruptions can be bothersome enough to get them off the subject, making it difficult to maintain the group mood.

## Considerations for the Group Leader

MacLennan and Dies (1992) asserted that working with adolescents is difficult, and it is essential for group leaders to have an understanding of self and to have worked through their personal adolescent issues. Katz (1990) noted that understanding, knowledge, empathy, warmth, and positive regard are essential when working with adolescents. He also pointed out that adolescents want a relationship with an adult who can be emotionally available, accepting and approving, nonjudgmental, and who has faith in the adolescent's potential.

Horton-Parker and Brown (2002) said the following characteristics and attitudes are helpful when working with adolescents. These are applicable for both individual and group work:

- Respect, genuineness, and honesty
- Clear about his or her personal standards
- A desire to work with adolescents
- Sensitivity to adolescents' moods and feelings
- Energy, vitality, and a sense of humor
- Willing to admit errors
- Nondefensiveness
- Open and willing to consider different perspectives

## A Sample Psychoeducational Group

The rest of the chapter is devoted to presenting a sample training group for adolescents. The focus is on academic skills, but the process can be adapted for other types of groups.

Program Study Skill Group for Adolescents
Focus: Improve Academic Performance

**Objectives:** To identify needed time management activities that will increase study skills; to increase awareness of time available for study and need for scheduling; to review or learn effective study skill habits; to identify personal study habits.

**Materials:** Copies of Handouts A, B, C, and D for each participant; name tags; pens or pencils; tables where groups of five can work and hold discussions.

**Time:** 6 to 12 hours (a 1-day workshop or a series of 1-hour sessions).

**Age/education:** Adolescents.

**Number of participants:** Upper limits of 5 to 10 members if used as a group over time; 30 to 35 members if used as a workshop.

**Preparation:** Review literature on study skills training and its effectiveness for the target group; survey or conduct interviews to determine the needs of participants; develop a schedule for presentation.

### Example of Topics and Strategies

| Topics | Strategy |
| --- | --- |
| Survey of study habits and skills | Program Exercise 1 and Handout A |
| Effective study skills | Program Exercise 2 and Handout B |
| Increasing academic effectiveness | Program Exercise 3 and Handout C |
| Tools for academic achievement | Handout D |
| Suggested additional minilectures (not included) | |
| Note taking | |
| Test-taking skills | |
| Reading improvement | |
| Memory systems | |

| Sample Schedule for a One-Day Session | |
|---|---|
| **Topic** | **Activity** |
| Introductions | Get acquainted ice-breaker (not included). |
| Overview | Review goal, objectives, and proposed schedule including breaks. Solicit input and additional objectives. |
| My study habits | Program Exercise 1. Survey of Study Habits and Skills. Handout A. |
| Results of survey | Discussion. |
| Break | |
| Tips for better study skills | Program Exercise 2. Effective Study Skills (and Handout B). |
| Personal barriers | Brainstorm personal barriers to effective study skills and post on newsprint. Discuss. |
| Break or lunch | |
| Study skills time management | Program Exercise 3. Increasing Academic Effectiveness, with discussion (and Handout C). |
| Break | |
| Tools for academic achievement | Handout D. Tools for Academic Achievement. |
| Termination | Closing exercise (not included). |

Program Exercise 10.1. Survey of Study Habits and Skills

> **Objectives:** To identify skills that need to be developed or increased; to
> identify habits that need to be decreased or eliminated.
> **Materials:** Handout A; pencils; large sheets of paper or newsprint; mask-
> ing tape.
> **Time:** 60 to 90 minutes.
> **Age/education:** Fifth-grade reading level and above.
> **Number of participants:** 35.
> **Preparation:** Gather materials and organize room.
> **Procedure:** Distribute Handout A and pencils. Tell participants that the
> first step in understanding their study habits and skills is identifying
> current behaviors. Ask them to fill out Handout A and add their ratings
> in each category. While they do this, post five sheets of paper with a
> category printed at the top of each: Environmental Concerns, Time Man-
> agement, Organizing, Controlling, and Communication.
>
> When participants have completed scoring, divide them into groups
> of four to six members. Ask groups to discuss the high and low catego-
> ries and to keep a list of the five items receiving the highest scores and
> the five receiving the lowest scores. Allow them 10 to 15 minutes to
> complete this.
>
> Ask each group in turn to report on the five highest rated items
> and write the item number on the appropriate category sheet of paper
> or newsprint. When an item is selected more than once, put a tally mark
> beside it. Draw a line across each sheet and have groups report the
> lowest rated number. Repeat the recording and tally. Part the combined
> ratings for each group.
> **Processing:** Lead a discussion on the habits and skills most frequently
> used. Focus on barriers or constraints that prevent participants from
> using certain habits and skills. Finally, have participants finish these
> statements by selecting one of the skills or habits: I need to increase . . . I
> need to decrease . . .

## Survey of Study Habits and Skills

**Directions:** Reflect on your usual study behavior and respond to the items using the following scale:

5 = Almost always, always;   4 = Usually;   3 = Sometimes;   2 = Seldom;
1 = Almost never, never

After you complete all the items, add your scores for each section and record them in the blanks.

### Environmental Concerns

| | |
|---|---|
| 1. I study in the same place (e.g., bedroom, library) each day. | 5  4  3  2  1 |
| 2. The place I study is quiet. | 5  4  3  2  1 |
| 3. I am free from interruptions when I study. | 5  4  3  2  1 |
| 4. I play background music or the television when I study. | 1  2  3  4  5 |
| Total: | ____ |

### Time Management

| | |
|---|---|
| 5. I schedule or arrange time for study each day. | 5  4  3  2  1 |
| 6. I read class notes shortly after class or before the next class meets. | 5  4  3  2  1 |
| 7. I study all night before a test. | 1  2  3  4  5 |
| 8. I read assigned chapters before class. | 5  4  3  2  1 |
| 9. I keep a calendar of assignments and tests. | 5  4  3  2  1 |
| 10. I do all assigned homework or more. | 5  4  3  2  1 |
| Total: | ____ |

### Organizing

| | |
|---|---|
| 11. I take notes in most classes each day. | 5  4  3  2  1 |
| 12. I read class handouts, syllabi, etc. | 5  4  3  2  1 |
| 13. I review tests on file in the library when available. | 5  4  3  2  1 |
| 14. I attend review sessions. | 5  4  3  2  1 |
| 15. I use different methods of study for different classes. | 5  4  3  2  1 |
| 16. I belong to a study group for difficult or demanding courses. | 5  4  3  2  1 |
| Total: | ____ |

## Controlling

17. I underline or highlight significant material in
the textbook.     5 4 3 2 1

18. I outline chapters in textbooks and read the outlines.   5 4 3 2 1

19. I make a list or flash cards of vocabulary used in
the course.     5 4 3 2 1

20. I memorize some content, such as formulas,
vocabulary, and sequential steps.     5 4 3 2 1

Total: _____

## Communication

21. I meet with the instructor to clarify or explain
material.     5 4 3 2 1

22. I get help from a tutor.     5 4 3 2 1

23. I ask the instructor or a class member for notes
when I am absent from class.     5 4 3 2 1

Total: _____

## Scoring
Write your scores in the designated spaces.

## Environmental Concerns: _____
(Scores of 12 or below indicate a need for attention.)

## Time Management: _____
(Scores of 18 or below indicate trouble with effective time use.)

## Organizing: _____
(Scores of 18 or below suggest that basic skills or behaviors need attention.)

## Controlling: _____
(Scores of 12 or below indicate that basic skills or behaviors are not used in an efficient way.)

## Communication: _____
(Scores of 9 or below indicate ineffective use of resources.)

I need to increase: _____
I need to decrease: _____

**Handout 10.A. Survey of Study Habits and Skills.** *Permission is granted to photocopy for group use.*

## Program Exercise 10.2. Effective Study Skills

**Objectives:** To increase awareness of effective study skill habits and techniques; to increase awareness of ineffective study habits and techniques.

**Materials:** Paper, pencils, large sheets of paper or newsprint. Masking tape.

**Time:** 60 to 90 minutes.

**Age/education:** Fifth-grade reading level and above.

**Number of participants:** 35.

**Preparation:** Gather materials; reproduce Handout B.

**Procedure:** Prior to distributing Handout B, have the group generate a list of ideas and the study practices it has found effective. It may be helpful to write these on large paper and post them on the wall with masking tape, or write them on a chalkboard.

**Processing:** After the list is generated, distribute Handout B. Effective Study Skills, and briefly discuss each item, giving the advantages of each and suggesting how it can be accomplished. The following can be used as a guide. It may be helpful to have examples of two or three different calendars:

## Effective Study Skills

Goals for Academic Achievement

 1. Keep a calendar of assignments and tests.

 2. Use different methods of study for different classes.

 3. Schedule a time for study every day.

 4. Have a quiet place for study that is free from distractions and interruptions.

 5. Read class handouts, syllabi, and so on.

 6. Read class notes immediately after class or before the next class period.

 7. Read assigned chapters or other material before class.

 8. Take notes in class or record lectures.

 9. Underline or highlight significant material in text.

10. Outline chapters and read outline.

11. Compile lists of vocabulary for courses.

12. Memorize content such as formulas.

13. Do *all* assigned homework.

14. Attend review sessions.

15. Seek help from a tutor.

16. Study with a group of students in the class.

17. Meet with the instructor to clarify class material.

18. Review tests on file in the library.

**Handout 10.B. Effective Study Skills.** *Permission is granted to photocopy for group use.*

## Program Exercise 10.3. Increasing Academic Effectiveness

**Objectives:** To develop awareness of current time use and what changes can be made to increase academic effectiveness; to develop an action plan for study.

**Materials:** Pencils, copies of Handouts C and D.

**Time:** 60 to 90 minutes.

**Age/education:** Fifth-grade reading level and above.

**Number of participants:** 35.

**Preparation:** Gather materials and reproduce Handouts C and D.

**Procedure:** Distribute Handout C and pencils. Tell participants you will guide them through the exercise. Ask that they move with you in working on items and ask questions. If they do not complete an item in the allotted time, they can return and complete it later.

Describe items 1 through 5, allowing enough time for participants to briefly reflect and write a response. Watch participants to get a sense of when most are ready to move to the next item.

When items 1 through 5 are completed, divide participants into groups of two or three to share their responses. Allow a brief period for sharing, then focus a discussion on what emerged for each item. Have members volunteer what they wrote, but do not judge or evaluate the responses.

The final part is the action plan. Follow the same process used for items 1 through 7.

Distribute Handout D for participants to read.

**Processing:** After participants have completed the task in Handout C, ask for volunteers to share their academic goal and what steps they can take to reach their goal.

## Increasing Academic Effectiveness

### Study Skills Time Management

1. List all classes and their time periods during the week (e.g., English 9 to 10 A.M. Monday through Friday). Total the number of hours for each, and overall.

| Class | Time | Days | Total hours for class |
|---|---|---|---|
| | | | Total hours:____ |

2. Rate the degree of difficulty you experience for each class using the following scale: 5 = extremely difficult; 4 = very difficult; 3 = difficult; 2 = not usually difficult; 1 = easy.

| Class | Difficulty Rating |
|---|---|

3. List other responsibilities (e.g., work), commitments (e.g., church), and meetings (e.g., club) you had during the previous week and an estimate of the amount of time each took. Include travel time if it applies.

| Event | Time Consumed |
|---|---|
| | Total Estimated Time Consumed:____ |

4. Estimate the amount of time you used for each of the following study-related activities during the previous week:

| Study Related Activity | Time |
|---|---|
| Planning (e.g., writing a to-do list) | ____ |
| Scheduling (e.g., writing specific times for events) | ____ |
| Organizing (e.g., review, reading) | ____ |
| Controlling (e.g., outlining, memorizing) | ____ |
| Communication (e.g., clarification of class material) | ____ |
| Total: | ____ |

5. Estimate the amount of time used the previous week for each of the following:

| | |
|---|---|
| Sleeping | ____ |
| Eating (include meal preparation time) | ____ |

6. How can you be more effective in using your time? Respond to each of the following with 3 or more ideas.

   a. I will reduce the time I spend

   b. I will stop or eliminate

   c. I will begin

**Handout 10.C. Increasing Academic Effectiveness.** *Permission is granted to photocopy for group use.*

## How I Can Achieve: Goals for Academic Achievement

| Skill | Advantage(s) | Tool/Strategy |
| --- | --- | --- |
| 1. Calendar of assignments | Not rushed to complete. Submitted on time. | Calendar, assignment book. |
| 2. Different methods of study | Give more time to more complex courses. | Rate, practice, work problems. |
| 3. Schedule study time | Breaks it into small manageable units; not as overwhelming. | Calendar, half-hour blocks. |
| 4. Quiet place | Free from distraction; better concentration. | List of quiet places. |
| 5. Read handouts, etc. | Understand expectations; gather information. | Read immediately, review periodically. |
| 6. Read class notes | Fix information in mind; reveal gaps in information. | Read immediately, review. |
| 7. Read assignments | Prepared for class; can focus on expanding. | Read prior to class. |
| 8. Take notes or record lectures | Have a record of material; can study for test. | Tape recorder, notebook. |
| 9. Underline material | Easier to review main points. | Highlighter. |
| 10. Outline material | Quicker review of main points, definitions, etc. | |
| 11. Vocabulary list | Learn words and concepts for subject. | Flash cards, memorization. |
| 12. Memorize content | Easier to recall | Rote, practice. |
| 13. Homework | Practice; reveal gaps and need for clarification. | |
| 14. Attend review sessions | Can get suggestion for test material or focus. | |
| 15. Tutors | One-to-one instruction. | |
| 16. Study groups | Have demonstrated usefulness; support. | Recruit two or three to study with regularly. |
| 17. Meet with instructor | Clarify material; shows interest. | Schedule an appointment. |
| 18. Review old tests on file | Understand test focus, kind of items, etc. | Ask for old tests or where available. |

**Handout 10.D. How I Can Achieve: Goals for Academic Achievement.** *Permission is granted to photocopy for group use.*

# Chapter 11

# Leading Psychoeducational Groups for Adults

Major Topics

*Knowledge Factor*
Examples and research for adult groups

*Science Factors*
Creating the adult group

## INTRODUCTION

Psychoeducational groups for adults have several advantages over groups for children and adolescents:

- Adults are less apt to be involuntary participants.
- Adults will more often have specific objectives or learning they expect from the group, and they are more aware of these expectations.
- Behavior, especially disruptive or aggressive behavior, is not usually a concern.
- Adults have life experiences that add to the richness of the group.
- Adults can be more task focused.

These traits can make the planning and facilitation of groups for adults much easier in some ways.

However, adults can also be more demanding and critical, impatient for results, desirous of more personalization and individualization, and very adept at resistance and defensive behavior. These traits can make the group leader's tasks more difficult.

Some groups for adults have another characteristic that is not generally found in children and adolescent groups: relevance to the world of work. Workshops, conferences, and other such venues use psychoeducational groups, and organizations spend a great deal of money on them.

## EXAMPLES OF GROUPS FOR ADULTS

Below are some examples of the variety of groups that are held for adults. They are but a few of the many such groups that are available, aside from psychoeducational support groups and therapy-related groups. They are categorized by the theme of the group.

### Self-Esteem

Swell (1992) studied an instructional program for college students that focused on self-esteem, values identification, conflict management, and positive reinforcement. Results of the study of 394 first-year students showed significant improvement for participants when matched with a control group.

McManus, Redford, and Hughes (1997) described a six-session psychoeducational group for women 18 years and older that focused on self-esteem issues or relationship difficulties. They used lectures, discussions, exercises, and homework to address these issues in the group.

### Social Skills

Stein, Cislo, and Ward (1994) reported that a one-semester course on developing social skills for undergraduates who would be working with psychiatrically disabled people increased the students' social networks, positive attitudes toward people with psychiatric disabilities, interpersonal self-efficacy, and social skills.

Martin and Thomas (2000) described a psychoeducational group for shy college students whose goals were to teach members how to relax in social situations. Additional topics were to develop and practice new socializing behaviors, gain confidence, and reduce self-defeating thoughts.

### Parenting

Morgan and Hensley (1998) conducted a pilot study on the effectiveness of a psychoeducational support group for working mothers. Goals were to achieve cognitive restructuring, reduce stress, and provide social support.

Vacha-Haase, Ness, Dannison, and Smith (2000) found that a

psychoeducational group for grandparents raising grandchildren was effective, and that learning and behavior increased significantly. The group was focused on parenting skills, personal well-being, relationships, managing finances, and legal issues.

## Stress

Ulman (2000) used a three-component psychoeducational group for stress reduction for women. The three components were teaching and practicing relaxation techniques, exploration of needed cognitive and behavioral changes, and discussion of members' life situations. Results indicated a significant decrease in symptoms of stress.

Jones (2001) investigated the effects of a psychoeducational group for undergraduate black college women. Results indicated a reduction in stress, an increase in active coping skills, and a decrease in external locus of control for the experimental group.

## Work-Related Groups

Hall and Cockburn (1990) reported on managers who had participated in a learner-centered modeling program to increase management skills. A 1-year follow-up study showed that the effectiveness of skills training was increased 10 to 70 percent. The focus for the action learning was interpersonal skills.

## CREATING THE ADULT GROUP

The advantages for adult groups mentioned earlier also carry some expectations for leaders. In order to meet these needs and expectations, leaders must be organized, plan well, and involve participants in setting goals.

Group composition and group size are of less concern than for children and adolescent groups. Helpers are useful for adult groups when group size rises above 20, however. It is generally most effective to divide a large group into small groups for discussion, exercises, and to promote interaction and involvement.

Length, duration, and number of sessions also are of less concern with groups for adults. Timing should be determined around availability of participants and the topic covered. Groups that have a topic of adequate interest for adults will attract and keep participants for a number of sessions over weeks and months.

## Setting Goals and Objectives

Spend some time in the beginning of the group clarifying participants' goals, objectives, and expectations so that you can accommodate as many as possible. One way is to have participants write their goals, objectives, and expectations on paper, then break into small groups, compile the lists on newsprint, post them on the wall, discuss them, and come to some agreement on the most important ones for the group. A variation would be to divide into groups; brainstorm goals, objectives, and expectations; prioritize and write them on newsprint; post them on the wall; and discuss.

You may accurately anticipate the major goals, objectives, and expectations, but the primary outcome for any exercise is to promote involvement and commitment. Getting participants involved and excited encourages participation and promotes learning.

## Environmental Concerns

Because adult group sessions tend to be held over a longer time span, you should pay attention to the comfort of participants. Adequate space for moving around and stretching is helpful, as is comfortable seating. Temperature control, a quiet atmosphere, adequate air exchange, and close availability of bathrooms also contribute to comfort.

Freedom from intrusion is as important for adults as it is for children and adolescents. Disruptions tend to focus attention away from the topic and interrupt input and interaction.

## Leader Tasks

Following is a short list of questions to explore when planning an adult group:

*What are the primary outcomes expected?* What are the participants to know or be able to do as a result of the group?

*Who are the participants?* You will need to know their ages, educational levels, and employment. You will want to know how many participants you will have and whether the group is homogeneous or a mix. One final consideration is whether there will be primarily males or females in the group, or a mixture.

*What time is available?* Be explicit about the number of hours the group will last—for example, say 3 hours rather than half a day, which could be either 3 or 4 hours. If there are several sessions planned, will there be a consistent time for the group to meet?

*What facilities will be used?* Will the group be held at an organization's facilities, at rented facilities such as a hotel, or in some other place?

*What are the funding concerns?* Will you have sufficient funds to cover helpers' stipends, the cost of materials, copying, renting movies or equipment, and refreshments?

Following are materials and a plan for a work-related group on time management. The program includes 5 exercises, 3 minilectures, and 7 handouts.

## PROGRAM TIME MANAGEMENT

**Objectives:** To learn effective ways to manage time and to increase achievement of tasks; to increase awareness of personal use of time and potential for more effective use; to learn to plan, prioritize, and stay focused on short-term and long-term goals; to identify personal time wasters and those related to managerial functions; to learn to plan and conduct meetings.

**Materials:** Paper, pens or pencils, newsprint, felt-tip markers and masking tape.

**Time:** Full day. 6–8 hours.

**Age/education:** Employed adults in managerial and supervisory positions.

**Number of participants:** 35.

**Preparation:** Gather materials; prepare examples; develop minilectures; organize space.

### Sample Schedule
### Time Management
(Each session is approximately 1 hour)

| Session | Activities/Handouts |
| --- | --- |
| Session 1 | Introductions, get acquainted exercise (not included), generation of lists of time management problems by participants. (Leader writes these on posted newsprint, or the chalkboard.) |
| Session 2 | Minilecture "Daily Planning," Program exercise 1, Handout 11.A, discussion |
| Session 3 | Program exercise 2, Handout 11.B, discussion |
| Session 4 | Program exercise 3, Handouts 11.C., discussion |
| Session 5 | Minilecture "Paperwork," Program exercise 4, discussion |
| Session 6 | Minilecture "Meetings," discussion |
| Session 7 | Handouts 11.E–11.H, Program exercise 5, Closing exercise (not included). |

## Minilecture: Daily Planning

In order to accomplish your goals, you need to plan on a daily basis. By planning on a daily basis, you will stay focused on your goals and engage in activities that will help you achieve them. Daily planning keeps you from getting bogged down in unproductive tasks. A daily plan is not rigid but allows for flexibility and change. Your daily plan should include the following:

1. *A list of things to do.* Do not trust your memory; write down what you need or want to do daily. Guard against listing trivia; list the major tasks to be done.
2. *Some prioritizing of tasks.* It helps to put a star beside the one task that must be accomplished that day. It may be a telephone call, information needed, a book to be checked out of the library, an appointment to be made, or a meeting to attend. While it may not be the most important task that day, it is the most imperative task.

   There are several systems for prioritizing lists of daily tasks. It does not matter what system you use, as long as it makes sense to you. Some hints on prioritizing follow this section.
3. *Flexibility.* Try not to have so many things on your list that the least little thing can throw your whole schedule off. Allow for tasks to take longer than anticipated, crises, and unexpected developments.

It is best to do your daily planning either first thing in the morning or just before going to bed. Planning in the morning organizes your day, and planning at night organizes the next day. Either way, you are not caught up in other activities at the time. Whenever you choose to plan, make it a part of your daily schedule. Plan at the same time each day. Remember, if you do not plan for something you want, you're unlikely to get it.

### Setting Priorities

There are times when it is difficult to set priorities because everything you have to do that day is important or even urgent. Or perhaps nothing seems particularly important. In these instances, there are two processes that may be helpful:

1. You can categorize your tasks and set priorities for them.
2. You can tap into your awareness to accomplish the same tasks.

To categorize and prioritize tasks, look at your entire list for the day. Put a 1 or a star by all the tasks that are *urgent*—that is, they must be done that day. Hopefully, you will have only one urgent task. However, if you have more than one, there may be a logical order for the tasks. If so, it becomes easier to decide which to do first. Label them 1a, 1b, and so on. Whatever else you have to do that day, these tasks will get done.

Label *semi-urgent* tasks 2a, 2b, and so on, in the same way. These are tasks that are important but may not have to be accomplished that day. It may be necessary to work on them, but it is not necessary to finish. These tasks usually require some thought as well as actions. Give them the attention they need.

Label *important* tasks 3a, 3b, and so on. These are tasks that are significant but do not have a sense of urgency. You do not want to delay working on them, but if you have to choose what to work on, these tasks should come after urgent and semiurgent tasks.

It is not necessary to label the last two categories of tasks, because you usually can choose to do or not do them. They are categorized as *busy work* and *wasted time*. You determine what tasks fall into these categories; they may be different for each individual.

The second process of prioritizing involves simply looking at the entire list of things to do and allowing the priorities to emerge. You do not analyze them in a cognitive way but rather in an intuitive way. This will accomplish the setting of priorities in a different way from consciously analyzing and categorizing tasks.

Sometimes our individual priorities are not congruent with the demands of the situation, and it may be necessary to switch and adhere to other priorities. Do not fret; if it must be done, you waste more time and energy fretting than you would if you just went ahead and did it. You can get back to your priorities; they will not disappear.

## Program Exercise 11.1. My Work Plan

**Objectives:** To schedule high-energy tasks around personal high-energy periods; to become aware of your own energy cycle; to develop strategies for coping when tasks and energy levels clash.

**Materials:** A copy of Handout 11.A and a pen or pencil for each participant; a schedule for a week, enlarged and posted where everyone can see it. The schedule should have all 7 days and the hours from 5 A.M. through midnight.

**Time:** 30 to 45 minutes.

**Age/education:** Eighth-grade reading level and above.

**Number of participants:** 35.

**Preparation:** Determine the usual working time frame for participants; develop the schedule and form for the chart based on those hours. For example, nurses working the late shift may have a working time of 10 P.M. to 6 A.M. Homemaker volunteers for an agency may have a working time of 10 A.M. to 2 P.M. While the schedule includes time before and after working time, the list of general activities and other times are built around working time. Once the intended audience is known, you can generate a list of major activities for the group. Another way to do this is to consult with someone who works in the area on usual tasks and those that present the most time management problems. The most effective way of generating the list is to survey the participants.

**Procedure:** Form small groups of five to seven members distributed around tables in the same room. Introduce the exercise by telling participants that we all have energy cycles and will find it easier to accomplish some tasks if we schedule them around those energy periods. Ask participants to reflect on when they find it easiest to do their most difficult tasks. Using the posted schedule for a week, show participants some examples of high-energy periods, such as the following:

- *Early morning:* Early-morning people have no trouble waking up; they can move rapidly, talk, jog, and so on.
- *Late morning:* Some people just drift through the morning; they do not want to talk or be faced with problems before 10 A.M.; they can function, but they do not want to.
- *Early afternoon:* This is the low period for early-morning people; some people actually function best during this time.
- *Late afternoon:* This usually is a rebounding time for early-morning people. Late-morning people begin to feel tired. Those who work 8 A.M. to 5 P.M. may find they are just getting into the swing about 2 hours before quitting time.
- *Early and late evening:* All of the above categories begin to wind down. People who become energized during this period can accomplish a lot.

    There also are individuals whose energy levels fluctuate over a period of days but remain constant during a single day. For example: *Early week:* These individuals can get a lot accomplished on Monday and Tuesday but are less energetic by Thursday and all but wiped out by Friday.
- *Midweek:* These individuals are somewhat slow to get into the job at the beginning of the week. However, by Wednesday their energy level has risen and they can get a lot done.
- *Late week:* These individuals have their highest energy levels when the usual work week is ending or has ended.

After describing these energy cycles, ask participants to fill out Handout 11.3. Allow 15 minutes for them to do so, then have them share in small groups.

**Processing:** Focus processing on new awareness. What emerged for participants that was new? What did they remember about their energy cycles? What changes could they make to better match energy levels and tasks?

## My Work Plan

**Directions:** List you major work activities in the first column. Then write the best time of day, and best day for you to complete that activity: that is when you have the most energy for the task. For example, an activity could be a meeting, and your best day and time is Wednesday at 10am. Next, write the day and time the activity usually happens, for example the meeting could happen at 8am on Mondays.

| Activity | Best Day | Best Time | Usual Day | Usual Time |
|----------|----------|-----------|-----------|------------|

**Handout 11.A. My Work Plan.** *Permission is granted to photcopy for group use.*

Program Exercise 11.2. Reconstructing a Day

**Objectives:** To increase awareness of the variety of feelings and moods experienced in a day; to focus on activities and their associated feelings, especially where possibilities for changes exist; to increase awareness of positive aspects of a day.

**Materials:** Copies of Handouts 11.B and 11.C, 11.D and 11.E for each participant; pens or pencils; large sheets of paper newsprint; felt-tip markers.

**Time:** 30 to 45 minutes.

**Age/education:** Eighth-grade reading level and above.

**Number of participants:** 35.

**Preparation:** Prepare three sheets of paper or newsprint for each small group titled Morning, Afternoon, and Evening, with subcategories of Feelings/Moods, Activities–Positive, Activities–Negative.

**Procedure:** Divide the group into small groups and ask each group to sit around a table. All groups should remain in the same room. Introduce the exercise by asking participants to get comfortable and to put down anything they may be holding. Tell them they will try to reconstruct the previous day. If it is helpful, they can close their eyes. Read the directions on Handout 11.B. Give examples and elaborations—for example, you could say after the first sentence, "There were many activities during your day, many feelings, many moods. You may have felt happy, rushed, frustrated, pleased, or satisfied. Try and recall all that transpired yesterday." Review your feelings and mood throughout the day and note the time frame for the most positive feelings/moods, and what category of activity was happening at this time. Note the time frame for the most negative feelings/moods, and the category of activity.

After reading the directions, instruct participants to complete the form with as much detail as possible. After forms are completed, allow time for small-group discussion.

**Processing:** Distribute the prepared sheets of paper or newsprint to each group. Within their groups, members are to list the primary feelings they experienced during the three periods. They also should list the kind of activities that produced the most positive and the most negative feelings. Kind of activity refers to categories such as commuting, socializing, or cleaning. After the small groups have completed the lists, post them on the wall and ask participants to look for similarities and differences. This is also an opportunity for participants to share suggestions for resolving difficulties—for example, what to do when stuck in traffic to avoid frustration.

A further step, if time permits, is to ask participants how they perceive their day after the exercise and if their perception has changed. Some participants will become more aware of how they have focused on the negative aspects and ignored many positive aspects.

## Reconstructing a Day

**Directions:** Begin when you arose and fill in the form for what happened with you yesterday.

| Time | Activity | Your feeling/mood |
| --- | --- | --- |
| Morning | | |
| 6 | | |
| 7 | | |
| 8 | | |
| 9 | | |
| 10 | | |
| 11 | | |
| 12 | | |
| Afternoon | | |
| 1 | | |
| 2 | | |
| 3 | | |
| 4 | | |
| 5 | | |
| 6 | | |
| Evening | | |
| 7 | | |
| 8 | | |
| 9 | | |
| 10 | | |
| 11 | | |
| 12 | | |

**Handout 11.B. Reconstructing a Day.** *Permission is granted to photocopy for group use.*

## Categories of Time Use

**Important and urgent:** Tasks that must be done either immediately or in the near future are important and urgent. These tasks are not usually a time management problem. An example would be setting up a meeting to consider an unanticipated problem.

**Important but not urgent:** Attention to this category is what divides effective individuals from ineffective ones. Most of the important things in life are not urgent but should be at the top of your task lists. If your activities are keyed to other people's priorities or to system-imposed deadlines that make things "urgent," you will never get around to your own priorities. An example might be a major written report or presentation.

**Urgent but not important:** In this category are things that clamor for immediate action, but you would assign a low priority if you examined them objectively. An example might be a request for information from someone.

**Busy work:** These tasks are marginally worth doing but are not urgent or important. They are diversionary: they provide a feeling of activity and accomplishment while giving you an excuse to put off tackling important but not urgent tasks, which have far greater benefit. Examples might include organizing and filing papers.

**Wasted time:** The definition of wasted time is subjective. How you feel afterward is the criterion. If you feel uncomfortable, the task probably wasted time.

---

Handout 11.C.  **Categories of Time Use.** *Permission is granted to photocopy for group use.*

## Program Exercise 11.3. Analysis of My Tasks

**Objectives:** To help participants determine if they are spending most of their time on their most important tasks; to increase awareness of where they spend time and energy; to identify possible changes.

**Materials:** Copies of Handouts 11.C for each participant; pens or pencils.

**Time:** 60 to 90 minutes.

**Age/education:** Eighth-grade reading level and above.

**Number of participants:** This exercise can be done in a large or small group. It is more effective in a small group where participants have an opportunity to interact with others.

**Preparation:** Gather materials; organize room.

**Procedure:** Distribute Handout. Ask participants to list the five most important tasks related to the topic of the group—after listing the most important tasks, participants should list their five most time-consuming tasks. If you are working with small groups, allow a short time for sharing in the groups.

**Processing:** Ask if there were any surprises in the lists—a show of hands for those whose lists were congruent—that is, the most time-consuming—were also the most important. It is unusual to find congruence for most participants. They may want to discuss some of the reasons for incongruence.

The next step is to identify the time-consuming tasks, or parts of tasks, over which participants have some control. These are the tasks that hold promise for changes. To identify possible changes, ask group members to consider the following:

- *Eliminate:* Do not do the task; consider both the positive and the negative consequences of elimination.
- *Delegate:* Give the task or part of the task to someone else.
- *Ask for help:* You do not always have the authority do delegate. In these instances, there may be someone who can help with part or all of the task.
- *Find another way:* Review the task and see if there are other ways to accomplish it. Often, time-consuming tasks are the results of habits that can be modified or changed—for example, you might pay someone to cut the grass; buy pies for special occasions instead of baking them; equip every PC or workstation with access to central information sources; or communicate information via a newsletter or memo instead of holding meetings.

Have participants write down a specific action for change—for example, ask a son to cut the grass.

## Program Exercise 11.4. Writing Myths

**Objective:** To determine how many myths participants have about writing that are time wasters.

**Materials:** A sheet of paper for each participant, and a pen or pencil.

**Procedure:** Ask participants to rate themselves on the following items as you slowly read them. Use ratings of 5 – always, or almost always; 4 – frequently; 3 – sometimes; 2 – seldom; and 1 – never, or almost never.

1. It is easier to collaborate than it is to write something by myself.

2. I need others to perceive what I write as "good."

3. I seek others' input on the validity of my ideas before I start writing.

4. I have to make an outline before I can begin writing.

5. I must write the sections, parts, and so on, in the order they will appear in the final document.

6. Each word, phrase, and sentence must be perfect in my thoughts before I write it.

7. I need long blocks of time to write.

8. It is futile to try and write anywhere other than on the computer.

9. I do not like to make revisions after I write something.

10. I cannot write before I have all the information I think I need.

11. Review each item, and ask for a show of hands for participants rating the item 3+.

12. Write the number of the items that have half or more participants rating it as 3+.

13. Once this list is generated, ask participants to brainstorm why these are constraints to their writing, and to generate possible solutions.

## Program Exercise 11.5. Managing My Time

**Objective:** To identify specific actions members can take to better control and manage their time.

**Materials:** Handouts 11.E and 11.F, pencils or pens, and a sheet of paper for each participant.

**Procedure:**

1. Present and discuss each point on Handout 11.E, and ask members to identify the things they already do, the ones they do not do, and the ones they could begin to do.
2. Have members write the things they do and could do on the sheet of paper.
3. Hold a discussion on the pros and cons of these tools.
4. Repeat the procedure for Handout 11.F, 11.G., and 11.H.

## Some Time Wasters Related to Time Management Functions

**Planning Function**

     Takes time and thought to plan

     Prefer to act or be spontaneous

**Prioritizing Function**

     Confusion about relative importance of tasks

     Shifting priorities

     No clearly defined goals and objectives

     Unable to distinguish between tasks

**Deciding Function**

     Lack of confidence in self or information

     Wanting *all* the facts before deciding

     Fear of making a mistake

     No decision-making process

**Delegating Function**

     Lack of confidence in abilities and competencies of others

     Assuming too much personal responsibility

     Failure to set priorities

     Not understanding how and when to delegate

**Organizing Function**

     Operating by crises

     Unrealistic time estimates

     Responding to the urgent

     Attempting too much

     Problem orientation

**Personal Competencies Function**

     Handling paper more than once

     Inefficient reading habits

     Lack of training

     Overanxious

     Refusal to delegate

     Enjoyment of socializing

     Inability to set priorities

**Handout 11.D. Some Time Wasters Related to Time Management Functions.** *Permission is granted to photocopy for group use.*

## Time Wasters and Management Functions

| If you find you are engaged in the following | The failure of management may be |
|---|---|
| Having to meet unrealistic time estimates; no deadlines; managing crises; having numerous tasks to do at the same time; no daily plan; shifting priorities | *Planning,* such as clear goals and objectives; priorities for tasks; communicated deadlines |
| Responding to multiple bosses; confused about responsibility and authority; duplication of effort | *Organizing,* such as a work plan with assigned tasks; agreed-upon priorities for tasks assigned to others; efficient work-space layout |
| Trying to do tasks for which you are not trained; unable to complete a task without interruptions, unless that is part of your job; missing time because of personal problems | *Staffing,* such as providing sufficient training and education; having sufficient staff; not being overstaffed; a process for helping workers cope with personal problems |
| Failure to cope with change; ongoing conflict; working alone when teamwork is called for; depressed motivation; uninteresting tasks; unimportant tasks; routine details | *Directing,* such as having a process to manage change; implementing conflict resolution skills; developing and supporting cooperation and teamwork; delegating important tasks; helping workers understand how what they do contributes to outcomes |
| Personal telephone calls many times during most days; chatting about personal topics constantly; visiting to or from others; not giving progress reports; being micromanaged; over-commitment because of an inability to say no; ineffective performance | *Controlling,* such as clear policies and expectations for conduct and performance; requesting progress reports; giving workers responsibility |
| Attending many meetings most days; having to ask for additional directions and clarifications; asking coworkers what is going on; constantly surprised by events; procrastinating; delaying or not making decisions | *Communicating,* such as giving clear directions for a task and checking to see if they were understood; keeping personnel up to date; involving personnel in making changes |
| Procrastinating; delaying by not making decisions | *Decision making,* such as understanding your decision-making style; knowing when you have sufficient facts to make a decision; knowing when to make decisions and when to involve others in the process |

**Handout 11.E. Time Wasters and Management Functions**. *Permission is granted to photocopy for group use.*

## Strategies to Address Time Wasters

| Function | Strategies |
|---|---|
| Planning | Recognize that planning saves time and concentrates energy on most important tasks; emphasize results not activity; set aside time for planning; make "to do" lists |
| Prioritizing | Set clear, achievable goals and objectives; prioritize "to do" lists; work on most important tasks first; shift priorities only when it is crucial to do so |
| Deciding | Develop a personal or team decision-making process; decide to forgive yourself for making mistakes; learn to make decisions without having to have all the facts; develop a network of reliable information sources |
| Delegating | Delegate tasks and give resources necessary to accomplish the tasks; set priorities daily and communicate them to others to whom tasks will be delegated; learn how and when to delegate |
| Organizing | Learn to distinguish between categories of tasks; set realistic time estimates; do not procrastinate; work on large tasks daily; organize your work space; make daily "to do" lists; develop a problem prevention orientation; have realistic expectations of yourself and others; allow for shifts in priorities |
| Personal Competence | Develop a "do it now" attitude for handling paper; try to handle each piece of paper only once; learn and practice speed reading; save socializing for after hours; learn to say no; concentrate on goals; work on important tasks first; group telephone calls; save junk mail and magazines to go through once a week; practice delegating |

**Handout 11.F.    Strategies to Address Time Wasters**. *Permission is granted to photocopy for group use.*

## Minilecture: Paperwork

Paperwork can be divided into roughly four categories; correspondence, reports, forms, and records. While the paperwork faced by workers in various settings may differ in quantity, all workers must complete some paperwork.
*Correspondence.*    Most workers, especially those in offices, will deal with correspondence. In fact, this is one task that can expand to fill entire days. You must respond to letters from customers, suppliers, and clients, of course, but there are ways to do it more efficiently.

1. Write a response on the bottom of the incoming letter or memorandum, make a copy, and mail.
2. Do not spend time writing a rough draft; just type a final copy and mail it. Most software will correct spelling and punctuation errors. After you frame your reply, you should only have to sign the letter.
3. Do not write a reply at all; instead, call or visit the individual and transact the business over the telephone or in person.
4. Use preprinted forms on which you write your letter at the top, and the bottom has space for a reply. These usually are on carbonless paper, which gives a copy without using either carbons or a copying machine.
5. Use dictating equipment. You can dictate letters in places or at times when you cannot write (e.g., in a car or on an airplane).

*Reports.*    Many workers must write reports at least monthly; some must do so weekly or even daily. Below are some tips for making the task go quickly.

1. When you learn that you must submit a report, begin gathering materials and data immediately.
   a. Make a folder to hold all materials relating to the report.
   b. Put the due date in bold letters on the outside of the folder and in at least two places on your desk calendar; include a reminder 1 month before it is due and the date it is due.
2. Make sure you know the correct format for the report as well as the information required. Put it in the folder.
3. Make an outline for the report. The outline can serve as your guide for collecting information and writing the report.
4. It may be useful to write a list of all bits and pieces of information you need for the report and staple it to the inside of the folder. That way, you can check off information as it is collected and have a reminder of what other information you need. You can then work on the report by gathering information each week, and you will not have to run around at the last minute trying to locate missing pieces.
5. The actual report writing can be done a little at a time or all at once. Most people typically use one or the other way and do not feel comfortable switch-

ing. Those who write a little at a time will work on the report off and on for several weeks and will not write the various sections in the order they appear in the report. Rather, they write the sections as they find the information for them. When they are ready to put the report together, it is just a matter of putting it in order.

Individuals who write all at once must have all of the information collected before they can begin writing. They prefer to start at the beginning and keep writing until they are through. It is terribly frustrating for them not to have all of their information.

Either method can be efficient and effective. The point is to avoid wasting time: gather your information and work on—not necessarily write—the report daily or weekly as you have time; do not delay. Procrastination is more time-consuming than writing.

*Forms.* There are few careers that do not require forms. There are also few forms that do not request unnecessary information. There are two primary time-saving procedures for forms: handle them only once and review them to eliminate unnecessary items.

1. Handle it only once: After you have read the form and understand its purpose, fill it out right away. Do not file it, put it in a pile, or otherwise delay filling it out. Most forms do not require a great deal of time to complete, and if you are interrupted, you can get back to them easily.
2. If you have forms in your office, review them with an eye toward simplifying them. Eliminate items that request unnecessary information. Ask these questions of each and every item: Why do we need this piece of information? How would it hurt to eliminate this piece of information? Is this item redundant—for example, asking for both age and date of birth?
3. Locate software that could be used to fill out forms on the computer. This is especially helpful if there are numerous forms to be filled out that require much of the same information.

*Records.* Keeping records can be very time consuming, particularly if you have not developed a system that allows for quick and easy retrieval. After all, one of the most important requirements for a record-keeping system is rapid access to needed information. Thus, it is crucial that the system be developed to allow you to get documents in a timely manner.

The suggestions that follow are based on the assumptions that you are keeping personal records and do not need a system for keeping records for others, that it is important in your work that you have documentation, and that you have a need for paper copies. Electronic record keeping is a separate topic; the focus here is on ways to handle paper.

1. Set up a system that makes sense to you. This will make it easier to retrieve needed information. One way to organize is by topic—that is, all documents relating to a particular topic are in one file. If this is a large file, you can have subtopic files—for example, if the topic "department budget" is too large for just one file, subtopics such as "department budget plan" and "budget by month" could be set up. In the particular file would be all documents, including memorandums, relating to that topic. Thus, when you need information, all of it would be in the single file.
2. Before filing a document, decide on its potential importance. Is it likely to be needed at some point in time? Some materials have a high potential for future importance, such as a memo assigning you a specific task with a due date. Memories can be unreliable, and this memo is a record for you and others of the stated requirements and expectations. Other documents, such as announcements, may never be needed and do not need to be filed.
3. Develop a time line for keeping categories of documents. Some documents, such as contracts, you would want to keep a long time, whereas a time schedule for a completed project could be discarded. Discard documents that have little or no potential for being needed or used in the foreseeable future. After all, space usually is limited. The one exception to this suggestion is when a law or regulation mandates the length of time documents must be kept.

### Minilecture: Meetings

Here are some questions to ponder and answer:

1. When you chair a meeting, do you prepare an agenda and distribute it prior to the meeting?
2. Is the meeting time set by you at your convenience?
3. Do you try to wait until all or most of the participants are present before beginning the meeting, even if it means not starting on time?
4. Do you let the majority rule even if you disagree?
5. Do you hold regular meetings (e.g., once a week)?

*Making meetings productive.* When time management workshop members are asked to list their concerns, many list meetings as time wasters. Meetings are perceived as wasting time for many reasons:

- They are not focused—that is, they have unclear goals and objectives.
- They begin and end late.
- The method of decision making leaves some feeling discounted.
- Members are not consulted about the time of the meeting.
- Nothing of importance is discussed; the meeting is focused on trivia or irrelevant issues.
- A few people dominate the meeting.

*Chairing meetings.* If you have the responsibility for chairing meetings, you can manage them so that your task is accomplished, relationships are enhanced, and time is well spent. Whether it is a committee meeting or a staff meeting makes no difference; either can be conducted with efficiency.

As in all time management processes, planning is of the utmost importance. Time spent in planning ensures that the meeting is focused and participants feel a sense of accomplishment. Planning includes these steps:

1. *Set the agenda.* Solicit ideas and suggestions from participants whenever possible. Using these suggestions promotes a sense of involvement. If the task is pretty clear-cut, have the agenda reflect the primary topics to be discussed and decided.
2. *Distribute the agenda prior to the meeting.* It puts people at a disadvantage when they do not have the agenda or topics beforehand. Many participants are reluctant to make decisions under these conditions because they have not had time to reflect and feel uncomfortable. They may need to gather information, consult with others, or just think things through before the meeting. It is not uncommon for participants to delay making decisions, necessitating another meeting.
3. *Distribute information pertinent to the agenda before the meeting.* If you want the discussion to be focused on the issues or decisions to be made at the meeting, make sure participants have related information beforehand. Most people cannot read, listen, and talk at the same time.
4. *Consult about setting the meeting time.* As much as possible, allow participants some say in when the meeting will take place. It makes people feel you respect them and their work when you try to plan meetings around their best time. It is not always feasible to do this; however, the attempt should be made.
5. *Begin and end on time.* Nothing is more annoying than making an effort to attend a meeting on time only to have the chairperson delay the start waiting for someone else to get there. It makes those who made the effort to get there on time feel less important than the one who is late. It also conveys a lack of respect for the time of others.
6. *Make sure the meetings are time-bound.* Meetings should have a definite beginning and ending time. If the meeting is to be 1 hour in length, make sure you end it when approximately 60 minutes are up. People appreciate being able to plan their activities, and meetings that run long can throw schedules off. It is always better to end early than to run overtime.
7. *Time discussions.* When issues are to be discussed, set a time limit. You might say, for example, "We will allow 20 minutes for the discussion on merit salary increases." If it appears that this time is insufficient to allow

everyone to have input, you can allow more time or table the issue until the next meeting. When discussions are protracted, more information, reflection, or consultation is needed. It becomes counterproductive to allow the discussion to continue. If it is unlikely that a satisfactory resolution can be reached, you should explore other alternatives—for example, you might assign a subcommittee to study the issue and provide information to the entire group; you might hold a special meeting to focus only on that issue; or you could generate a list of solutions to be discussed.

8. *Focus meetings.* Keep the discussion focused on the main topics; stick to the agenda as much as possible. Use your facilitation skills to keep the discussion focused and to make participants feel heard. Skills that help include reflection, summarizing, linking, and identification of primary issues or concerns. Do not allow extraneous questions, comments, or statements to deflect the discussion.

There are times when important events or issues emerge after the agenda has been set. You should be flexible enough to adjust to the new situation, but make sure the new issues are more important than the items on the agenda.

9. *Involve everyone.* As chair, you should solicit input and opinions from everyone, and you should make sure that everyone feels involved. Before accepting a decision, ask if anyone has a question or comment. You may find that the quiet individual has an important point that changes everything. Individuals who are not involved in the discussion and the decision may not feel committed to implementing the decision.

10. *Take minutes.* If there is a secretary responsible for recording the minutes, make sure he or she notes *what* was done—that is, the important points made, issues raised, and all decisions should be in the minutes, not who said what, who made or seconded motions, and so on. The minutes should be distributed to all participants.

If there is no secretary, the chairperson or a designated individual should make notes on the decisions made and important issues or concerns raised. These should be approximately one page in length, typed, and distributed to all attendees, with the understanding that they can be corrected if in error. You will find that it saves time if what was said is in writing rather than in an individual's memory. Avoid hurt feelings and misunderstandings by distributing minutes and listing attendees in alphabetical order. Any time a list of names appears on anything, order the list alphabetically, regardless of the status of the individuals.

*Participating in meetings.* As a participant, you can help to make meetings productive and not time-wasters. Although you cannot do many of the things already noted, there are several other things you can do.

1. If an agenda has not been set or distributed, ask for one. Make it a request, not a demand, and put it on the basis of being helpful to all the participants.
2. Once you know the topics on the agenda, prepare for the meeting. Do not wait for information to be disseminated; it may not be. Seek information and *read it* before attending the meeting.
3. Make a list or note any points that you want clarified. It may be useful to note any points you want to make.
4. Arrive on time and be ready to begin. Do not let socializing interfere with the meeting. If the chairperson does not begin on time, request that the meeting start. Sometimes, all it takes is a reminder.
5. Keep your input focused on the topics at hand.
6. Use your facilitation skills: reflection, linking, clarifying, and questioning.
7. Be concrete; do not waffle or be ambiguous.
8. Be assertive, not aggressive or apathetic.

## Tools for Time Management

1. *Set goals* (objectives) and establish priorities, and work on them daily.

2. *Plan.* Nothing is more important!

3. *Schedule your time.* Recognize and accept that there is some time over which you have no control.

4. *Reschedule your time.* Your schedule will be interrupted continually. People will have needs that must be met now. Work out ways to reschedule things you have been forced to postpone.

5. *Write it down!* Do not trust your memory; if something is important, put it in writing.

6. *Have follow-up systems.* Being accountable and holding others accountable are great time savers and help eliminate procrastination.

7. *Delegate.* Do only what you can do best and delegate whatever you can; but do not delegate your job—that which you are supposed to do or only you can do.

8. *Use different reading techniques for different material:* scan, speed read, study, analyze.

9. *Assume interruptions.* Do not make your schedule too tight; set aside time to return calls and to see people.

10. *Communicate.* Nothing wastes time more than misunderstandings. Be clear and concise, get feedback, and establish regular information flow systems.

**Handout 11.G. Tools for Time Management.** *Permission is granted to photocopy for group use.*

## Some Basic Time Management Strategies

**Planning**

Plan each day and try to plan at the same time each day.
Make a daily "to do" list.
Prioritize the list and work on the most important items first.
Set life goals and objectives, and work to achieve them.

**Organizing**

Schedule your tasks.
Plan for interruptions. Do not schedule too tightly.
Plan ahead for recurring tasks, such as meals.
Organize materials before you need them (e.g., pack the night before a trip).
Anticipate delays.
Delegate wherever possible and feasible.

**Controlling**

Distinguish between tasks that are urgent and important and those that are just urgent.
When needed, eliminate all tasks that are not urgent and important.
Practice a "do it now" attitude. The price of procrastination may be too high.
Ask yourself this question frequently: What is the best use of my time at this moment? Act on the answer.

**Directing**

For any 10- to 15-minute period, ask yourself: What can be done?
Here are some possible answers:
Go through a pile of papers on the desk and sort and throw some away.
Clear the desk.
Return a call.
Request needed information.
Dust a room.
Read a page, a paragraph, an article, or a brochure.
Plan a task into its components.
Work on a piece of a larger task.
Make an appointment.

**Handout 11.H. Some Basic Time Management Strategies.** *Permission is granted to photocopy for group use.*

# Chapter 12

# Psychoeducational Support Groups

Major Topics and Concepts

*Knowledge Factors*
    Support and self-help groups
    Description of support groups
    Background for psychoeducational support groups

*Science Factors*
    Guidelines for structuring learning
    Designing support groups

*Art, Skills, and Techniques Factors*
    Facilitating factors

## INTRODUCTION

Support groups are often thought of as self-help groups, but they differ in some important ways: leadership, focus, goals and objectives, and structure. Support groups generally have a leader who is trained in leading groups as well as having knowledge about the condition or circumstance that is being addressed. Self-help groups quite often do not have a formally trained leader. Many self-help groups use a rotating peer leader instead of a consistent group leader.

The focus for support groups also differs from that for self-help groups. Support groups have a primary focus on educating members about the condition or circumstance, whereas self-help groups' primary purposes are mutual assistance and support. This difference is not as clear-cut as other differences, as both self-help and support groups focus on education and on mutual assistance and support but have them as different priorities. Understanding your primary focus keeps the group on track for accomplishing its goal.

The goals and objectives can also differ in important ways. Support groups' goals and objectives are more specific and short term than those of self-help groups. The educational component drives the objectives and strategies for support groups, whereas self-help groups tend to stay focused on mutual assistance and are more peer facilitated.

The major differences between the two can be found in the structure for the groups. Many support groups are time bound, in that there are a specific number of sessions. Self-help groups tend to not have a specific number of sessions and can continue for many years. Many support groups described in the literature are closed, and new members are not added. Self-help groups, for the most part, are open groups with members leaving and new members constantly added. Another structural difference is the curriculum for support groups can be formal, written, and followed. This structure makes the group more like an academic course. Self-help groups tend to either not have a curriculum or to develop one in response to members' needs specific for that group.

It can be confusing to try to distinguish between support and self-help groups as there are numerous similarities.

Similarities between support and self-help groups include paying attention to emotions, providing a source of social support, imparting information and guidance, emphasizing similarities among members, and having an underlying theme that provides evidence of commonalities among members. Both kinds of groups recognize that the *emotional content* is very important, even when the primary focus is on providing information. Considerable attention is given to helping members sort through conflicting feelings and expressing them, providing a venue for catharsis, and giving encouragement and support for difficult feelings.

Social support has been found to be beneficial for people's feelings of hope, well-being, and efficacy. The quality of interpersonal relations and social support does much to assist people in coping with disease and conditions, and both groups recognize its importance. This is one reason why these groups tend to be homogeneous around the disease or condition.

Both types of groups provide information and guidance. This is one of the therapeutic factors that members find helpful in all types of groups, and support and self-help groups have it as a major focus.

Members maintain their uniqueness while searching for similarities. The emphasis is on similarities around a common concern. As in any group, situations and individuals differ, but similarities tend to be more easily discernible in self-help groups, and members begin to look for these similarities from the first session.

It seems to be therapeutic for members to actively interact with other members who have benefited from being in the group and dealing with the problem or concern. Seeing others who have been in similar circumstances and hearing how they coped or dealt with the situation promotes hope and provides encouragement.

Universality is a therapeutic factor and appears to be strong in support and self-help groups. There is a conscious search for common underlying themes to unite members. A kind of "we are all in this together" attitude reduces isolation and helps form supportive connections.

Support and self-help groups allow members to try new behaviors and skills, encourage them, cheer them if they are successful, and support them if they are not. This support encourages members to continue trying, modifying, and changing until they are successful. Members learn that goal setting and achievement is an ongoing process and that failure is not the worst thing that can happen—giving up is.

## DESCRIPTION OF PSYCHOEDUCATIONAL SUPPORT GROUPS

Psychoeducational support groups are defined as having

- A strong and formal educational component
- A trained group leader
- A specific number of sessions
- The tendency to be a closed rather than an open group
- A unifying theme and purpose
- Structure and direction

The main goals for psychoeducational support groups are the following:

- To provide information and guidance about the disease, condition, or circumstance
- To empower and encourage members to obtain control over and improve the quality of their lives, relationships, and self-acceptance
- To provide an emotional support system that decreases alienation and isolation, moderates despair, and increases hopefulness and personal responsibility
- To help members derive a greater sense of joy and satisfaction from life as it is with all of its barriers, constraints, setbacks, and disappointments
- To practice and learn new ways of behaving and relating

A major responsibility for the leader is to learn about the disease, condition, or circumstance, or to locate other professionals who can provide members with needed information. A review of the literature is essential, and it is suggested that you get in the habit of searching the literature for available information.

You must decide how you will impart this information as well, and should follow guidelines provided in Chapter 5. You need to know enough about the condition to facilitate groups even when the in-depth knowledge comes from an outsider who will probably attend only one or two meetings.

## GUIDELINES FOR STRUCTURING LEARNING

The primary guidelines are to

- Emphasize education and therapeutic alternatives
- Teach members how to relieve anxiety and stress
- Identify needed lifestyle changes
- Teach behavioral steps to achieve these changes
- Provide emotional support.

### *Emphasize Education*

Members probably do not have sufficient and accurate information about their conditions. They may not have encountered the circumstance before and have no idea what are expected behaviors or feelings. If they are dealing with an acute or chronic illness, they may have little knowledge about the etiological factors, expected treatment, or potential outcomes. If the group members are family members of someone who is ill, they need this information in order to best care for and react to the illness. The leader should obtain reading materials and a list of questions about the condition; talk with a professional about optimum treatment, as well as about what the individual can do to help him- or herself; and/or secure the services of someone to teach a session on these topics.

Anxiety and stress often contribute to the condition, illness, or circumstance. Stress reduces immunity, thereby giving rise to infections; can increase blood pressure and constriction of the arteries; and increases muscle tension, leading to pain, such as lower back pain and headaches. Relaxation moderates reactions to stress, reduces anxiety, and allows the individual to feel more in control. The sample psychoeducational self-help program in this chapter focuses on stress reduction.

Teaching members the benefits of life changes, such as diet, exercise, work habits, and use of leisure, is another task for the leader. Understanding the effects of their present lifestyle and setting reasonable goals for changes can improve their attitudes as well as their physical health. A leader needs to be knowledgeable in these areas.

## Emotional Expression

Self-help groups are developed around a problem, condition, or concern: Something is awry or wrong. Whatever the situation, intense feelings usually are aroused. These feelings can be openly expressed and dealt with in self-help groups. Facilitating expression of feelings is a primary goal for these groups.

There are conditions, characteristics, and events that contribute to increased potential for stress when we are faced with a life condition over which we have little or no control. These risk factors range from manageable to unmanageable, and differ in their extent and intensity—that is, you may be able to tolerate more of a particular factor than others, or you may be prone to responding to even a slight presence of a factor where others can accept and deal with more of the same factor.

The factors associated with increased potential for uncomfortable stress are categorized as existential, work related, stress management skills, negative stress management behaviors, personal characteristics, and uncontrollable events. Examples of each are provided in Table 12.1.

## BACKGROUND FOR PSYCHOEDUCATIONAL SUPPORT GROUPS

A review of literature from 1997 to 2002 on support groups, revealed a considerable number of articles on studies that were labeled specifically as psychoeducational support groups. These studies were on a wide variety of conditions and circumstances that were conducted for children, adolescents, and adults. For purposes of discussion, these studies are categorized as support groups for medical conditions, caretakers, families, psychiatric conditions, life transitions, and trauma.

It is not unreasonable to conclude that the value of psychoeducation is perceived for many conditions and circumstances. A brief description of the literature follows, and readers are encouraged to read the full text, especially for those conditions of interest either personally or professionally.

### Medical Conditions

Many local daily newspapers provide a listing of available support groups in their regions, and many of these are focused on medical conditions. In addition, many physicians' offices and hospitals have literature and announcements about support groups they sponsor. There seems to be a recognition that psychoeducational support groups can make a difference in the recovery and treatment of medical conditions whether they are acute and short term, such as surgery for cancer, or chronic and long term, such as Parkinson's disease.

Roberts, Piper, Denny, and Cuddeback (1997) worked with young adults who were diagnosed with cancer. The psychoeducational support group component was designed to help members accept and adjust to the diagnosis. Topics

TABLE 12.1

Stress Risk Factors

| Categories | Examples |
| --- | --- |
| Existential/spiritual | Lack of purpose in life<br>Unclear, unattainable goals<br>Conflicting values<br>Confused beliefs |
| Work elated | Boring tasks<br>Conflict with coworkers<br>Conflict with boss<br>External pressure to do more, succeed, etc.<br>Ambiguous or uncertain environment<br>Responsibility without authorization<br>Inadequate resources to get the job done (e.g., time, equipment, personnel)<br>Feeling unappreciated or devalued<br>Confused lines of authority<br>Multiple bosses |
| Inadequate stress | Rigidity versus flexibility in attitude |
| Management skills | Refusal to change or seek new ways to cope<br>Neglecting emotional support systems<br>Poor health management and habits; neglect (e.g., lack of exercise, eating on the run) |
| Negative stress | Alcohol abuse |
| Management behaviors | Drug abuse<br>Overeating<br>Undereating<br>Frequent temper tantrums |
| Personal characteristics | Need for perfectionism<br>Pessimistic in outlook<br>Sense of overresponsibility for others' well-being<br>Suppressing, denying, or repressing emotions |
| Uncontrolled or uncontrollable events | The economy<br>Bad weather (e.g., hurricanes)<br>Taxes<br>Accidents<br>Death<br>Severe or chronic illness |

such as fertility, finances, health and well-being, and relationships were addressed.

Karp, Brown, Sullivan, and Massie (1999) conducted a study with women who had a high genetic risk for breast cancer and were considering the possibility of prophylactic mastectomy. This was a pilot study to determine the usefulness of a psychoeducational support group with this population. The authors concluded that such groups are cost-effective and beneficial when used with individual counseling.

Payne, Lundberg, Brennan, and Holland (1997) studied the effectiveness of a modified thematic counseling model for patients successfully treated for soft tissue sarcoma. The results showed that members' feelings of isolation, anger, depression, and anxiety significantly decreased, and self-confidence increased.

## Caretakers

This category of psychoeducational support groups is focused on the people who must provide extensive and long-term everyday living assistance for another person who is not expected to recover full function or to significantly improve. It is now recognized that there are many physical, emotional, and psychological impacts on caregivers, and that few people understand the demands that their caregiving exerts on their well-being, or how to cope with the many uncomfortable feelings that can emerge.

Bultz, Speca, Brasker, Geggie, and Page (2000) conducted a pilot study on the effects of a brief psychoeducational support group for partners of women who had early-stage breast cancer. Assessment at pre-, post-, and 3-month follow-up showed that the intervention helped both the patient and the partner; there was less mood disturbance for both and greater support and relationship satisfaction.

Cummings, Long, Peterson-Hazan, and Harrison (1999) present a model for caretakers of people who have early-stage Alzheimer's. The model was developed from a study on the effectiveness of a psychoeducational support group for this audience. Posttest measures showed that the group intervention could assist caregivers to be better prepared for the emotional and physical effects of the caregiving role.

## Families

Although caregivers are usually family members, a separate category is described for families, since the psychoeducational groups described here are for the family members of someone who does not need the extensive care provided by caregivers. Some are groups to help family members understand the condition, treatment options, the impact of the condition on functioning and relationships, supportive strategies that family members can provide, and the process for recovery. Other groups are conducted to improve the quality of family life and to help family members learn new coping skills.

Lefley (2001) describes the psychoeducational support groups conducted by the University of Miami–Jackson Memorial Medical Center for families of people who have severe psychiatric illnesses and are also criminal offenders. Members are referred by the hospital, other mental health facilities, or private psychiatrists.

Morgan and Hensley (1998) conducted a study to determine the efficacy of a psychoeducational support group for helping working mothers manage their roles. The group was designed to reduce stress, provide social support, and achieve different cognitions about self.

Arledge (1997) studied the effectiveness of a psychoeducational support group intervention for young children of alcoholics. These children were ages 6 to 12 with a parent who attended a private alcohol and drug treatment center. Follow-up results showed that the intervention to provide education and support was effective, and that these results continued to have a positive effect on the children's lives.

## Psychiatric Conditions

Psychoeducational support groups are provided for a wide range of diagnosed psychiatric conditions for the person, caregivers, and/or family members. These groups are usually designed to provide information about the condition, treatment, and how to cope with expected behaviors. Evidence is increasing that these psychoeducational support groups can make a significant difference in stress levels, coping, functioning, and relapse prevention.

Misri, Kostaras, Fox, and Kostaras (2000) conducted an experimental study on the effectiveness of a psychoeducational support group and a control group for women suffering from postpartum depression, and their partners. Results showed that members of the support group had a significant decrease in depressive symptoms and other conditions.

In their analysis of an integrated therapy program for schizophrenic patients that included a psychoeducational group, Vallian-Fernandez and colleagues (2001) found a significant difference between the experimental group and the control group on clinical status, stress level, family functioning, coping styles, and problem-solving skills. The improvement of the experimental group members persisted through the 9-month follow-up period.

## Life Conditions and Transitions

This category of psychoeducational support groups incorporates a wide range of topics for all ages. Topics such as grandparents raising grandchildren, dating violence prevention for teens, gay men, menopausal women, and multiracial children are in the following review. The theme for some groups is prevention and preparation for life's tasks, while for other groups the theme is remedial to learn how to cope with one's condition as it exists. This category is very broad in terms of topics and audiences.

Caluza (2000) described the 12-session curriculum used for psychoeducational support groups for multiracial adolescents, and the qualitative study used to derive the themes for the curriculum. Themes include ethnic identity, physical appearance, family, socialization and marginalization experiences, historical context, and contact with other multiracial groups.

Diegel (1999) conducted a qualitative study on the efficacy of a dating violence prevention psychoeducational support group on a sample of high school female students. Eight core themes were derived: healing wounds, belonging, trust, holistic involvement, education, increased awareness, empowerment, and appreciation.

## Trauma

This last category begins a bridge to counseling or therapy as trauma victims may often receive these more in-depth services. However, there are also psychoeducational support groups for victims and family members. These groups provide an educational component to give information about potential physical, psychological, and emotional effects; and to guide members in understanding how to cope with their reactions. These support groups can reduce isolation and alienation that can result from being a trauma victim. Interpersonal relationships can be impaired, and both victims and their families can be educated and supported about challenges and changes that will result in certain behaviors and relationships.

Zamanian and Adams (1997) described a 16-week group for sexually abused boys that incorporated the eight goals of the Specialized Treatment and Rehabilitation Service program developed by the community health department of Merced County California. The program uses exercises, art work and role-play, and discussion of the topic of the week.

Mara and Winton (1990) described a parent support group for parents who had a sexually abused child. Topics presented and discussed were child sexuality, normal child development, stress management, managing difficult feelings such as guilt, behavior modification, and problem solving. An evaluation by the authors found that there was a decrease in the associated children's dysfunctional behaviors.

## DESIGNING PSYCHOEDUCATIONAL SUPPORT GROUPS

There are a few general guidelines for designing psychoeducational support groups for all target audiences regardless of age, gender, condition, disease, or circumstance. The guidelines presented here are divided into two categories: factors for planning and factors for facilitation.

Factors for Planning

These factors include the following:

- Understanding major background factors of the target audience
- Sensitivity to the participants' emotional states
- The role of fear
- The impact of a sense of personal inadequacy and failure
- Loss and grief issues
- Dealing with feelings of powerlessness and loss of control

Major background factors are demographics, such as age, gender, educational level, and occupation. These factors play major roles in decisions about content, instructional strategies, and other activities—for example, you will want to gear your content to the lowest reading level of participants, since some materials will require reading. Presenting material that is too advanced or too elementary can alienate your audience.

Background factors can play a part in deciding the sequence for material, illustrations, and examples, terminology, and many other instructional strategies. If members are to learn, apply, and retain the material, the leader has to present it in the most effective way. Knowing your audience helps.

The emotional state of members is important, because anxiety, shame, embarrassment, and other emotions can interfere with learning and participation. Members may feel stigmatized, socially alienated, and angry that they are singled out to carry the burden of the disease, condition, or circumstance. The leader's sensitivity to members' emotional states can play a major role in establishing safety and trust, facilitating learning, and members' willingness to self-disclose.

Fear can play a role in the quantity and quality of members' participation. Members can bring fears to the group about any or all of the following:

- Potential and possible personal death
- An inability to care for self and having to rely on others
- Financial concerns
- Loss of function
- Deterioration of the quality of life
- The negative impact on relationships

The fears may not be openly disclosed, but that does not lessen their impact on group members. These fears are in addition to the following common fears about group experiences that many members bring to the group:

- Being excluded or rejected by other members and/or the group leader
- Losing control

- Getting worse by being in contact with sick, or emotionally disturbed people
- Being attacked
- Catching other members' emotions
- Losing individuality
- Lacking of sufficient boundaries for the group

There are many fears, and all members will have some level of most of these fears, even if they do not speak of them. Leaders need to be aware that the fears exist and take steps to address them.

Some group members will perceive their disease, condition, or circumstance as a personal failure *or* inadequacy on their part. This is an irrational reaction that is buried in the unconscious; incorporated from messages received in childhood from parents, religious teachings, or the culture; and/or a part of their self-perception that they should have prevented this from happening.

This perception can be a belief for children, parents, and immature adults who have not developed to the point where they clearly understand their boundaries and acceptance that there are forces beyond their control. These people believe that they can and should control what happens to them. Group leaders will have to choose their words carefully to prevent any hint of blame or criticism of members for the disease, condition, or circumstance. The art of group leadership is especially important in addressing this concern.

Loss and grief will be large issues in support groups, as all members will be facing them on some level. There can be, among many others,

- Loss of innocence
- Deterioration of function
- Reduction in quality of life
- Actual loss of a physical part of the person
- Loss of some quality or trait for the person
- A realization of impending doom and/or death
- Loss of meaningful connections to others
- A sense of vulnerability, as safety has been compromised
- A realization of helplessness and powerlessness to help or to save oneself

These feelings can be intense for members, and much of their emotional reactions can be traced to dealing with grief and loss.

The overwhelming feelings of powerlessness and loss of control have to be addressed before members can move on and start to take action. This depressive state can be real depression or it can be a realistic appraisal of group members' inability to return to a previous state, to change themselves or what happened to them, and to significantly impact their future around whatever brought them to group.

Group leaders need to expect that the depressive state will manifest itself in different ways, such as increased activity and acting out, apathy, or an inability to connect to others. It could be helpful to bring these feelings out at some point and make them visible for everyone—that is, the leader could say that some people might feel powerless and a lack of control when faced with the situations of group members, and the leader could open the floor for members who want to connect or verbalize such feelings. Just do not ignore them.

### Factors for Facilitation

Leaders can take pains to promote certain factors. They are facilitative for both individual members and for the group as a whole. These factors can work to

- Reduce guilt and shame feelings
- Increase connectedness to others
- Provide a reality check
- Mobilize helpful but unrecognized strengths
- Help members recognize stress and its impact
- Show and guide members in planning for the future
- Teach members a self-care focus rather than having a self-absorbed one

These factors are incorporated in the helpful group factors described in Chapter 4.

Members can have considerable feelings of shame and guilt for needing care, not being perfect or healthy, using family resources, and so forth. Never underestimate the importance and impact of these feelings, since they do affect behavior, reactions, and even healing. Although the primary focus for psychoeducational support groups is education, the emotional state of members plays an important role. It is helpful when group leaders remain aware of the possibility that members have guilt and shame feelings, recognize the indirect ways these can be expressed, help members identify commonalities and feelings, and work to reduce the negative impact these feelings can have.

The importance of interpersonal connections in assisting people to heal, get better, remain hopeful, and effectively cope cannot be overestimated. For example, a longitudinal study of more than 7,000 people over 9 years found that the "common denominator that most often led to good health and long life [was] the amount of social support a person enjoys" (Blai, 1989, p. 261). The report goes on to note that people who had strong ties to other people were better able to stay well.

The psychoeducational support group can be one source for making meaningful connections and can help members recognize and/or build other sources of support. This is accomplished when group leaders identify commonalities, promote interactions among group members, give constructive feedback, and model and foster altruism.

Group members are helpful in providing each other with a reality check. Although members are concerned with their personal situation, they are also able to see what other members are discounting, overlooking, or minimizing. The reason for the support group can be overwhelming for some members, which can make it difficult for them to see unrecognized and unused resources, understand what outside resources are available, and focus on hopeful factors. Other group members can be more realistic about someone else and provide a needed reality check.

Mobilizing unrecognized strengths of members can do much to instill hope. This would be a realistic hope, not a fantasy, that all will be well. When people are in a crisis, pain, or lack sufficient information, they tend to focus more on deficits than strengths. Psychoeducational support groups are a rich source for helping members to identify their strengths.

Capitalizing on strengths is more effective and satisfying than trying to remediate deficiencies. Further, many members' perceived deficiencies are a part of what brings them to the group, and little can be done to remedy these deficits. Members can be taught to focus on what they can do or be, not what is lost or not possible under the current circumstances.

Most everyone accepts that stress exists and that it can have a negative impact on physical, emotional, psychological, and relational functioning. Indeed, some physical conditions that bring members to psychoeducational groups have a strong stress-related component. Conditions such as hypertension, asthma, substance abuse, and heart conditions are some examples.

The group can be a place where members allow themselves to become aware of the impact that stress is having on them, learn ways to reduce and cope with stress, and practice relaxation techniques. Staying in a state of tension does not aid recovery, nor does it help in everyday living and relating.

On the other hand, there are constructive ways to handle stress, and some members may have mastered that process. Not only can the leader recognize this as a personal strength for those members but the members can be models to help fellow group members learn new ways of coping with stress.

Many, if not most, members in psychoeducational support groups will be stuck in the disease, condition, or circumstance, and will find it difficult to visualize their futures. The group can be an excellent resource to introduce short- and long-term planning. Members can learn more about the limitations of what brought them to the group and how to overcome or compensate for these constraints.

Members can also gain hope, optimism, and determination that can be valuable in recovery, compensating, and/or making life decisions. There is considerable evidence that these mental states play an important role in the quality of life, physical and psychological health, and connectedness to self and others.

Reducing self-absorption and promoting a self-care focus may need more time and effort than what a psychoeducational group can provide. It is not realistic to think that the group will bring about a deep characterological change for the member who is very self-absorbed. However, all members can become more aware of how their self-absorbed behaviors and attitudes can negatively affect their relationships through interactions among group members and through feedback from members and the leader.

Although they may seem similar, self-care is vastly different from self-absorption, and group leaders are encouraged to read the literature on self-psychology and narcissism to gain a fuller understanding of self-absorption. Self-care requires an understanding of psychological boundaries, the limits for taking responsibility for the care of others, and an ability to reach out to others when needed. In other words, you do not exploit others, feel that others exist to serve you, manipulate and/or seek to control others; nor do you let others do these things to you.

Following are some exercises that could be useful in a support group. This presentation is for an adult group but can be modified for adolescents and children.

### Exercise 12.1. My Existential/Spiritual Self

**Objectives:** To increase awareness of personal involvement with existential/spiritual issues; to identify existential/spiritual strengths.

**Materials:** A sheet of paper with a large circle drawn on it for each member; markers or pencils; glue sticks; magazines or catalogues; copies of Handout 12.A, which lists the following categories:

- Lack of purpose in life
- Encounter(s) with death
- Present conflicts in values
- A few awe-inspiring experiences
- Present status of religious beliefs
- Extent of major commitments
- Difficult choices being faced
- Presently held doubts

**Time:** 60 to 90 minutes.

**Age/education:** Sixth-grade reading level and above.

**Number of participants:** Works best with a group of 10 or fewer members but can be used with a larger group of 20 to 25.

**Preparation:** Gather materials; reproduce Handout 12.A.

**Procedure:** Explain the focus for this exercise—existential/spiritual issues. Include these points: healthy people realize that there is a continuing search for truth and purpose in life; know that values must be examined; commit to causes and services; seek hope and meaning; experience despair; define faith as acceptance of the unknown and unknowable.

For some, religion is the source of spirituality. This exercise puts spiritual life in focus and identifies potential spiritual concerns that may contribute to stress, as well as strengths that can be used.

Pass out materials and explain to members that they are to write words or phrases associated with each of the categories on Handout 11.1. Next, they are to place symbols for each of the categories in the circle, forming a seal. They are free to draw the symbols or to find pictures in the magazines and catalogs that symbolize the categories.

Allow 20 to 30 minutes for completion of the seals. Depending on the time available, sharing of the seals can be done in the entire group or in small groups. Seals can be posted on the wall. Allow enough time for each person to describe his or her seal.

**Processing:** The focus for processing emphasizes unused spiritual resources. Ask if any surprises emerged, new awarenesses, remembered satisfactions, or directions for the future. Members can write their answers down so that they can refer back to them. Writing also ensures that each member has an opportunity to make associations.

## Existential/Spiritual Risk Factors

Lack of purpose in life:

Encounter(s) with death:

Present conflicts in values:

A few awe-inspiring experiences:

Present status of religious beliefs:

Extent of major commitments:

Difficult choices being faced:

Presently held doubts:

**Handout 12.A Existential/Spiritual Risk Factors.** *Permission is granted to photocopy for group use.*

## Exercise 12.2. Demands and Rewards

**Objectives:** To increase awareness of demands or requirements placed on you and another person in a relationship; to make explicit your expectations/needs/desires for rewards from this person; to develop an awareness of the other's expectations/needs/desires for rewards from you; to assess the stress factor.

**Materials:** Pencil or pen for each member; one or two sheets of paper for each member.

**Time:** 60 to 90 minutes.

**Age/education:** Ninth-grade reading level and above.

**Number of participants:** 20 to 25.

**Preparation:** Gather materials.

**Procedure:** Introduce the exercise by telling members the objectives for the exercise. Ask them to select one relationship with which to work. This may be a relationship that is satisfying or one that is troublesome. A neutral or indifferent relationship will not produce much awareness or learning. Ask participants to write the person's name or role at the top of the page. Ask members to write their responses to the following items. Allow time for them to write down their responses:

1. Write all words or phrases that come to mind when you think of this person.
2. List the person's negative traits or qualities.
3. List his or her positive qualities.
4. Identify demands or requirements this person places on or expects from you.
5. Label the items in step 4 **E** if the demand or requirement is explicit and **I** if it is implicit.
6. Identify demands or requirements you expect of this person.
7. In step 6, label the items **E** if explicit and **I** if implicit.
8. List the rewards you expect from the person and estimate the percentage of time you receive each.
9. Review what you have written and write a paragraph describing the stress you experience in the relationship due to the other person's implicit demands and requirements.

**Processing:** Help members identify implicit demands and encourage them to formulate steps to make these explicit, if the reward would be worth the effort. Members can be encouraged to decide how they can let go of unrewarding demands or behavior, thereby reducing stress.

Exercise 12.3. Emotional Risk Factors

**Objectives:** To increase awareness of the wide variety of feelings experienced; to identify major blocks to feeling expressions; to enhance expression and awareness of pleasant feelings.

**Materials:** A sheet of paper with a circle drawn on it for each participant; crayons, felt-tip markers, or oil pastels in sufficient number so that each member has access to a variety of colors; a blank sheet of paper for each member; pens or pencils.

**Time:** 60 to 90 minutes.

**Age/education:** Fourth-grade reading level and above.

**Number of participants:** 20 to 25.

**Preparation:** Gather materials; organize room.

**Procedure:** Introduce the exercise by telling members that healthy people feel deeply, are sensitive to feelings in themselves and in others, are able to experience a wide range of feelings, and are able to access their feelings easily. Sometimes even healthy people try to block or deny unpleasant feelings, cannot find words to express their feelings, confuse experiencing a feeling with acting on it, or become so mired in a feeling that they block out other feelings.

Distribute the blank sheet of paper and pens and ask participants to mentally divide the sheet into four sections. In the upper left section (#1), ask them to list all unpleasant feelings they experienced in the previous week. Allow time for them to construct their lists. In the upper right section (#2), ask them to list all pleasant feelings they experienced in the same time period. After both lists are completed, have them put the sheet aside.

Distribute the paper with a circle and markers. Ask members to examine their lists of feelings and to select a color for each. They are to use the color to fill in the circle in the shape and to the extent that they experienced the feeling. For example, if sadness was the strongest and most persistent feeling, they could use a dark blue or gray to color in a large cloud shape in the circle. Members should look at both lists and make choices before beginning to fill in the circle.

When the circles are finished, have members show theirs and describe what feelings the colors illustrate.

Return to the sheet with the lists. In the lower right section (#3), have members list steps they can take to decrease the level and frequency of the unpleasant feelings. In the lower right section (#4), have members list what they can do to increase the level and frequency of pleasant feelings.

**Processing:** Allow time for sharing and focus processing on awareness that has emerged during the exercise.

# Chapter 13

# Therapy-Related Psychoeducational Groups

Major Topics

*Knowledge and Science Factors*
  Planning and forming the group

*Art and Skills Factors*
  Members' factors, such as emotional intensity
  Members' attitudes and behaviors

## INTRODUCTION

Many therapies now include a component for psychoeducational groups where participants receive information specific for the condition that is under treatment along with the other treatment modalities. This approach is used in both outpatient and inpatient settings. Examples of this use include the following:

* Relapse prevention—Sandahl and Ronnbers, 1990
* Dual diagnosis—Pressman and Brook, 1999
* Obsessive-compulsive disorder—Fals-Stewart and Lucente, 1994
* Wife abuse—Pressman and Sheps, 1994
* Agoraphobia and panic disorder—Belfer, Munoz, Schachter, and Levendusky, 1995
* Traumatized women—Lubin and Johnson, 1997

These are but a few of the many conditions and treatment programs that incorporate psychoeducational groups as part of an array of modalities for intervention and treatment. These groups are characterized by

- Having a specific focus and theme
- An emphasis on information relative to the goal
- Narrowly defined goals
- Homogeneity of group members
- Being time specific or time bound
- Opportunities to consult with other professionals treating the same person on a more regular basis

## REMEDIATION

One basic characteristic that can have an impact on the group and the leader is the remedial focus for the group, even when the group is categorized as prevention, such as relapse prevention. Participants have a condition, problem, or concern that is negatively affecting their lives. This condition can be physical, emotional, relational, or any combination of these. It is important to remember that what affects one part of a person's life generally has implications for other parts of his or her life. This interaction is one reason why planning groups for a target population with a common concern cannot be entirely pro forma, in that you cannot readily predict the needs of a particular group or for a particular group member. However, there can be some certainty for the target group, as they will have some commonalities, which can be very helpful for the group leader.

The remedial nature of the group is one commonality that is important. It is considerably harder to overcome a deficit, weakness, ignorance, or the like, than it is to learn something new, such as prevention strategies. In addition, for many of these therapy-associated psychoeducational groups, you are also dealing with members whose basic condition will not change—for example, alcoholism—no matter what the treatment. The group leader must maintain an awareness of the hopelessness for changing the condition and not hold out false hope of overcoming or eliminating it.

The condition also should not be ignored because of its hopeless nature. Although the tendency may be to want to move beyond what cannot be fixed and focus on what can be done, care should be taken not to move too fast. Group members need to know that the leader understands much about their condition and its impact before they can trust that what the leader is trying to do will be beneficial for them. Leaders need to remember that group members' goals may differ from leaders' goals, but members' goals will determine their behavior and the success or failure of the group.

## EMOTIONAL INTENSITY

Another commonality may be the emotional intensity of members and the defense mechanisms used to mask this intensity. Members will differ in their emotions and in their intensity, and each will use a variety of defense mechanisms to try and manage them. However, the group leader should expect that members will have many of the following:

- Anger—"Why me?"
- Resentment—"It isn't fair."
- Despair—"I'll never get better."
- Fear—"I'll be abandoned and/or destroyed."
- Envy—"Others are not more worthy than I am."
- Rage—"I'll make someone pay (suffer) for this."
- Dread—"I won't be able to cope."
- Shame—"I am so flawed and I cannot do anything about it."
- Humiliation—"I can't look out for myself. I have to be dependent (ask for and take help from others).
- Alienated—"No one can understand what I'm going through."
- Isolated—"No one will be able to tolerate being around me."
- Anxiety—"Can I survive?"

The difficulty for the leader is that these feelings may not be openly expressed, acknowledged, or even in members' awareness. The feelings may be masked, hidden, denied, repressed, and/or expressed in indirect ways. The trust and safety you as the leader can develop is dependent on your understanding of members' feelings and how they are expressed in indirect ways, or are being denied and repressed.

## SIMILARITIES OF MEMBERS

The paradox for members of these psychoeducational groups is that they have similar conditions, issues, concerns, and experiences, but all these can also differ in significant ways. Members may tend to focus on these differences, which will prevent the group from becoming cohesive. Groups become cohesive around similarities and dissolve or fail to become cohesive around differences. Thus, in order to build universality and promote cohesiveness, the leader must seek out and highlight similarities among members.

Leaders need to be aware that similarities are not always evident and observable. Some are subtle and must be teased out from the information that members share. This is where the skill of linking can be important, as the leader can perceive the similarities for two or more members and can speak about them to the group. While members tend to perceive visible similarities, such as age, race, and gender, leaders can become experienced at perceiving deeper and more meaningful similarities, such as values and family of origin experiences.

Differences are important to members, as each wants to be perceived as a unique individual, and leaders must be careful not to forget these individual differences in the effort to highlight similarities. It can be very threatening to some members when the leader does not appear to perceive their differences from other members. However, other members may prefer that the leader view them as similar to other members, as being different means exclusion from the group.

The most obvious similarity is the common problem, issue, concern, or condition that brought members to the group, and this is a good starting point to emphasize similarities. Leaders should not take for granted that members know the rationale for the group. Stating the rationale can emphasize that members are similar in important ways.

## HOMOGENEITY

Many therapeutic groups will be homogeneous around one or more of the following: age, gender, educational level, and other demographics. This homogeneity can be both a strength and a weakness. Members can feel safe when it is evident that they are like other group members. They can have more certainty, assurance, and understanding of other group members. Leaders will find that they do not have to work as hard to show members their similarities. Research tends to show that members in homogeneous groups will have positive feelings about the group quicker than members of heterogeneous groups (Yalom, 1995).

On the other hand, heterogeneous groups tend to have a wider range of resources because members differ. Members can get a variety of perspectives, experiences, and feedback that are not available when members are homogeneous. This is enriching to the group process, and members can increase their self-understanding and understanding of others when this variety is available.

## PLANNING AND FORMING THE GROUP

The process for planning a therapeutic psychoeducational group is almost the same as the planning for other categories. There are a few differences, and these are important:

- The possible direct involvement of other treatment professionals
- The effects of other therapies and/or medication on members

- Reporting responsibilities for the leader
- Outside-group socialization
- Physical, psychological, and emotional states of members
- Effects of the condition on members' functioning

While most of these can be present for one or more members of other types of groups, they differ in that any one or all of them can exist for every member of a therapeutic group. Thus, leaders should plan the group assuming that all members will have a common effect, state, or reaction—for example, to medication, a situation, and so on—around the particular condition that defines the group. There will be individual differences, of course, but leaders need to plan for an overall possibility.

## Other Professionals

Therapeutic psychoeducational groups are likely to be a part of treatment programs for both inpatient and outpatient groups. Treatment programs usually include a variety of modalities, such as medication, individual therapy, group therapy, art therapy, family therapy, and so forth. Even when the condition is medical, such as cancer and heart attacks, there are several treatment modalities involved, and these professionals may be an integral part or have roles in planning the psychoeducational group. The group leader may need to consult with the other professionals and get their input on

- How other treatments may have an effect on members and what these effects are
- What information is essential or critical for members to have
- Characteristics of group members that may be important for the group's functioning
- Expectations for the leader for case management, reporting, and so on

Consulting with other professionals involved in treatment of group members helps to foster a team approach to providing valuable information for planning and conducting the group.

## Other Therapies

It can be very helpful to know and understand what is being provided by other therapies—not so much the content for particular members, which may be confidential, but knowing what areas are being explored. For example, if impulse control is the focus for individual therapy for many group members, the psychoeducational group could have a session on a related topic.

Understanding the purpose, process, and effects of other therapies can help provide a more integrated experience for members of the psychoeducational group. The leader can expand, enhance, compensate, and enrich other therapies through the group experience, but this is unlikely to occur if the psychoeducational group is isolated from members' other therapeutic treatments.

## Reporting Responsibilities

The usual constraints for reporting confidential material may not apply to your therapy psychoeducational group, and you must determine the extent to which they do apply. You have certain reporting responsibilities that should be communicated to group members at the first session. The treatment program, agency, or hospital and/or the lead professional for the treatment team may require reporting of

- Attendance
- Extent of participation
- Major personal issues discussed
- Violations of the facilities' rules and regulations
- Disclosures of illegal acts
- Suspicions of child abuse and child neglect
- Drug and alcohol use
- Violent acts in the group
- Sexual assault or rape
- Harassment
- Stalking behavior
- Threats against staff

These are simply examples for what can be mandated reporting. It is only fair that members understand the limits on what can be kept confidential and what has to be reported.

Reporting responsibilities also include case notes where the group leader has to submit regular reports for each group member and/or for the group session. The facility generally has a format and guidelines for this reporting. An additional concern can be the legal implications for written case notes. Each state can differ in the legal requirements, and group leaders should determine what the legal requirements are for their states. Leaders should be aware that personal notes can be subpoenaed in some states, and these may not remain confidential. A good guideline for case and personal notes is to not write anything you do not wish the client or an open court to read.

## Outside-Group Socializing

Members who socialize outside the group run the risk of becoming a clique and of revealing confidential material. These are two undesirable outcomes, but it may be impossible to prevent outside-group socializing. For example, members from inpatient treatment may live together in the facility and have other shared activities. It would not be reasonable to expect that there would be no outside-group socializing under these circumstances.

The best that a group leader may be able to do is remind members not to discuss group material outside the group, and when socializing or other interactions do take place outside the group, the interaction should be brought back to the group—for example, if two or three members meet for lunch, this would be reported in the next session. Outside-group socializing can foment distrust when it seems secretive, which is why it is important for members to openly acknowledge it.

## Members' States

Each member's physical, psychological, and emotional states are dynamic and can even change by the moment. It is important for the group leader to know in advance the current and/or expected states for each member—for example, members who had recent heart attacks may be expected to have some level of depression; members who are taking tranquilizers may be lethargic; men arrested for spouse abuse may be hypersensitive and angry. These states will have an impact on the process and progress for the group.

Members' states can also impact how much material can be learned and what instructional strategies to use. It does no good to present information if the audience cannot take it in and remember it. It is not helpful to lecture to sleeping or zoned-out members. Choosing an activity or exercise that could produce acting-out behavior, either verbally or physically, is not advisable. These are some of the reasons why a group leader would want to get as much information as possible in advance about expected effects of the condition and treatment in general, and specifically for members attending the group.

## Effects of Medication

Although the effects of medication are associated with the previous section, this factor is listed separately to highlight its importance. Medication can affect members' ability to pay attention, nonverbal behaviors, and concentration. Some effects can be subtle and others can have a major impact. The group leader should learn the expected effects for any usual medication provided for the treatment of a specific condition, as it can have implications for behavior in the group.

It can also be important to understand food and drug interactions, especially if the group allows food and drink during sessions. Food and drink are not recommended, but some group leaders do permit them. The interaction of food and medications is often overlooked. Group leaders should not provide anything that could produce an adverse reaction with known medications. It may be too much to expect leaders to know about other medications and food interactions, as these can be varied. But knowing this for the specific treatment medications for the particular condition could be helpful.

### Effects of the Condition

Understanding what and how members are affected by the condition are essential when planning therapy psychoeducational groups. This understanding includes a literature review to get as much comprehensive information as possible. It is probably not wise to totally rely on your experience, even when it is extensive. It is also not advisable to think that you know the effects because you too experienced the condition. New information is constantly emerging and can be helpful in guiding selection of material to present, instructional strategies, and other planning. When you rely heavily on your personal experiences for guidance, you run the risk of omitting relevant material and using only anecdotal evidence that may not be fully understood. There are some similarities among people with the same experiences, but there can be significant differences—for example, gender or age could produce different effects.

Attention should be given to as many areas of functioning as possible. It is not sufficient to just know some physical effects; it is much more helpful to also know the psychological, emotional, and relational effects, since they can play a major role in members' needs, extent and kind of involvement in the group, ability to attend to and learn the material, developing relations in the group, interactions among members, and other group dynamics.

## MEMBERS' ATTITUDES AND BEHAVIORS
## THAT CAN AFFECT THE GROUP

Members of therapy-related psychoeducational groups may have some characteristics, behaviors, and attitudes that will impact the leader and the group's functioning in important ways:

• Self-absorbed behaviors and attitudes
• Less reaching out and connecting to others
• Easily triggered defenses
• Intense fears of contamination, loss of control, incompetence, and shame
• Displaced hostility
• Depressed state, resignation, and giving up

These characteristics, behaviors, and attitudes can make it more difficult for the leader to form a therapeutic alliance and can negatively impact the amount of information that members can incorporate, learn, and retain. The leader who is aware of these potential characteristics, behaviors, and attitudes is better able to address them, cope when they emerge, and be more secure in his or her ability to manage them in a constructive way.

## Self-Absorption

The nature of the condition and the client's personal level of development can interact to produce more self-absorbed behaviors and attitudes. Even members who have an age-appropriate level of developed narcissism may regress to an earlier level when faced with the condition that brought them to treatment—for example, people faced with a life-threatening condition, such as a heart attack or cancer, could regress to a more dependent state and become more self-absorbed. This self-absorption can

- Make it more difficult for members to be interested in the group and other members
- Prevent emergence of therapeutic factors such as altruism
- Impair, or make difficult, constructive interactions among members and with the leader
- Produce more acting-out behavior
- Increase resistance
- Block the ability and willingness to learn new material

These issues can be significant forces in the group, and there will not be much the leader can do to effectively address them. It takes time to build a therapeutic relationship, and the psychoeducational group usually does not last long enough to address these intense and important items. There are other reasons why the leader has few options, but it is important that leaders neither blame themselves for not being effective nor blame members for being self-absorbed.

What are some self-absorbed behaviors and attitudes?

- Wanting to be considered as unique and special
- Attention-seeking behaviors
- Admiration-seeking behaviors
- Lack of empathy
- Entitlement attitude
- Grandiosity, arrogance, and contemptuous attitude
- Everything seen and related to in terms of self

Self-absorption is differentiated from self-care by its intensity and frequency. In addition, the self-absorbed person has a cluster of these behaviors and attitudes, not just one or two of them. A self-care focus is expected and understandable for adults, just as self-absorption is for children. This is known as age-appropriate narcissism. However, the self-absorption of children and adolescents is not expected to be manifested in adult behavior and attitudes.

## Reaching Out and Connecting

Group interactions and relationships are important indices of the quality of the group's process. Process is defined as the here-and-now interactions among group members and with the leader. Although the primary focus for psychoeducational groups is on presenting and learning information, it is also important to attend to the emotional and relational components. Indeed, the feelings that group members bring to the group, past and present associations for these, and how these feelings are expressed and received can play major roles in the effectiveness of the group and the positive impact on group members.

Interactions among group members that are genuine, respectful of differences, caring, and constructive are enriching to the group and to members. Positive interactions promote self-learning, self-reflection, and self-understanding while reducing defensiveness, resistance, isolation, and alienation. Thus, it can be vitally important for the group leader to conduct the group in ways that foster interactions among members. Group members can be valuable resources for each other, and group leaders should plan to capitalize on these.

## Easily Triggered Defenses

Members of therapeutic psychoeducational groups can be emotionally fragile, and their defenses can be easily triggered. They are confronted with

- Loss of control, or an inability to control major parts of their lives
- Powerlessness
- Helplessness
- A realization of their mortality
- Dependence, whereas before there was some or considerable independence
- Shame, embarrassment, or humiliation
- Fear of the unknown
- Ambiguity and uncertainty

These are both internal and external assaults on the self, and the usual response is to defend against them. Leaders must realize that members may be constantly on edge and alert for potential attacks from either direction. Some members may be so well defended that they never let down their guard.

Leaders should recognize the defense and *leave it alone*. There is not enough time to build the necessary therapeutic relationship that will enable members to feel safe, trust each other, or trust the leader sufficiently to lower or explore the defense. It is there to protect the member, and you are well advised to leave it in place. The most you can hope for is that there will be some moderation of defenses for some members.

## Intense Fears

It is not unusual for group members to have intense fears that

• They will catch something from other members that will make them worse
• The sessions will be constructed so as to make them lose control of their emotions or their resistance to self-disclosure, or the leader will push them to lose control
• Other members and the leader will perceive them as incompetent, or their incompetence will be revealed
• They will be shamed

These fears are intensified because members can feel emotionally fragile and worried that they will not be able to maintain their defenses.

Leaders cannot relieve these intense fears. The more you try to show members that they are needlessly worrying, the more anxious they may become. Expecting members to trust you because you are a trustworthy person is an exercise in futility. It is not about you; it is about them. The best you can do is be yourself, make empathic responses, block other members' aggression, and foster expression of feelings. It takes time to build trust, and your understanding of their fears, conditions, and emotions helps to develop trust. Many members will not be able to reduce or eliminate their intense fears because of other longstanding deep-seated issues.

## Displaced Hostility

Fears, anxiety, other emotional states, transference, and unfinished business can play roles in how members handle their anger and hostility related to their condition and to other aspects of their lives. How other treatment professionals interact and relate with them, insurance and HMO policies and procedures, the treatment facility, and other external forces also contribute to displaced hostility. Leaders must remain aware that the hostility directed at them or at other members may be the outcome of that member's external and internal experiencing, not the current experience or the people who are present.

It can be very disconcerting when members are hostile, attack you, remain detached, and/or cannot be satisfied with anything or anyone. After all, you are cordial, warm, caring, and all that good stuff. You also are trying to be helpful, and that should be obvious and accepted in the spirit with which it is given. You may even be expecting hostile behavior but thought that it would occur in the second stage of group development. However, there are times when it is present from the first moment.

Your initial response may be to try harder to please, or to become defensive, or to go on the offensive. When you realize that you may respond in these ways, it will be more helpful to reflect on whether the hostile behavior and attitudes are being displaced on you and/or other members. This realization can do much to allow you to stop trying so hard to please, since this cannot be done; to be less defensive or not defensive at all, since you are not in the wrong; and to not go on the offensive. As a matter of fact, it is never acceptable for you as the leader to go on the offensive.

Once you realize you are experiencing displaced hostility, you can take some constructive steps. However, you must also realize that

- It is not your role or responsibility to make members feel better
- You cannot take care of outside-group concerns
- You are not suffering as they are, and they are aware of the difference
- You can only present; you cannot force acceptance or learning

The most constructive step is to not take the hostility as a personal attack or failure. It is also helpful to stick to your plan and at the same time be empathic and understanding of members' conditions, concerns, and fears. Modeling how to contain and manage anxiety, refusing to retaliate, and continuing to show caring, warmth, and acceptance can help members learn other ways to respond to hostility. Most displaced hostility will be eliminated by these actions and attitudes.

## Depressed State, Resignation, and Giving Up

Some members may be resigned to what they know or think is their fate. They do not have hope, and without hope there is no reason to work, continue suffering, or connect to others. There are many levels or variations of this state ranging from mild to severe. If there is a severe depressed state, the member should immediately be referred for a mental status assessment. If the member is already on medication and under treatment for depression, you need not refer.

We are not really sure what causes it, but the presence of a depressed group member can dampen the group's mood and interfere with learning. The depressed person does not intend this and is usually helpless to do anything about how he or she feels. It may be important for the leader to block any behaviors that tell or suggest that the depressed person "look on the bright side," attack the person for being down or feeling hopeless, and seek to exclude the depressed person.

There may be outside concerns that contribute to this depressed state, such as family and financial concerns. You cannot be expected to address or solve these. However, it can be useful to allow expression of these concerns and to show your understanding of their impact on the group member. If you feel uncomfortable or alarmed about a member who seems resigned, depressed, hopeless, or makes statements about "giving up," you have a responsibility to check out his or her suicidal ideation. Directly ask if the person is considering suicide or has made plans to commit suicide. If either answer is yes, you have an ethical obligation to report this to your supervisor or to whomever your site has designated as leader of the treatment team.

# References

Arledge, S. (1997). An evaluation of For Kids Only: An intervention, education, and support program for children of alcoholics. *Dissertation Abstracts International 57* (12-A) 5310 US: University Microfilms International.

Aronson, S. (1995). Five girls in search of a group: A group experience for adolescents of parents with AIDS. *International Journal of Group Psychotherapy, 45*(2), 223–235.

Association for Specialists in Group Work (1990). *Ethical guidelines for group counselors and professional standards for the training of group workers.* Alexandria, VA: Author.

Association for Specialists in Group Work (1991). *Ethical guidelines for group counselors.* Alexandria, VA: Author.

Baker, S. (2001). Coping-skills training for adolescents: Applying cognitive-behavioral principles to psychoeducational groups. *Journal for Specialists in Group Work, 26*(3), 219–227.

Bandura, A. (1977). *Social learning theory.* Englewood Cliffs, NJ: Prentice-Hall.

Beeferman, D., & Orvaschel (1994). Group psychotherapy for depressed adolescents: A critical review. *International Journal of Group Psychotherapy, 44*(4), 463–474.

Belfer, Pl, Munoz, L., Schachter, J., & Levendusky, P. (1995). Cognitive-behavioral group psychotherapy for agoraphobia and panic disorder. *International Journal of Group Psychotherapy, 45*(2), 185–206.

Benjamin, A. (1987). *The helping interview.* Boston: Houghton Mifflin.

Berenson, B. G., Mitchell, K. M., & Laney, R. C. (1968). Therapeutic conditions after therapist-initiated confrontation. *Journal of Clinical Psychology, 24,* 363–364.

Bion, W. (1961). *Experiences in groups and other papers.* London: Tavistock.

Bird, C. (1940). *Social psychology.* New York: Appleton-Century-Crofts.

Bloom, B. S., Krathwohl, D. R., & Masia, B. B. (1956). *Taxonomy of educational objectives: Handbook 1—Cognitive domain.* New York: David McKay.

Brabender, V. (2002). *Introduction to group therapy.* New York: Wiley.

Brown, N. (1994). *Group counseling for elementary and middle school children.* Westport, CT: Praeger.

Brown, N. (1996). *Expressive processes in group counseling.* Westport, CT: Praeger.

Brown, N. (1998). *The destructive narcissistic pattern.* Westport, CT: Praeger.

Bultz, B., Speca, M., Brasker, P., Geggie, P., & Page, S. (2000). A randomized controlled trial of a brief psychoeducational support group for partners of early stage breast cancer patients. *Psycho-Oncology, 9*(4), 303–313.

Caluza, K. (2000). A psychoeducational support group for multiracial adolescents: A twelve session treatment manual. *Dissertation Abstracts International* 61(1-B). Ann Arbor, MI: University Microfilms International.

Campbell, D. (1974). *If you don't know where you are going, you'll probably end up somewhere else.* Niles, IL: Argus Communications.

Carnegie Council on Adolescent Development (1995). Report of the Carnegie task force. New York: Author.

Catalano, R. F., & Hawkins, J. D. (1996). The social development model: A theory of antisocial behavior. In J. D. Hawkins (Ed.), *Delinquency and crime: Current theories* (pp. 149–197). New York: Cambridge University Press.

Coie, J., Miller-Johnson, S., Terry, R., Maummary-Gremaud, A., & Lochman, J. (1996). The influence of deviant peers on types of adolescent delinquency. *Symposium conducted at the meeting of the American Society of Criminology.* Chicago, IL.

Corey, G. (1995). *Theory and practice of counseling and psychotherapy* (5th ed.). Pacific Grove, CA: Brooks/Cole.

Corsini, R., & Rosenberg, B. (1955). Mechanisms of group psychotherapy: Processes & dynamics. *Journal of Abnormal Social Psychology, 51,* 406–411.

Cummings, S., Long, J., Peterson-Hazan, S., & Harrison, J. (1999). The efficacy of a group treatment model in helping spouses meet the emotional and practical challenges of early stage caregiving. *Clinical Gerontologist, 20*(1), 29–45.

Devine, E. C. (1992). Effects of psychoeducational care for adult surgical patients: A meta-analysis of 191 studies. *Patient Education and Counseling, 19*(2), 129–142.

Diegel, R. (1999). Participation in a dating violence prevention psychoeducational support group for adolescent females: A phenomenological inquiry. *Dissertation Abstracts* 60 (6-B). Ann Arbor, MI: University Microfilms International.

Dishion, T., McCord, J., & Paulin, F. (1999). When interventions harm. *American Psychologist, 54*(9), 755–764.

Dishion, T. J., Reid, J. B., & Patterson, G. R. (1988). Empirical guidelines for the development of a treatment for early adolescent substance use. In R. E. Coombs (Ed.), *The family context of adolescent drug use* (pp. 189–224). New York: Haworth.

Dollard, J., & Miller, N. E. (1950). *Personality and psychotherapy.* New York: McGraw-Hill.

Douglas, M., & Mueser, K. T. (1990). Teaching conflict resolution skills to the chronically mentally ill: Social skills training groups for briefly hospitalized patients. *Behavior Modification, 124*(4), 519–547.

Durlak, J. A., Fuhrman, T., & Lampman, C. (1991). Effectiveness of cognitive-behavior therapy for maladapting children: A meta-analysis. *Psychological Bulletin, 110,* 204–214.

Egan, G. (1975). *Exercises in helping skills.* Pacific Grove, CA: Brooks/Cole.

Fals-Stewart, W., & Lucente, S. (1994). Behavioral group therapy with obsessives-compulsives. *International Journal of Group Psychotherapy, 44*(1), 35–51.

Fawzy, I., & Fawzy, N. W. (1994). A structured psychoeducational intervention for cancer patients. *General Hospital Psychiatry, 16*(3), 149–192.

Fawzy, I., Fawzy, N. W., Aront, L. A., & Pasnau, R. O. (1995). Critical review of psychosocial interventions in cancer care. *Archives of General Psychiatry, 52*(2), 100–113.

Fiedler, F. (1978). Recent developments in research on the contingency model. In L. Berkowitz (Ed.), *Group process* (pp. 62–78). New York: Academic Press.

Fine, S., Forth, A., Gilbert, M., & Haley, G. (1991). Group therapy for adolescent depressive disorder: Comparison of social skills and therapeutic support. *Journal of the American Academy of Child and Adolescent Psychiatry, 30*, 79–85.

Forester, B., Cornfield, D. S., Fleiss, J. L., & Thomas, S. (1993). Group psychotherapy during radiotherapy. *American Journal of Psychiatry, 150*(11), 1700–1706.

Franklin, R., & Pack-Brown, S. (2001). Team brothers: An Africentric approach to group work with African American male adolescents. *Journal for Specialists in Group Work, 26*(3), 237–245.

Gagné, R. M. (1965). The analysis of instructional objectives for the design of instruction. In R. Glaser (Ed.), *Teaching machines and programmed learning II: Data and directions.* Washington, DC: Department of Audio-Visual Instruction, National Education Association.

Gamble, E. H., Elder, S., & Lashley, J. K. (1989). Group behavior therapy: A selective review of the literature. *Medical Psychotherapy: An International Journal, 2*, 193–204.

Garrett, M., & Cruchfield, L. (1997). Moving full circle: A unity model of group work with children. *Journal for Specialists in Group Work, 22*(3), 175–188.

Garrison, K. D., & Magoon, R. A. (1972). *Educational psychology.* Columbus, OH: Charles E. Merrill.

Gladding, S. (1995). *Group work: A counseling specialty* (2nd ed.). Englewood Cliffs, NJ: Prentice-Hall.

Gladding, S. (1999). *Group work: A counseling specialty.* (3rd ed.). Upper Saddle River, NJ: Merrill/Prentice Hall.

Goldstein, A. P., & Glick, B. (1987). Aggression replacement training. *Journal of Counseling and Development, 65*, 356–367.

Gough, H. (1975). *Manual for the California Psychological Inventory.* Palo Alto, CA: Consulting Psychologist Press.

Hafen, B., Karren, K., Frandsen, K., & Smith, N. (1996). *Mind/body health.* Boston: Allyn & Bacon.

Hall, D., & Cockburn, E. (1990). Developing management skills. *Management Education and Development, 21*(1), 41–50.

Hanna, F., Hanna, C., & Keys, S. (1999). Fifty strategies for counseling defiant, aggressive adolescents: Reaching, accepting, and relating. *Journal of Counseling and Development, 77*, 395–404.

Heise, D. (1970). The semantic differential and attitude research. In G. Summers (Ed.), *Attitude measurement* (pp. 235–253). Chicago, IL: Rand McNally.

Hershey, P., & Blanchard, K. (1977). *Management of organizational behavior: Utilizing human resources* (3rd ed.). Englewood Cliffs, NJ: Prentice-Hall.

Holland, J. (1973). *Making vocational choices: A theory of careers.* Englewood Cliffs, NJ: Prentice Hall.

Horton-Parker, R., & Brown, N. (2002). *The unfolding life: Counseling across the life-span.* Westport, CT: Praeger.

Hull, C. L. (1943). *Principles of behavior.* New York: Appleton-Century-Croft.

Jakobovits, L. A. (1966). Comparative psycholinguistics in the study of cultures. *International Journal of Psychology, 1,* 15–37.

James, W. (1890). *The principles of psychology.* New York: Holt, Rinehart & Winston.

Johnson, D., & Johnson, F. (2003). *Joining together: Group theory and group skills* (8th ed.). Boston: Allyn & Bacon.

Jones, L. (2001). Enhancing psychosocial competence among black women through an innovative psychoeducational group intervention. *Dissertation Abstracts* 61 (11-A) 4550. Ann Arbor, MI: University Microfilms International.

Judd, C. H. (1908). The relation of special training to general intelligence. *Educational Review, 36,* 36–37.

Kamps, D. M., Leonard, B. R., Vernon, S., & Dugan, E. P. (1992, Summer). Teaching social skills to students with autism to increase peer interactions in an integrated first-grade classroom. *Journal of Applied Behavior Analysis, 29*(2), 281–288.

Karp, J., Brown, K., Sullivan, M., & Massie, M. (1999). The prophylactic mastectomy dilemma: A support group for women at high genetic risk for breast cancer. *Journal of Genetic Counseling, 8*(3), 163–173.

Katz, P. (1990). The first few minutes: The engagement of the difficult adolescent. In Sherman Feinstein (Ed.), *Adolescent Psychiatry.* Chicago: University of Chicago Press.

Khattri, N. (1991). *An assessment of the social validity of cooperative learning and conflict resolution programs in an alternative inner city high school.* New York: Columbia University Press.

Kiselica, M. (1994). Preparing teenage fathers for parenthood: A group psychoeducational approach. *Journal for Specialists in Group Work, 19*(2), 83–94.

Kohut, H. (1977). *The restoration of the self.* New York: International University Press.

Kuder, F. (1963, 1987). *Kuder General Interest Survey.* Chicago, IL: Science Research Associates.

Kurtz, R. R., & Jones, J. E. (1973). Confrontation: Types, conditions, and outcomes. In J. W. Pfeiffer & J. E. Jones (Eds.), *The 1973 annual handbook for group facilitators.* LaJolla, CA: University Associates Publishers.

la Salivia, T. A. (1993). Enhancing addictions treatment through psychoeducational groups. *Journal of Substance Abuse Treatment, 10*(5), 439–444.

Lefley, H. (2001). Helping families of criminal offenders with mental illness. In G. Landsberg & A. Smiley (Eds.), *Forensic Mental Health.* 40-1-40-13. American Psychological Association.

Lubin, H., & Johnson, D. (1997). Interactive psychoeducational group therapy for traumatized women. *International Journal of Group Psychotherapy, 47*(3), 271–289.

MacLennan, B., & Dies, K. (1992). *Group counseling and group psychotherapy with adolescents* (2nd ed.). New York: Columbia University Press.

Malekoff, A. (1997). *Group work with adolescents.* New York: Guilford.

Mann, R. (1959). A review of the relationship between personality and performance in a small group. *Psychological Bulletin, 56,* 241–270.

Mara, B., & Winton, M. (1990). Sexual abuse intervention: A support group for parents who have a sexually abused child. *International Journal of Group Psychotherapy, 40*(1), 63–76.

Martin, V., & Thomas, C. (2000). A model psychoeducation group for shy college students. *Journal for Specialists in Group Work, 25*(1), 79–88.

Maslow, A. (1943). A theory of human motivation. *Psychological Review, 50,* 370–396.

McCord, J. (1992). The Cambridge-Somerville study: A pioneering longitudinal-experimental study of delinquency prevention. In J. McCord & R. E. Tremblay (Eds.), *Preventing antisocial behavior: Interventions from birth through adolescence* (pp. 196–206). New York: Guilford Press.

McManus, P., Redford, J., & Hughes, R. (1997). Connecting to self and others: A structured group for women. *Journal for Specialists in Group Work, 22*(1), 22–30.

McMillan, J. H., & Schumacher, S. (1997). *Research in education* (4th ed.). New York: Longman.

Misri, W., Kostaras, X., Fox, D., & Kostaras, D. (2000). The impact of partner support in the treatment of postpartum depression. *Canadian Journal of Psychiatry, 45*(6), 554–558.

Moreau, A. S. (1994). Improvising social skills of third grade students through conflict resolution training. *ERIC,* ED 375. 33 4.

Morgan, B., & Hensley, L. (1998). Supporting mothers through group work: A multimodal psychoeducational approach. *Journal for Specialists in Group Work, 23*(3), 298–311.

Mowrer, O. M. (1960). *Learning theory and behavior.* New York: John Wiley.

Murray, B. (2002, April). Tech enrichment or overkill? *APA Monitor.* 42–44.

Murray, H. (1938). *Explorations in personality.* New York: Oxford University Press.

Newstrom, J., & Scannell, E. (1991). *Still more games trainers play.* New York: McGraw-Hill.

Osgood, C. E., Tannenbaum, P. H., & Suci, G. J. (1957). *The measurement of meaning.* Urbana: University of Illinois Press.

Patterson, G., Dishion, T., & Yoeger, K. (1999). Adolescent growth in new forms of problem behavior: Macro- and micro-peer dynamics. Manuscript submitted for publication.

Pavlov, I. (1927). *Conditioned reflexes.* New York: Oxford University Press.

Payne, D., Lundberg, J., Brennan, M., & Holland, J. (1997). A psychosocial intervention for patients with soft tissue sarcoma. *Psycho-Oncology, 6*(1), 65–72.

Powers, E., & Winter, H. (1951). *An experiment in the prevention of delinquency: The Cambridge-Somerville Youth Study.* New York: Columbia University Press.

Pressman, B., & Sheps, A. (1994). Treating wife abuse: An integrated model. *International Journal of Group Psychotherapy, 44*(4), 477–498.

Pressman, M., & Brook, D. (1999). A multiple group psychotherapy approach to adolescents with psychiatric and substance abuse comorbidity. *International Journal of Group Psychotherapy, 49*(4), 486–512.

Roberts, C., Piper, L., Denny, J., & Cuddeback, G. (1997). A support group intervention to facilitate young adults' adjustment to cancer. *Health and Social Work, 22*(2), 133–141.

Rotter, J. B. (1959). Substituting good behavior for bad. *Contemporary Psychology, 4,* 176–178.

Salvendy, J. (1999). Ethnocultural considerations in group therapy. *International Journal of Group Psychotherapy, 49*(4), 429–463.

Sandahl, C., & Ronnbers, S. (1990). Brief group psychotherapy in relapse prevention for alcohol dependent patients. *International Journal of Group Psychotherapy, 40*(4), 453–476.

Schulz, C. (1993). Helping factors in a peer-developed support group for persons with head injury, Part 2: Survivor interview perspective. *American Journal of Occupational Therapy, 48,* 305–309.

Schwartzberg, S. L. (1993). Helping factors in a peer-developed support group for persons with head injury. Part 1: Participant-observer perspective. *American Journal of Occupational Therapy, 48,* 297–304.

Sheckman, Z. (1994). Group counseling/psychotherapy as a school intervention to enhance close friendships in preadolescence. *Journal for Specialists in Group Work, 44*(3), 377–391.

Sheckman, Z. (2001). Prevention groups for angry and aggressive children. *Journal for Specialists in Group Work, 26*(3), 228–236.

Shure, M. B. (1993, December). I can problem solve: Interpersonal cognitive problem solving for your children. *Early Childhood Development and Care*, 49–64.

Skinner, B. F. (1953). *Science and human behavior.* New York: Macmillan.

Stein, C. H., Cislo, D. A., & Ward, M. (1994, July 18). Collaboration in the college classroom: Evaluation of a social network and social skills program for undergraduates and people with serious mental illnesses. *Psychosocial Rehabilitation Journal, 1,* 13–33.

Stern, M., Lawrence, M., & Duluy, J. (1992, October). *Groups for the medically ill.* Paper presented at the Mid-Atlantic Group Psychotherapy Society Conference, Williamsburg, VA.

Stogdill, R. (1959). *Individual behavior and group achievement.* New York: Oxford University Press.

Stogdill, R. (1974). *Handbook of leadership.* New York: Free Press.

Swell, L. (1992). Education for success: A program to enhance the self-concept of freshmen on a large college campus—An evaluation. *Canadian Journal of Higher Education, 22*(2), 68–72.

Thompson, C., & Randolph, L. (1983). *Counseling children.* Monterey, CA: Brooks/ Cole.

Thorndike, E. L. (1913). *Educational psychology.* New York: Columbia University Press.

Ulman, K. (2000). An integrative model of stress management groups for women. *International Journal of Group Psychotherapy, 50*(3), 341–362.

Vacha-Haase, T., Ness, C., Dannison, L., & Smith, A. (2000). Grandparents raising grandchildren: A psychoeducational group approach. *Journal for Specialists in Group Work, 25*(1), 67–78.

Vallian-Fernandez, O., Lemos-Giraldez, S., Roder, V., Garcia-Saiz, A., Otero-Garcia, A., Alonso-Sanchez, M., & Gutierrez-Perez, A. (2001). Controlled study of an integrated psychological intervention in schizophrenia. *European Journal of Psychiatry, 15*(3), 167–179.

Vitaro, F., Tremblay, R., Kerr, M., Pagani, L., & Bukowski, W. (1997). Disruptiveness, friends' characteristics, and delinquency in early adolescence: A test of two models of development. *Child Development, 68,* 676–689.

Walton, R. (1987). *Managing conflict.* Reading, MA: Addison-Wesley.

Weist, M. D., Vannatta, K., & Wayland, K. (1993). Social skills training for abused girls: Interpersonal skills training for sexually abused girls. *Behavior Change,* *10*(4), 244–252.

Wertheimer, M. (1959). *Productive thinking* (2nd ed.). New York: Harper & Row.

Wolpe, J. (1958). *Psychotherapy by reciprocal inhibition.* Palo Alto, CA: Stanford University Press.

Worchel, S., & Shebilske, W. (1992). *Psychology principles and applications* (4th ed.). Englewood Cliffs, NJ: Prentice Hall.

Yalom, I. (1985). *The theory and practice of group psychotherapy* (3rd ed.). New York: Basic Books.

Yalom, I. (1995). *The theory and practice of group psychotherapy* (4th ed.). New York: Basic Books.

Zamanian, K., & Adams, C. (1997). Group psychotherapy with sexually abused boys: Dynamics and interventions. *International Journal of Group Psychotherapy,* *47*(1), 109–126.

# Index

Adolescent groups
  characteristics, 178–180
  goals, 177
  guidelines, 181–183
  planning, 180–181
  sample group 183–193
Adult groups
  advantages, 195–196
  creating, 197–198
  examples, 196–197
  leader tasks, 198
  sample, 199–220
Art factor, 2

Caretakers, 227
Children groups
  confidentiality, 162
  differences, 156–158
  first session, 161
  guidelines, 158–160
  plan, 163
  purpose and goals, 162
  questions and comments, 164
  research, 156
  rules, 162
  sample, 165–176
  sample procedures, 160–165
  types, 154–156
Confrontation
  fundamentals, 150–151

  guidelines, 147–148
  major types, 145–147
  variables, 148–150
Conflict
  characteristic behavior, 140–141
  management strategies, 141–142
Countertransference, 27–28
Cultural factors, 19–21

Developing the group
  goals and objectives, 78
  participants' characteristics, 78
  pregroup, 77–78

Ethical issues
  guidelines, 15–19
  involuntary members, 123–125
Evaluation
  assessing learning, 111–112
  formative evaluation, 112
  instruments, 112–113
  process of evaluation, 110
  questionnaires, 113–114
  rationale, 108–109
  rating scales, 114–117
  semantic differential, 117–118
  summative evaluation, 110
  terms, 109–110
Experiential activities
  goals, 103
  materials, 105–106

Experiential activities (*continued*)
  participants, 103–104
  planning, 103–106
  time and group size, 104

Families, 227–228

Group dynamics, 70–72
Group leadership
  art factor, 3–4
  group level skills, 35–36
  knowledge factor, 2–4
  leader characteristics, 30–33
  model, 1–5
  science factor, 4
  skills, 4, 33–34, 36–46
  techniques, 5
Group stages
  stages and dynamics 72–77

Helpful group factors, 79–86

Ineffective communication, 40–41
Instructional strategies
  exercises and games, 99–100
  lectures, 98–99
  media, 100–102
  mini-lectures, 94–98
  role play, 102–103
  simulations, 102
  techniques, 79, 98–103
Instructional styles, 52–53

KASST model, 1–5

Leadership strategy clusters
  advice giving, 136
  feeling responses, 135
  personal relationship, 53–56
  resistance, 135
  specific strategies, 134–136
Learning levels
  low, 50–51
  low to moderate, 51
  high, 53
Life conditions, 228–229
Listening and responding, 37–40

Meaningfulness of material, 57
Medical conditions, 225
Members
  attention seeking, 127
  constraints to active participation, 121
  disengaged, 128–131
  ethical guidelines, 123–125
  involuntary, 120–121
  leader's role, 122–123
  over-participation, 126
  physical distractions, 127
  problem behaviors, 125–131
  socializing, 128
  storytelling and monopolizing, 126
  strategies, 129
  under- or nonparticipation, 127
Membership skills
  expressing feelings, 134
  feelings, thoughts, and ideas, 131–132
  general designations, 132
  identifying feelings, 133
  mind reading, 132–133
  nonverbal communication, 133–134
  personal statements, 132
  teaching, 131
Methods, 57

Narcissism
  underdeveloped, 28–30

Personal development
  exercises, 22–23, 46, 67, 86, 106, 136–137, 152
  rationale, 26–27
Planning groups
  guidelines, 89–94
Principles of instruction
  active versus passive, 63
  comprehension, 63–64
  goals, 60–61
  motivation, 62
  organization, 63
  readiness, 62
Principles of learning, 56
Psychiatric conditions, 228
Psychoeducational groups
  basic characteristics, 10–12

categories, 13–15
classification, 12–13
definitions, 5–10
planning, 86

Questioning
closed, 42–43
direct, 42
double, 43
inappropriate, 45
open, 42
receiving, 44
skill development, 41–46

Resistance, 135
Retention of material, 59

Self-help groups, 221–223
Stress risk factors, 226
Support groups
background, 225–229
description, 223–2224
design, 229–232
facilitation, 232–234
guidelines, 224–225

Taxonomy of educational objectives, 64–65
Techniques
exercises and games, 66
discussion, 66
lectures, 65–66
media, 66–67

Theories
distributed actions/functions, 49
group leadership, 48–50
situational leadership, 49–50
styles, 49
traits and characteristics, 48
Therapy-related groups
attitudes, 246
defenses, 248
depressed state, 250–251
effects of condition, 246
emotional intensity, 241
fears, 249
homogeneity, 242
hostility, 249–250
medication, 245–246
members, 241–242
members' states, 245
other therapies, 243–244
planning, 242
professionals, 243
reaching out, 248
remediation, 240
reporting, 244
self–absorption, 247
socializing, 244–245
Transfer of learning, 58
Trauma, 229

Variable conflict management
expertise, 143
management strategies, 141–142
model, 143–145
responsibility, 142

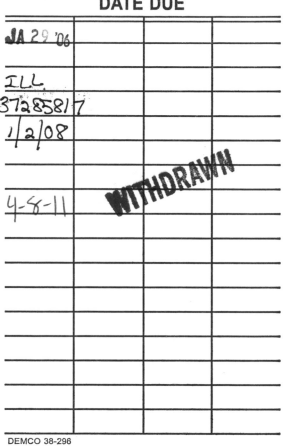